The Sound of Architecture
Acoustic Atmospheres in Place

The Sound of Architecture

Acoustic Atmospheres
in Place

Edited by
Angeliki Sioli and
Elisavet Kiourtsoglou

Leuven University Press

The work has benefited from the support of AMUP Research Unit (UR7309), a joint unit of the National School of Architecture in Strasbourg (ENSAS) and INSA Strasbourg, as well as from the University of Thessaly and the Delft University of Technology, Department of Architecture.

Strasbourg,
école d'architecture

UNIVERSITY OF
THESSALY

Delft
University of
Technology

ISBN 978 94 6270 321 6
e-ISBN 978 94 6166 456 3
D/2022/1869/23
NUR: 648
https://doi.org/10.11116/9789461664563
Cover design: Daniel Benneworth-Gray
Cover illustration: Jef Aerosol, Chuuuttt !!! 2011 © SABAM Belgium 2021 / Image by rbrudolph from Pixabay
Lay-out: Crius Group

Every effort has been made to contact all holders of the copyright to the visual material contained in this publication. Any copyrightholders who believe that illustrations have been reproduced without their knowledge are asked to contact the publisher.

to those who look for ways to listen…

Table of Contents

Echoes

Acknowledgements

Angeliki Sioli and Elisavet Kiourtsoglou

For *The Sound of Architecture* to be heard, many voices have tuned in with our own and supported us generously over the last four years. This book emerged from a session we co-chaired at the 72nd Annual International Conference of the Society of Architectural Historians in April of 2019, in Rhode Island, USA (https://www.sah.org/2019). We are grateful to the organizers, especially Victoria Young, the Conference Chair, and Chris Kirbabas, the director of SAH programs, for accepting our call for papers and giving us an ideal place for a conversation on acoustic atmospheres. The School of Architecture at Louisiana State University and the École Nationale Supérieure d'Architecture de Strasbourg, where we were respectively teaching at the time, generously supported and encouraged our participation in this academic event. We will always be grateful to Directors Marwan Ghandour and Sara Reichert—no matter how far away our paths have now taken us—for listening attentively to our ambitions and fueling them with genuine encouragement.

Our call for papers did not only attract interested conference participants: Mirjam Truwant, the acquisitions editor at Leuven University Press, envisioned—before we ever did—the possibility of a book related to our topic and thankfully knocked on our electronic doors. Ever since that first inquiry e-mail, Mirjam has been the "good fairy" of this project. Her patience, kindness and humorous disposition have supported all our attempts and facilitated the many stages of the publication process. Our e-mails titled "Happy Friday", communicating good news on Friday afternoons along the way, quickly became a tradition among us—and one we will greatly miss.

For responding to our call for papers with enthusiasm and academic rigor, we are immensely grateful to this volume's contributors. Without their strong voices we could not have studied in such meticulous detail the acoustic atmospheres you will find in the pages to come. Anna Ulrikke Andersen, through e-mails always filled with positivity and joy, shared with us fascinating stories from her archival research and earlier years as a doctoral candidate. Michael Windover and James Deaville overcame with utmost determination the closing of libraries and archives that the pandemic imposed and worked with us through challenging timeframes without the slightest complaint. Timothy Carey many times spontaneously shared how happy he felt working on his article and what joy gave him searching for images that could accompany his finely tuned words. Clemens Finkelstein, who without exception was always first to answer our e-mails with the kindest of words, generously shared vibes of friendly collegiality from wherever in the world his research took him. Ross El-fline discussed the wonderful responsibility of administrative academic duties during our communications, and proactively started planning possibilities for distributing the book before we even thought about it ourselves. Paul Holmquist sent the most kind, eloquent and impossible-to-deny requests for deadline extensions, only because his piece had to be absolutely perfect—an exaggeration that only Paul is capable of. Carlotta Darò, whom we personally invited to join our project, fought with all her strength against Kafkaesque bureaucratic hurdles regarding issues of copyright per-missions and managed to win, so that this book can have an e-version as well. Joseph L. Clarke, who used to call us A+E and always informed us about new publications related to architecture and sound, responded to our questions on race with utmost sensitivity and profound historical knowledge. Federica Goffi, with her kind and gra-cious disposition, worked tirelessly to overcome creatively the obstacles the pandemic created, denying her the possibility to visit the archives of the composer and architect she examines in her work. Cécile Regnault was always willing to examine all the pos-sible nuances between the French and English language in order to make Kircher's words resonate with contemporary architectural discourse. Karen Van Lengen, who was always just a phone call away, in case any details needed to be discussed, patiently bore with our million decisions and indecisions regarding where best to place her work in the structure of our book. Pamela Jordan, whose capacity to orally present at a conference can make everyone jealous, always made us smile by constantly thanking us for the transparency of our communication. Klaske Havik and Michael de Beer sent kind requests to include additional images in their contribution, believing pas-sionately in the importance of giving space to students' work and the inner workings of the pedagogical process.

Immense gratitude will always fill our hearts for the last two contributors in this book's table of contents, both invited by us to join this fascinating group of people above. Alberto Pérez-Gómez discussed passionately with us questions that triggered the creation of this book but also offered guidance on theoretical and historical doubts that we faced along the way. Ricardo Castro, who we still need to meet in Greece for some sardines, tirelessly inspired our work, particularly in moments of hesitation, re-counting in his e-mails moments of silence in Montreal during the pandemic.

For their care with words and copy-editing work we were happy to have in our corner Rebecca Bryan and Vincent Cellucci. Their love of language and precision of expression have made many of the articles in this volume "speak" sharply and loudly.

None of the above voices would find a presence in the pages of this book without the generous support of the Research Laboratory AMUP (Strasbourg), the University of Thessaly and TU Delft's Faculty of Architecture and the Built Environment, in partially covering the costs of production. The possibility for an offset print and a section with color images was made possible only because Denis Bocquet and Florence Rudolf, the directors of AMUP, along with Lise Lançon, the administrative research manager, believed in the importance of the project. Professor Dimitris Zoumboulakis, who is in charge of the University of Thessaly Press, and Professor Klaske Havik, Chair of Methods of Analysis and Imagination, of TU Delft readily agreed to cover additional costs of the publication.

Last but not least, we would like to thank deeply and wholeheartedly our professors at the Department of Architecture of the University of Thessaly in Volos, where the two of us first met in 1999. They taught us, in their diverse, unique ways, that the world around us is a miraculous place and that being sensible to its many wonders is *the* architectural way to live life.

Introduction

01.

Atmospheres that Touch

Angeliki Sioli and
Elisavet Kiourtsoglou

Hearing about the death of Fernando Pessoa, the famous Portuguese poet, Ricardo Reis returns to Lisbon from Brazil. He wanders the streets of the city, lost in his thoughts, during the day, and then retreats to a small hotel. One of the first nights, he notices that "when one awaits to sleep in the silence of a room that is still unfamiliar, listening to the rain outside, things assume their real dimension, they all become great, solemn, heavy."[1] He lies in bed in an attempt to fall asleep, surrounded by his small hotel room and its basic amenities, immersed in the room's silence as disrupted by the sound of the rain, attuned to the felt impressions these acoustic dimensions create, receptive of the emerging atmosphere of an unfamiliar place: great, solemn, heavy. Although a fictional character—the product of the imagination of the author José Saramango—Ricardo Reis' thoughts connect eloquently the actual elements that inspired the creation of this book: the embodied experience in a place of a given scale, the prevalent acoustic conditions and the perceived atmosphere.

This collection of essays explores how sound and architecture work together in creating acoustic atmospheres that influence our embodied experience of place. In doing so it discusses how acoustic experience and atmosphere are connected with the scale of the place itself, scale understood in this context as the relative size of the place. The contributors to this volume look at three main scales of the built environment—rooms, buildings and cities—and examine acoustic atmospheres within domestic environments, private spaces, public institutions, urban monuments and cityscapes, and how these are experienced by inhabitants and users. The case studies discussed span from the end of the 17th Century to the beginning of the 21st, with the majority belonging to the 20th Century. The authors demonstrate how acoustic atmospheres can be tangible architectural phenomena, not because they can be measured or quantified, but because they "touch" the embodied active participant, agreeing with Murray Schaffer's poetic assertion that "hearing is a way of touching at a distance."[2]

The Atmospheres of Place

The notion of atmosphere in architecture has lately been attracting considerable attention. Theoreticians and practitioners of architecture, especially within a Western context, refer to the growing awareness of the role atmospheres play in design as the "atmospheric turn" in the field.[3] A number of architectural publications and conferences have attempted to bring to the fore a discussion on atmospheres and places as vital for our contemporary architectural world.[4] This shift seems to respond to the concern, raised by both academics and practitioners, that in recent decades architecture has been in a state of crisis, a victim of design trends that focus on form or function but fail to prioritize the users and the actual experience of place.[5] Approaching place through the design of atmospheres seems to expand the conversation beyond these trends. As Christian Borch characteristically argues, "an atmospheric perspective pays attention to how architecture and urban planning are able to provide nourishment to the multisensory experiences."[6]

The study of what exactly constitutes a spatial atmosphere, however, is not straightforward. Atmospheres have an elusive and temporal character and their perception can be at times subjective. Voices from the contemporary continental philosophical discourse attempt to tackle these noted difficulties. Gernot Böhme's *Atmospheric Architectures: The Aesthetics of Felt Space* (2017) and Tonino Griffero's *Atmospheres: Aesthetics of Emotional Spaces* (2016) constitute foundational texts for understanding the experience of a place's atmosphere, as discussed in this book. Böhme's philosophical claim that sound is among the objective means by which atmosphere can be generated, is the basis from which this book evolved.[7] His definition of atmosphere as "attuned space" and "a shared reality of the perceiver and the perceived," underpins our approach. Griffero's focus on patterns of emotional tones in different places and their impact on the felt body supports our investigations. He unpacks how atmospheres affect our emotions, our bodies' reactions, our state of mind and, as a result, our behavior and judgments, a topic of concern for architecture and one our book looks at carefully.[8]

More recently, Bruce Bégout, through his work *Le Concept d'Ambiance* (2020), argues that atmospheres can demonstrate how absolute immersion in the environment that surrounds us takes place. Paying attention to the atmospheres of a place—in our case the acoustic atmospheres—opens us up to perceiving the vibrancy of the environment we are part of, he explains, making us aware in the most convincing way that there is no division between the self and the world.[9] For Bégout moreover, the elusive character of atmospheres should not be seen as a problem but rather as a condition which merits further study.

The Scale of Place

Our joint project, as editors, on architecture and sound began with a session we chaired at the 72nd Annual International Conference of the Society of Architectural Historians in 2019. We believed that sound could offer a tangible parameter in the study and understanding of spatial atmospheres, because sound has the capacity to actually create a unique space of its own, or even endow space with a character of its own that at times may be difficult to escape.[10] Our main interest was how architects and designers could approach acoustic atmospheres by recounting the experience of place. We asked for compelling case studies of architectural design, urban planning and art installations in which either the acoustic atmospheres were an integral part of the design or the place's acoustic properties were consciously incorporated into the design itself. Our approach was grounded on the theoretical frameworks of phenomenological hermeneutics and sound studies.

Through the contributors' suggested topics, it became evident that the case studies were defined by the scale of the places under examination. This observation aligned with the recent literature on architecture and sound that poses scale as a defining parameter when it comes to the experience of place. For example, Michel Fowler, in his *Architectures of Sound* (2017), posits that sound offers an embodied understanding of the limits and boundaries of physical space, in terms of both the infinitesimally small and the extraordinarily large. More specifically he explains that people "sense the auditory dimensions of architectural space through (…) a sum of vibrations that each approach the ear at slightly varied time distributions."[11] These varied time distributions and delays "are the result of sound waves essentially mapping out the physical boundaries, the tangible architectonics of the reflective surfaces that surround us."[12] The scale of the place that envelops us acts as a pivot between the acoustic qualities, geometry and dimension of place as gauged against its auditory qualities and characteristics.[13] In more experiential terms, Griffero adds to this conversation that "geometry is incapable of justifying the (not only metaphorical) volume of a Sunday silence or the narrowness of a living room, perhaps metrically identical to another which is yet perceived as more spacious."[14] In other words, the limits of our surroundings influence our perception of sound, and vice versa, the perception of sound affects our impression of our environment's dimensions.

The Sound of Place

Sound studies have expanded in scope beyond the purely musicological paths, employing methods and epistemological tools from diverses disciplines, such as architecture, acoustics, history and psychology. Most importantly, sound studies have focused on analyzing sound through space (rather than through time metrics as used to be the case for music) and have underlined the societal forces and cultural backgrounds that interact with and define sonic environments. Sound has progressively become an element of analysis of human culture. Starting with R. Murray Schafer's iconic work *The Soundscape* (1977), sound was understood as an element of separation between culture and nature. Schafer merged music and noise, studying sounds produced by humans, animals, machines and nature.[15] Following in his path, the French research laboratory CRESSON coined the term "sonic effects" to describe dimensions of soundscapes in cities and architectural spaces, arguing that both the production and perception of sonic effects are related to specific temporal circumstances and human intentions. For historians, this interest in the sonic environment added another element to the analysis of human society: sound can actually function as a cultural mode of perception and knowledge. For example, Alain Corbin argued that a soundscape is constructed and perceived inside a historic timeframe, exactly like a landscape.[16] Active listeners actually choose the point of audition, loading with meaning and emotion the sounds heard, while also appreciating and understanding them.

Moreover, the history of science has shown that even the "physicality" of sound is socially and historically constructed. Emily Thompson, in *The Soundscape of Modernity* (2002), argues that the rise of the science of acoustics at the beginning of the 20th Century had a major impact on the culture of listening in America and the development of a certain architectural design that privileged "dry" sound.[17] Interested in the relative nature of sound perception and appreciation, sensory archeology had as an objective the understanding of human activity through the reconstruction of sensory experiences. Excellent examples of this kind of scholarship, such as Bissera V. Pentcheva's *Hagia Sophia* (2017), Deborah Howard and Laura Moretti's *Sound and Space in Renaissance Venice* (2010) and Niall Atkinson's *The Noisy Renaissance: Sound, Architecture, and Florentine Urban Life* (2016), aim to reconstruct the original conditions that influence the interaction between sound, space and people.[18] What was heard and how played an important role in the encounters of the members of society with the divine and the political power of the time, setting a rhythm for everyday life. Sonority was a dimension of the experience of place, not an element of a neutral Cartesian space.

The importance given to active listeners in terms of creating and perceiving sonic environments has also changed their role in the design of architectural space. As Barry Blesser and Linda-Ruth Salter argue, experiencing space by attentive listening allows perception of an aural architecture, beyond three dimensions. In a way, subjects function as "aural architects" whose individual psychology and social backgrounds interfere with the available technology and create an "aural representation" of the place they are in. As subjective as this version of space can be, aural architecture underlines the familiarization and appropriation of the space through sound.[19]

The Experience of Place

One could of course argue that the embodied perception and felt atmospheres in a place can be subjective and thus not of great value for a study such as the one we wish to carry out. However, we believe that beyond the subjectivity of any experience—conditioned by countless parameters like gender, race, ethnicity, education, disposition or context—architecture and the acoustic atmospheres it encompasses have the potential to reveal elements of place that can be sensed and shared by a wide and diverse audience. These atmospheres have the potential to touch chords that transcend our subjective experiences. In line with phenomenological hermeneutics, the contributions to this volume focus on acoustic phenomena and attempt to explain them though an empirical study of place and sound, showing that sound asks us to investigate architecture not as an intellectual but as an embodied experience. Phenomenological hermeneutics, in Heidegger's own words, strives for interpretations that are "not grounded in human consciousness and human categories but in the manifestness of the things encountered, the reality that comes to meet us."[20]

The contributors to this book study in close detail precisely this "reality that comes to meet us" and moreover exemplify that atmospheres are culturally and historically defined. Indeed, as Richard Palmer explains "phenomenological hermeneutics believes that understanding is a historical act and as such is always connected to the present. (...) From this point of view to speak of 'objectively valid interpretation' is naïve, since to do so assumes that it is possible to understand from some standpoint outside of history."[21] The articles demonstrate how each time period's cultural norms, spatial discourse, and available technology allowed architects, interior designers and composers to prioritize the creation of specific acoustic atmospheres. Many times, it was the creation of these very atmospheres that ensured the programmatic success of the architectural or urban design.

Prioritizing the embodied experience and the subsequent interpretation of architectural acoustic atmospheres, the contributors also seem to align with the intentions set recently by what philosophers Richard Kearney and Brian Treanor call carnal hermeneutics. Carnal hermeneutics propose, "at a moment when questions of matter, flesh, and body call out for new rethinking, to revisit the deep and inextricable relationship between *sensation* and *interpretation*."[22] Such a move, the philosophers believe, "may help us better understand how we are constantly *reading* flesh, *interpreting* senses, and *orienting* bodies in passion and place even as we symbolize and dream."[23]

The Acoustic Atmospheres in Place

The case studies presented in this volume refer to and are analyzed from a Western perspective. The feelings, sensations and types of hearing discussed reveal primarily Western theoretical and practical preoccupations. The emotional power of sound in the living rooms of North America, the dramatic nature of sound in European theaters and concert halls, the metaphysical echoing of sound in Medieval and Renaissance churches, the social or celebratory sonic environment of exhibition spaces or public urban environments fill the pages of this book. Many of these architectural typologies dependent heavily on sound in order to immerse their audience in a specific mood, and it is through specific acoustic atmospheres that architectural space is experienced at its fullest, creating a meaning related to each culture and historical time. The case studies presented and analyzed are either not widely known in the literature or well-known ones which have not been studied from the perspective of acoustic atmospheres.

Although not the main focus of this book, we would be remiss not to acknowledge that "the production of architectural atmospheres amounts to a subtle form of power that aims to achieve its effects by working on a nonconscious level."[24] Shops using Muzak or modern drone (or atmospheric) music invite customers to stay longer and consume more. In less radical examples, we can claim that every encounter with architecture may influence or affect the mood of the user in a subtle, unconscious way. Entering a well-furnished room, running through an empty building or walking around narrow, echoing medieval streets create a certain atmosphere that affects us.[25]

The authors of this book listen attentively to how the experience of place was imagined, conceived, designed and produced by architects, artists, musicians and engineers in order to provoke a certain feeling or impression. Specific qualities of sound or soundscapes were orchestrated, more or less consciously, to create or work with a certain atmosphere. The contributors amplify with their work the role of sound's embodied effect on the user or inhabitant of a place. They focus on sound's capacity to influence the mood, emotions and intellect of an engaged participant, even guide their behavior consciously or unconsciously.

The Sound of Architecture

The book's sections are titled: "Room Vibrations," "Building Pitches" and "City Tunes" respectively, and each section opens with a chapter that examines acoustic atmospheres at the given scale, as they are discussed in a theoretical or historical treatise. Following this chapter, each section includes four articles that discuss specific case studies at the same scale.

Room Vibrations

The first section opens with a piece by Anna Ulrikke Andersen, who illuminates the role of sound and music in Norberg-Schulz's renowned *Genius Loci: Towards a Phenomenology of Architecture* (1980). She examines the rooms in which the architectural theoretician wrote one of the most influential treatises of the 20th Century. She discusses how specific sounds and musical pieces related to these rooms sparked ideas of embodied experience in place that were incorporated in the author's work. The piece has a speculative nature, trying to imagine the sounds heard inside and outside the environments in which the theoretician worked.

Following this imaginative opening, the section features four articles on rooms where architectural atmospheres and recorded music co-exist, moving from the private realm of the home to the public realm of public installations. The focus is twofold: how the recorded music resonates in space, altering the atmosphere in the rooms in which it is performed, and how the design of specific atmospheres in a room influences the creation and recording of music.

Focusing on the middle-class North American living room at the turn of the 20th Century, Michael Windover and James Deaville consider how musical instruments like the piano affected interior design decisions and the acoustic experience of early 20th-century homes. The next two articles of "Room Vibrations" study analogue and digital possibilities for the creation and recording of music. Timothy Carey traces the history that led to the design and creation of the first professional recording studios. He shows how impromptu solutions to harness the acoustic qualities of promising reverberant rooms were gradually codified in the design of recording studios. Diving further into the topic of studios and their atmospheric qualities, Clemens Finkelstein examines in detail Jimi Hendrix's facility Electric Lady. The article unpacks the technological advances in the creation of different atmospheres in the studio room, which affected the composition and recording of music. In the last piece of this section, Ross Elfline shows how modern composers Alvin Lucier and La Monte Young play with the materiality of specific rooms in order to create and record unique sound atmospheres.

Building Pitches

The book's second section shifts the scale of the conversation from the room to the public building. The opening piece studies Claude-Nicolas Ledoux's Theater of Besançon (1784) as presented in his treatise *L'architecture considérée sous le rapport de l'art, des moeurs et de la législation* (1804). Examining the architect's intentions for the acoustic performance of the theater, Paul Holmquist discusses the creation of a synesthetic architectural atmosphere shared by the spectators, an atmosphere which according to Ledoux was meant to offer moral guidance.

Echoing this piece on theater, the articles in "Building Pitches" examine three building typologies that are highly dependent on sound: concert halls, religious buildings and exhibition spaces. Carlotta Darò presents a method that allows architects to predict the acoustic atmosphere of a concert hall during the design process. It is an analogue technique based on large-scale models that work in parallel with computational design and help correct and attune the atmosphere of the building that is under construction. Joseph L. Clarke and Federika Goffi examine, in their respective contributions, specific acoustic atmospheres in two well-known historic churches. Through archival work, Clarke imagines the sound of the chapel of Le Corbusier's Notre-Dame du Haut in Ronchamp (1955). Although the chapel's campanile was never built, as Le Corbusier had hoped, the article shows clearly the architect's intentions and attempts to design a specific sound atmosphere. Goffi explores the collaboration between architect Renzo Piano and avant-garde composer Luigi Nono for Nono's last composition, *Prometheus: Tragedy of Listening* (1981–1985). Both architect and composer emphasized the creation of an acoustic experience that would achieve the aural immersion of participants in the socio-cultural and political conditions of the world around them. The section closes with Elisavet Kiourtsolgou's article on the renowned Philips Pavilion (1958) and the embodied experience of its audience. Designed by architect and composer Iannis Xenakis in collaboration with Le Corbusier, the pavilion offered a unique acoustic environment for the performance of two specially composed pieces of electroacoustic music. The article analyzes the relation between the representation of sound by the composers and the acoustic atmosphere perceived by the audience.

City Tunes

The last section of the book opens with an article that examines what is considered to be the first treatise on acoustics, Athanasius Kircher's *Phonurgia Nova* (1673). Cécile Regnault unpacks connections between sound city, landscape and outdoor large-scale spaces by looking into Kircher's concept of the "sounding city" and his various "city instruments." She concludes her contribution by connecting Kircher's thinking to the contemporary discourse on the aesthetics of atmospheres.

"City Tunes" then presents four distinct aspects of acoustic atmospheres in the city: the psychological, aesthetic, political and pedagogical aspects of city-sounds. Angeliki Sioli focuses on the random, insignificant sounds of modern London and examines the effect they have on citizens' consciousness and actions. Looking in detail at Virginia Woolf's *Mrs Dalloway* (1925), she demonstrates how sound influences our perception and appropriation of urban space, and why literature is an ideal tool to study this topic. Karen Van Lengen discusses urban sound installations and how they can either reveal historical aspects of a site or create new and unexpected space in the public domain. She examines how sound installations can foster communicative relationships among citizens and reveal sonic elements of the city's architecture. Pamela Jordan continues the conversation on sound's power to influence our conduct in a city by analyzing the Berlin Wall as a sonic infrastructural space. She looks into the acoustic environment the Wall created in the heart of the city and how citizens reacted to it. She then examines the acoustic environment of the contemporary memorial of the Wall and the dramatic shifts in sound atmospheres it has led to, emphasizing constantly the political nature and power of sound. The last article takes the reader to the Latin American cities of Bogotá, Colombia and Valparaíso, Chile and unpacks pedagogical approaches focused on the study of sound in the urban environment. Klaske Havik and Michael de Beer argue for the need to raise sound awareness in architectural pedagogy. They present writing assignments that can train students to sense and capture acoustic urban atmospheres, and elaborate on how such training can enhance students' design abilities, leading to projects attuned to the sounds of the environment they are conceived for.

Echoes

Instead of a formal afterword, the book concludes with two pieces that tune the readers to the palpable voice of two academics. The interview with Alberto Pérez-Gómez touches on many topics unpacked in the various articles in this collection, adding how sound has been treated in the Western architectural discourse historically, how contemporary theories look at the act of hearing and listening in place, and how atmospheres, acoustic or not, can be approached within an educational setting. The piece by Ricardo Castro narrates moments of eloquent silences in unique architectural places around the world. It is a piece containing the personal reminiscences of a dedicated architectural traveler, which hints poetically at the fact that not only the experience of place but also the memory of this experience is basically just an atmosphere.

We hope that the pages of *The Sound of Architecture* recount what was heard and felt in specific historic moments in different scales of places, making louder the importance of acoustic atmospheres for the study and understanding of our wondrous built environment and the difficult task of architecture. With this hope in place, we leave the act of reading and *listening* to you.

Notes

1. José Saramango, *The Year of the Death of Ricardo Reis*, transl. Giovanni Pontiero (Orlando; Austin; New York; San Diego; London: Harvest Book Press, 1991), 23.

2. R. Murray Schafer, *The Soundscape: Our Sonic Environment and the Tuning of the World* (Vermont: Destiny Books, 1994), 12.

3. A-Chr.Engels-Schwarzpaul, Böhme's translator in English, mentions in the introduction of *Atmospheric Architectures* that the works of Böhme contribute in this atmospheric turn. [Gernot Böhme, *Atmospheric Architectures: The Aesthetics of Felt Spaces* (London; Oxford; New York; New Dehli; Sydney: Bloomsbury, 2017), 5.]

4. In 2013 the journal *OASE* published the issue *Building Atmospheres*. The publication dealt with the noted difficulty in defining atmospheres. It presented theoretical perspectives on the topic, Zumthor's creative design process and positions by the Finish architect Juhani Pallasmaa. Pallasmaa continues publishing on the topic. His piece "Place, Space and Atmosphere: Peripheral Perception on Architectural Experience," (2014) discusses the necessity to finally abandon a visual approach to architecture and focus on embodied synesthetic atmospheres. Similarly, the volume "Atmospheres" by *The Journal of Architectural Education* (2019) discusses the need for an "atmospheric turn" in architecture and architectural education, focusing on the political dimension of atmospheres. The annual international conference "Atmospheres organized by the Faculty of Architecture, University of Manitoba since 2008 (atmos.ca) and the conference of the Ambiances network (once every 4 years) are important factors in the ongoing discourse. More tightly connected to our acoustic emphasis, the architectural journal OASE published in 2009 an issue on Sound and Architecture, titled "Immersed." The volume examined the auditive dimensions of various cultural practices in space, from the multifarious standpoints of the hearing subject. The *Journal of Architecture* with the issue "Sound Modernities" (2018) brought to the foreground the epistemological dimension of acoustics for the history of modern architecture.

5. Alberto Pérez-Gómez's *Architecture and The Crisis of Modern Science* (1985), Dalibor Vesely's *Architecture in the Age of Divided Representation: The Question of Creativity in the Shadow of Production* (2006), Juhani Pallasmaa's *The Eyes of the Skin, Architecture and the Senses* (2005) and *The Thinking Hand: Existential and Embodied Wisdom in Architecture* (2009), David Letherbarrow's *Architecture Oriented Otherwise* (2008), are only some of the most representative studies on the issue.

6. Christian Borch (ed.), *Architectural Atmospheres: On the Experience and Politics of Architecture* (Basel: Birkhauser, 2014), 15.

7. Gernot Böhme, *Atmospheric Architectures,* 3.

8. Tonino Griffero, *Atmospheres: Aesthetics of Emotional Spaces* (Abingdon Oxfordshire, UK: Routledge, 2016).

9. Bruce Bégout, *Le Concept d'Ambiance* (Paris: Seuil, 2020), 32.

10.   Gernot Böhme, *Atmospheric Architectures,* 76.

11.   Michel Fowler, *Architectures of Sound: Acoustic Concepts and Parameters for Architectural Design* (Basel: Birkhäuser, 2017), 44.

12.   Ibid.

13.   Ibid., 9.

14.   Tonino Griffero, *Atmospheres: Aesthetics of Emotional Spaces,* 36.

15.   By analyzing such diverse soundscapes Schafer offered the first "sonic ecology," appreciating the diversity and aesthetics of natural sounds while almost demonizing the postindustrial sonic pollution. (R. Murray Schafer, *The Soundscape,* 71–102.)

16.   Alain Corbin, *Les Cloches de la Terre. Paysage sonore et culture sensible dans les campagnes aux XIX siècle* (Paris: Albin Michel, 1994).

17.   Emily Thomsphon, *The Soundscape of Modernity. Architectural Acoustics and the Culture of Listening in America, 1900–1933* (Cambridge, Mass: The MIT Press, 2002).

18.   For more see: Bissera V. Pentcheva, *Hagia Sophia: Sound, Space, and Spirit in Byzantium,* (University Park, PA: Penn State University Press, 2017); Howard Deborah and Laura Moretti, *Sound and Space in Rennaissance Venice: Architecture, Music, Acoustics* (New Heaven: Yale University Press, 2009); Niall Atkinson, *The Noisy Renaissance Sound, Architecture, and Florentine Urban Life,* (University Park, PA: Penn State University Press, 2016).

19.   Barry Blesser, Linda-Ruth Salter, *Spaces Speak, Are You Listening? Experiencing Aural Architecture,* (Cambridge, Mass: The MIT Press, 2006).

20.   Martin Heidegger, *Time and Being,* trans. Joan Stambaugh, red. ed. (Albany, N.Y.: State University of New York Press, 2010), 26–37.

21.   Richard E. Palmer, *Hermeneutics, Interpretation Theory in Schleiermacher, Dilthey, Heidegger, and Gadamer* (Evanston, IL: Northwestern University Press, 1969), 46.

22.   Richard Kearney and Brian Treanor (eds.), *Carnal Herrmeneutics* (New York: Fordham University Press, 2015), 27.

23.   Ibid.

24.   Examples of designing and staging events that can affect massively emotions and opinions can be recounted in Hittler's reflections on mass propaganda or the first celebration of Fete de la Féderation in Paris where spectacles directed the attention of the crowds. [Christian Borch, "The Politics of Atmospheres: Architecture, Power and the Senses," in Christian Borch (ed.), *Architectural Atmospheres,* 73–77.]

25.   Ibid., 80–82.

_____

Room Vibrations

02.

Listening with Christian Norberg-Schulz: Sonic Experience and Music Theory in his Writings

Anna Ulrikke Andersen

'Before I die, I *must* write a book on music!'[1] the Norwegian architectural theorist Christian Norberg-Schulz once told his daughter Elizabeth Norberg-Schulz, a renowned soprano and professor of music. Although this wish was expressed towards the end of his life, his keen interest in music could be traced back to his youth. Growing up he wanted to pursue a career in music and he was also a talented pianist. According to his daughter though he never managed to express himself fully through the instrument, and his technical skills were simply not good enough to excel as a pianist, his daughter explained.[2] At the age of 19 years old he decided instead to study architecture. His true talents lay in the writing, thinking and teaching of architectural history and theory.

Norberg-Schulz never wrote that book on music but when he died in 2000, he left behind an impressive oeuvre of books, articles, essays, book chapters and edited volumes on architecture, place and urban planning. Whereas his book *Intentions in Architecture* (1963) awarded him a role within the international scene of architectural theory, it is *Genius Loci: Towards a Phenomenology of Architecture* (1980) that is considered to be his landmark treatise. In this book, first published in Italian in 1979, he develops Martin Heidegger's phenomenology into the field of architecture. He builds upon Heidegger's understanding of *Dasein*—being-in-the-world—to explain how our being is formed in relation with a surrounding world.[3] Norberg-Schulz discusses the phenomenon of place, which he defines through its character, structure and spirit, and argues that the architect should incorporate this into the design process. Vital to his thesis is the concept of dwelling: that certain architectures allow for dwelling while other buildings or places do not. "The place is a concrete manifestation of man's dwelling, and his identity depends on his belonging to places,"[4] he argues. Thus, it is paramount for the architect to design in a way that manifests dwelling. Norberg-Schulz exhibits his argument through three case studies, the cities of Prague, Karthoum and Rome, outlining how each place and their architecture express the *genius loci*. He demonstrates how the character, structure and spirit of these cities are specific to each place, and offers examples of architecture and city planning which allow for dwelling.

Although the literature discussing Norberg Schulz's take on Heidegger's phenomenology and his concept of place is rich,[5] little attention has been awarded to his interest in music. I have previously argued that sound and music do play a role in Norberg-Schulz's theory of place, particularly evident in his suggestions for the soundtrack of the TV documentary *Livet finner sted* (1992) which portrays his life and work.[6] Expanding upon these findings, this chapter tackles the theme of sound and music by focusing on the sonic environments in which he worked and lived when he was writing *Genius Loci*. My approach is inspired by architectural historians such as Adam Sharr, Diana Fuss and Jane Rendell, whose focus on the specific rooms where the thinking took place, links environments with the work of the thinker who inhabits or inhabited these spaces, such as Heidegger, Sigmund Freud or the author herself, as in the work of Rendell.[7] Taking aboard Gernot Böhme's attention to the sonic aspects of architecture and place, as articulated in *Atmospheric Architectures: The Aesthetics of Felt Spaces* (2017), this article moves through a series of sonic atmospheres, both exterior and interior ones, demonstrating how they influenced Norberg-Schulz's writings. Unpacking these sonic environments sheds new light on Norberg-Schulz's theoretical writings on sound and music. Allowing itself to be speculative, at times, this chapter considers these sonic environments as seen in the context of his theory of architecture and place. What role does sound and music play in both conceiving the notion of *genius loci* and explaining it in his writings? When listening with Norberg-Schulz, what room vibrations comes forth?

The Sounds Surrounding Home: From Snow and Church Bells to Site-specific Music

Where did Norberg-Schulz write his book *Genius Loci*? The answer is not necessarily straight forward. The actual process of researching and developing his thinking was a process that involved extensive travelling. In order to be able to describe the spirit of *one* place, Norberg-Schulz had to have other places to compare it with, and travelling became key to his process. His first international journey out of Oslo took place in 1945 as he moved to Switzerland to study architecture. He lived in Zürich until 1949, and in the next decades he moved frequently, and lived in Norway, USA, Italy and Germany. The period 1973-74 he was based in Rome, as part of a research stay related to *genius loci*.[8] His travel journal from that year shows how much he traveled in Europe, the Middle East and the USA. His entries include his observations, highlighting the importance of experiencing place first hand.[9]

The photographs he took during his travels made it into his books and articles, illustrating his many international examples. Whereas the photographs in *Genius Loci* show architecture, place, and landscapes from Italy, Jordan, USA or Sudan, the very first photograph of the book shows the view from inside his own house at Ris in Oslo.[10] In this photograph, located on the page seven of the book,[11] the window sills are clearly visible, behind which appears a winter landscape covered in snow along with Ris Church, erected between 1919-32 and designed in Romanesque revival style by the architect Carl Berner. Norberg-Schulz discusses this view in reference to the German poet George Trakl's poem "A Winter Evening," where the poet describes concrete phenomena such as windows and snow to say something more profound about belonging and place.[12] "A winter evening…is something more than a point in the calendar,"[13] Norberg-Schulz writes. "As a concrete presence it is experienced as a set of particular qualities, or in general as a *Stimmung* or 'character' which forms the background to acts and occurrences."[14]

Although the theory articulated in *Genius Loci* (1980) was very much formed on the move, I wish to speculate how the view out of this particular window, with its specific qualities, character and *Stimmung* did play an important role in the theorist's writing process. What were the spatial preconditions of his working environment? A map from the Oslo City Archive dating 1974, offers a clear idea of what this view was when he came back to Oslo in the summer of the same year, after his research stay in Rome (Figure 1). The house where Norberg-Schulz lived, a large 1926 villa, is marked with the number 100, colored yellow because it was built in wood, whereas the church, *Ris Kirke,* is colored in orange signalling a concrete or brick structure, here visible in a darker shade of gray. Above the church, another orange building is marked *Helsestasjon.* This was the local health centre. The tramline, is marked with double lines and passes closely by both the villa and the health centre, while beyond the tramline the main road *Slemdalsveien* runs parallel to the railway tracks.

The atmosphere outside Norberg-Schulz's window, was that of a quiet suburb. The tram line would have been as distinctly audible from the villa in the 1970s, as it is still these days, something that my recent visits to the area has confirmed.[15] Passing by at regular intervals, the proximity between the villa, the tramline and tram stop cannot be overlooked. The sound of the tram carriages passing on the railway, squeaking as the operator steps at the breaks to slow down for passengers at Ris, must had become part of the everyday acoustic atmosphere for the inhabitants in the area. Cars passing on the main road would have been audible from the villa, but there would not have been that many in the mid 1970s. Another regular sonic event would

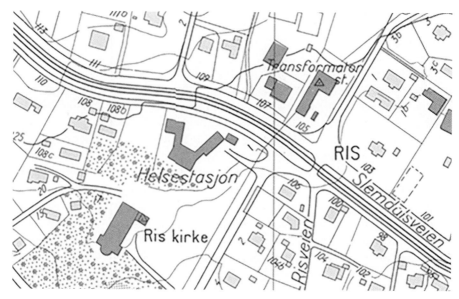

Figure 1: Map of Smedstad –Vindern, 1974. Oslo oppmålingsvesen og Aker oppmålingsvesen.

have been the church bells ringing from the clocktower of Ris church. The largest bell weights 1746kg and is tuned in D♯, a smaller bell weighing 892kg is tuned in F♯, and an even smaller bell of 550kg is tuned in A♯.[16] Together these bells would form a D♯ minor chord, creating a dark and melancholic reverberation in the air. In the winter this sound would have traveled freely through the naked trees, carried over by the snow-covered landscape and the cold winter winds characteristic of Oslo.

Describing the Norwegian *genius loci* Norberg-Schulz writes: "Nordic man has to be friend with fog, ice, and cold winds; he has to enjoy the creaking sound of snow under the feet when he walks around, he has to experience the poetic value of being immersed in fog."[17] A similar statement occurs in the TV documentary *Livet finner sted*: "One cannot live in Norway without being friends with the snow, without enjoying skiing, or liking the sound of snow squeaking under one's feet."[18] The sound of walking on cold, packed snow, thus, influences his understanding of *genius loci*. Yet, his writing did not take place outdoors in the cold. Although thinking might have taken place on the move, walking across the cold snow-covered pavements or skiing in the nearby woodlands, his typing occurred by the window. The theorist included a photograph of a winter evening in his book, and according to his writing outlined above, a winter evening was not merely an experience of temperature, eye sight or touch: sound was also involved. The sonic environment that Norberg-Schulz observed beyond the window pane enriches the elements that constitute *genius loci* in the theoretician's thinking, foregrounding sound as vital in the argument on belonging, place and the relationship between being and worlds.

These site-specific sounds and acoustic atmospheres, might have further influenced the theoretician's thinking, inspiring him to look into place-specific compositions when trying to grasp the particularities of a given place. In *Nightlands: Nordic Building* (1996) for example, Norberg-Schulz aims to describe and discuss the specificities of Nordic building practices and the specific atmosphere of Nordic countries. He references the Finish composer Jean Sibelius and the Finish national epic *Kalevala* first published in 1835. With a distinct rhythm and musicality, the poem reveals a series of myths, involving exciting battles and challenging quests. Norberg-Schulz writes: "Here are interwoven natural forces, divine manifestation, and the role of humans in a total, functioning world-picture that gave upon its publication in the 19th Century, an entire people an understanding of their identity."[19] The poem is considered as related to a Finish national identity, and the formation of this identity thereof.

Yet Norberg-Schulz's interest in the epic poem considers the human being in relation to the world, a central trait of phenomenology. He refers to a specific section of the poem, where the first man, Väinämöinen, is comparing his strength to the much younger Joukahainen. Challenged to describe his surroundings, the rather rationalist Joukahainen explains how the water springs from the rock, or copper is to be found in the hills. Yet, Väinämöinen shows his strength in a different and more profound manner. Instead of describing the functions of things, he *sings* the earth, rocks and mountains. With his song he engages the world around him so strongly and effectively that earth, rocks and mountains start trembling and swallow Joukahainen who must beg for his life.[20] "As Väinämöinen sang the world, it achieved immediate presence, and logical order ended up in the swamp,"[21] argues Norberg-Schulz. Here, it is song that truly engages and resonates with the world, not rationalist description.

To Norberg-Schulz, Sibelius "realizes life and natural forces in sound."[22] With this, he means that Sibelius not only was inspired by *Kalevala*, but that his music embodies the same attention to being and place as expressed in the epos. The specific spatial structures described in *Kalevala*—earth, rocks or mountains—correspond to musical forms in Sibelius' work:

> Sibelius's characters remain undisclosed, fragments emerge and withdraw, scraps of 'something' comes to light and dissolve again. What is primary is mood as rhythm (Third Symphony), or as atmosphere (*Tapiola*). And even though characters remain hidden, they are nonetheless expressed as beings, for it is only that which *is* that may hide itself.[23]

For the theoretician the fragmented and undisclosed elements of music, evident in Sibelius' *Symphony No.3* (1907) and *Tapioloa* (1926), correspond with a form of being

in Nordic landscapes. Being in a Nordic world can similarly be marked by fragmenta-
tion and lack of disclosure. To Norberg-Schulz thus, this specific site-inspired music,
has the capacity to "express the Nordic world."[24] This suggests that music influenced
Norberg-Schulz's vision on the *genius loci* of Norway.

The Sounds of Home: From the Grand Piano and the Record Player to "Frozen Music"

Norberg-Schulz's process of writing, did, however, take place indoors. When the family first moved into the house at Ris, the daughter, Elizabeth Norberg-Schulz, describes how her father used to work from the living room, while she was playing the
piano or her younger brother was drawing besides him.[25] She recalls:

> We had a grand piano in the living room. I began playing the piano when I was
> ten, eleven years old. I would sit and rehearse, and play exercises for an hour a
> day. I played scales and simple pieces. I sat there and played, and [next to me]
> was my father's desk, where he sat and wrote his influential books. But he always
> paid attention to the music that I played. 'Ah! That was not good – repeat that
> exercise!' he would say.[26]

Although immersed in his work, Norberg-Schulz would still comment on his daughter's technique and offer his advice. The space for writing was placed in the midst of
the family life, and his work routine was accompanied by the music coming from the
grand piano as his daughter played.

Ground plans kept in the *Oslo Plan- og Bygningsetat* [Oslo Agency for Planning and
Building Services] show the original planning application for the villa, as submitted
on June 4, 1926 by Johan Hansen, Henny Hansen and Birger Hansen, presumably
the family who had the villa designed, planned and built.[27] A ground plan from a later
date, 13 October 1926 shows the original plans with the heating system included.
The first floor consists of a large hall, kitchen, dining room, and a living room large
enough to indeed house a grand piano, heating coming from the radiators below the
windows on cold winter nights. It is not far-fetched to imagine that the music coming
from the piano would resonate with the wooden structure. Doors could be opened
to the hall and dining room which would have allowed the music to also resonate
throughout the house, up the wooden staircase to the second floor (Figure 2).

After the eldest son Erik moved out, his bedroom in the second floor was transformed into a small library and study for Norberg-Schulz. This must have happened
around 1974, when Erik turned 19 and Norberg-Schulz returned to Norway after his
stay in Rome. "He had a small library and a desk in front of a window overlooking Ris.

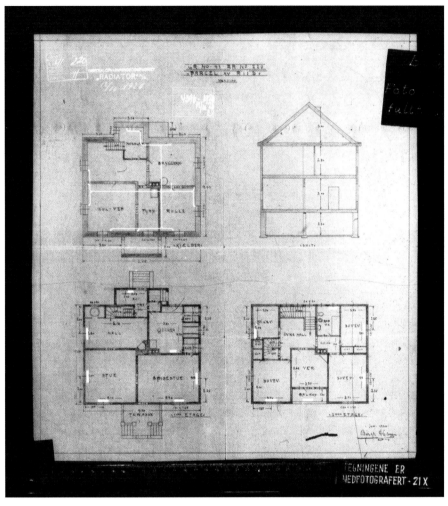

Figure 2: Norberg-Schulz's former home, built in 1926. 192600551. Oslo Agency for Planning and Building Services.

He could see the trees and the skies. But he wrote from home, constantly listening to music,"[28] Elizabeth Norberg-Schulz recalls. She remembers how music flowed from her father's workspace. If she knocked on his door to ask for help with her homework, he would ask her to name the composer before offering his help. She remembers standing in the hallway, listening to the music coming from his office, trying to remember the name of the composer in question before she knocked. "He was a good teacher. He

taught me to listen. And I started to recognise Mozart. This must be Mozart! This must
be Stravinsky! This must be Bach! This must be Brüchner!"[29] she explains.

Norberg-Schulz listened to most classical composers: "everything from Stravinsky, to Schönberg, and Mozart."[30] Elizabeth Norberg-Schulz specifically remembers
her father listening to Igor Stravinsky's *Petrushka* (1910-11) and explains how he introduced her to Arnold Schönberg's *Gürrelieder* (1900-03). Coming from the grand piano
or his record player, classical music filled the rooms in which he wrote.

Classical music filled also many of the pages he wrote. Richard Wagner's *Tristan
and Isolde* (1859) for example plays an integral role in Norberg-Schulz's article
"Frossen musikk" [Frozen Music] (1996;1997), an article that was published twice
in its original Norwegian, but has never been translated to English.[31] Here, Norberg-
Schulz begins by referring to a long tradition of architects, philosophers and poets,
from Plutarch, to Schelling and Goethe, who have described architecture as frozen
music. But where these authors use this concept in passing, Norberg-Schulz wishes to
delve more deeply into the issue and asks how a theory of architecture and a theory
of music might inform each other.

In his article, Norberg-Schulz outlines a set of principles taken from music theory,
arguing that the basic principles of architecture could be compared to certain basic
principles of music. This is evident in the way different tones relate to each other. He
outlines how western music is based upon a system of scales consisting of seven tones.
Each scale has a tone that functions as the root and each of the other tones stands in a
specific relationship to this root. The most prominent relationship is between the root
and the fifth note, as well as the root and the seventh. The fifth and the seventh lead to
the root, and if left unresolved produce sense of longing. A scale using all twelve tones,
instead of the seven, is called the chromatic scale. Here the relationship between
the intervals can create dissonance also creating a sense of longing. In the opening
of *Tristan and Isolde* (1859), Wagner includes a dissonant chord based on this theory,
which creates this effect of longing and that which is unresolved, suitable to the opera's thematic of impossible love. Schönberg later became widely known for utilising
all twelve tones of the scale in his compositions such as *Erwartung* (1909). In his article
Norberg-Schulz describes the earlier *Gurrelieder* (1900-03) from Schönberg's romantic period, as an early example of the intensity that can be expressed in the chords,
and how the relationship between tones creates a sense of a whole.

Norberg-Schulz compares the relationship between notes in Wagner's opera and
the upwards and downwards movements in music to the vertical dimensions of a
building. In Norberg-Schulz's writings, the horizontal and vertical aspects of architecture is a common theme. Building upon Heidegger's phenomenology, he understood
horizontality linked with earth and sky, with architectural and human beings standing
in between vertically. In fact, the only version of *Genius Loci* published in Norwegian
in 1978 was titled *Mellom jord og himmel* which translates to: Between Earth and Sky.[32]

In the article "Frozen Music" (1996;1997) the resemblance between the structures of architecture and that of music are even more explicitly linked. Rhythm and melody in music, are compared with *omriss* [outline] and *oppriss* [elevation] in architecture.[33] The elevation rises vertically comparable to a melody, whereas the outline of a building can express playful rhythms. The way the music rises and the intervals relate to each other, are, according to Norberg-Schulz, relatable to the architectural elements base, column and cornice. A chord—such as D♯ minor—consists of a root, a third and a fifth. A D♯, F♯ and A♯ form a triad that sounds together as a whole: D♯ minor. The combination of architectural elements—such as base, column and cornice—are, in Norberg-Sculz's article, comparable with the combination of notes into an accord, where different combinations create different wholes. He writes:

> Both in its origin and its historical manifestations, music and architecture 'mirrors' each other. When architecture is closer to music than painting and sculpture, it is because our relationship to both artforms is 'within' the event. We never stand *before* a piece of music, and we are always surrounded by an architectonic whole, even when standing 'before' a facade. 'The whole' reminds the keyword, which means that music and architecture disseminate a *whole* world that we stand within.[34]

Both architecture and music create a whole that we can inhabit, which must be experienced.[35] In Norberg-Schulz's writing, a theory of music offers a way to understand the way different parts in architecture create a whole, and how this world can be inhabited. Understanding architecture in relation to a whole is a central theme in *Genius Loci* (1980), particularly evident in Norberg-Schulz's chapter on Rome. He describes how the eternal city itself consists of a number of buildings, sites, streets, *piazzas,* as well as larger structures in the landscapes such as the Roman *campagna* surrounding the city. These parts create a greater whole: the spirit of the place.[36] These ideas are above all most evident when Norberg-Schulz discusses the Roman *piazza*. About *Piazza Navona* in Rome, he writes:

> At Piazza Navona we are really "inside", close to the earth, close to the palpable things of everyday existence, at the same time as we feel ward of a comprehensive cultural totality. No wonder that it has become the popular place of Rome *par excellence.* The synthesis of nature and culture is condensed and visualized in Bernini's great fountain, where natural elements such as water and rocks are combined with human figures and religious symbols, as well as the *axis mundi* of the obelisk.[37]

Here Norberg-Schulz argues how the spirit of the place consists of a cultural totality, in close contact with natural and man-made structures. Here, one is "inside" and close to earth, whereas the obelisk rises tall, vertically and up towards the sky.

His chapter on Prague conveys similar ideas. He writes: "We may very well say that the inhabitants of Bohemia loved the *genius loci*; the country was theirs because they identified with its qualities. Their love has been expressed in literature and music and not least in building."[38] Thus, Norberg-Schulz argues that the spirit of the place is expressed through music, and in the context of Prague, this spirit of the place is characterised by "an expressive interplay of horizontal and vertical 'forces.'"[39] He believes that these forces are evident in Peter Parler's design for *St. Vitus Cathedral* in Prague, where a contrast can be identified between "the 'massive' arcade and the dematerialized upper wall and vault."[40] Norberg-Schulz highlights more examples in Prague where the horizontal and vertical interplay in architecture are evident and discusses them in reference to similar structures in music.

Conclusion

In his book *Acoustic Atmospheres* Böhme encourages the reader to "ask which acoustic characters the spaces we live in should have,"[41] emphasising the importance of sound, music and voice in our experience of place and its atmosphere. In relation to Norberg-Schulz's *Genius Loci* (1980), I attempted to answer this question by "listening" to the specific sounds and music that created the acoustic environment inside and outside his writing room, albeit a symphony by Sibelius, or the sound of cold snow under one's feet while walking. When listening with Norberg-Schulz, I allow myself to speculate and bring my own experiences into the discussion, in order to unpack both the writing process and Norberg-Schulz's theorical oeuvre in relation to the acoustic atmosphere of his rooms and the near surroundings. I imagine how the writing process could be related to specific music and acoustic atmospheres outside and inside the place of writing. By related I mean, how these atmospheres could affect his descriptions or provide an example for his writings while trying to prove an argument. Atmospheres and *genius loci* are anyhow more tangibly understood through examples, although in essence felt and experienced rather than reduced to mere descriptions. In this way, the characteristics of the rooms in which he wrote, seem attuned to what he writes and argues. And here sound, plays an integral role, both in his own experience of dwelling, and how he suggested others—architects included—could approach and understand dwelling. Analysis of place-specific musical compositions and theory of classical music gave him elements to build his own theory of architecture. From the ideal dimensions of buildings, connecting them with the rhythm and the melody of music, to experiencing architecture as a whole, in the same way we do when immersed into listening a music symphony, Norberg-Schulz continues the long tradition of western architectural theory related to music.

Today, most readers might encounter the photograph at page 7 of *Genius Loci* at the library. The book is out of print, and second-hand copies are expensive. Most library copies can only be looked at in the library, or taken home on short loan. Like my first encounter with Norberg-Schulz's book—that was before I invested in an expensive hardcopy—most readers will open the book sat at a desk, or between the shelves of a quiet university library. Looking at the photograph nowadays is a rather silent experience. As the reader's eyes are drawn towards the snow-covered landscape, a photograph captured from a room in which the theorist wrote, the typing by other students, or the occasional shuffling of papers or photocopier, might softly break the silence. But this chapter encourages the reader to listen with Norberg-Schulz, imagine, speculate, and look for the references to music and sound. What comes forth is a series of sonic environments that are of relevance for the architect reading Norberg-Schulz's theory. When Norberg-Schulz discusses music or draws upon music theory, it is to say something about architecture. Elizabeth Norberg-Schulz explains: "He loved music… He found music to be the highest mode of expression. It is a mode of expression that does not need word."[42] This aspect of his theory, which has so far been overlooked by scholars, is what I wish to make resonant.

Notes

1. Elizabeth Norberg-Schulz (daughter of Christian Norberg-Schulz), interview and translation by Anna Ulrikke Andersen, Rome, September 2014.

2. Elizabeth Norberg-Schulz (daughter of Christian Norberg-Schulz), interview and translation by Anna Ulrikke Andersen, Rome, September 2014.

3. Christian Norberg-Schulz, *Genius Loci: Towards a Phenomenology of Architecture* (London: Academy Editions, 1980). Firstly published in Italian *Genius Loci: Paesaggio, Ambiente, Architettura* (Milan: Electa editrice, 1979).

4. Ibid., 6.

5. See: Mari Hvattum et.al. eds, *An Eye for Place: Christian Norberg-Schulz: Architect, Historian and Editor* (Oslo: Akademisk publisering, 2009); Jorge Otero-Pailos, *Architecture's Historical Turn: Phenomenology and the Rise of the Postmodern.* (Minneapolis; London: University of Minnesota Press, 2010); Hilde Heynen, *Architecture and Modernity: A Critique* (Cambridge, Mass: MIT, 1999); Rowan Wilken, "The Critical Reception of Christian Norberg-Schulz's Writings on Heidegger and Place" in *Architectural Theory Review,* 18: 3 (December 2013) 340–55.

6. Anna Ulrikke Andersen, "The Death of the Chemist: the role of sound in the life and work of Christian Norberg-Schulz explored through the essay form in film and writing" in *InForma Journal,* 12 (2019)176–187.

7.   Diana Fuss, *The Sense of an Interior: Four Writers and the Rooms That Shaped Them* (New York; London: Routledge, 2004); Jane Rendell, *The Architecture of Psychoanalysis: Spaces of Transition* (London: IBTauris, 2017); Adam Sharr, *Heidegger's Hut* (Cambridge, Mass: MIT Press, 2006).

8.   Christian Norberg-Schulz, CV. Box: Diverse uregistrerte fra den sorte pulten. The Norberg Schulz Archive, The Architectural Collections, The National Museum of Art, Architecture and Design, Oslo.

9.   Christian Norberg-Schulz, Travel Journal, Box: 2002:15 Arkivstykke 2F notatbøker/ notater, The Christian Norberg-Schulz Archive, The Architectural Collections, The National Museum of Art, Architecture and Design, Oslo.

10.   This photograph is included in an article by Jorge Otero-Pailos from 2006. The article discusses the relationship between Norberg-Schulz's design in an earlier home, Planetveien 14, and his theoretical authorship with an emphasis on his book *Intentions in Architecture* (1963). The rooms and villa at Ris, is only discussed in a caption to the illustrations. Jorge Otero-Pailos, "Norberg-Schulz' hus: en modern søken etter hjemmets visuelle mønstre» in *Arkitektur-N* (21 February 2017) https://arkitektur-n.no/artikler/norberg-schulz-hus. Accessed 23 September 2020. First published in *Arkitektur-N,* 7 (2006).

11.   Norberg-Schulz, *Genius Loci,* 7.

12.   Ibid., 8.

13.   Ibid.

14.   Ibid.

15.   Visit to Risveien 2, 7 september 2014.

16.   Jan Høeg and Ola Rypdal, *Ris kirke 1932–2007* (Oslo: Ris Menighetsråd, 2007) 9.

17.   Ibid., 21.

18.   "Opplevelsen på toget lærte meg at det vi er, er det vi er blitt kjent med fra barnsbena. Vi Nordmenn er den tette skogen og den myke skogbunnen. Derfor skifter alltid folkearkitekturen uttrykk, selv om funksjonen er den samme. For det å bo betyr å respektere omgivelsene. En kan ikke bo i Norge uten å være venner med sneen. Uten å like å gå på ski, eller like lyden av snøen som knirker under føttene." My translation, *Livet finner sted,* Sven Erik Helgesen, 1992. 10:38-11:19. https://tv.nrk.no/program/ FKUR30002291

19.   Christian Norberg-Schulz, *Nightlands: Nordic Building,* Translated by Thomas McQuillan (Cambridge, Mass; London: MIT Press, 1996) 9.

20.   Ibid., 10.

21.   Ibid.

22.   Ibid., 11.

23.   Ibid.

24.   Ibid.

25.   Elizabeth Norberg-Schulz (daughter of Christian Norberg-Schulz), interview and translation by Anna Ulrikke Andersen, Rome, September 2014.

26.   Ibid.

27.   Planning application dated 4 June 1926 by Johan Hansen, Henny Hansen and Birger Hansen. Kept in the Oslo Agency for Planning and Building Services.

28.   Ibid.

29.   Ibid.

30.   Ibid.

31.   Christian Norberg-Schulz, "Frossen musikk," in *Christian Norberg-Schulz: Et Festskrift På 70års Dagen*, eds. Guttorm Fløistad, Thomas Thiis-Evensen, and Kjetil Moe, 8–15 (Oslo: Norsk arkitekturforlag, 1996); Christian Norberg-Schulz, "Frossen musikk," *Øye og Hånd: essays og artikler*, ed. Gordon Hølmebakk, 40–48 (Oslo: Gyldendal, 1997).

32.   Christian Norberg-Schulz, *Mellom jord og himmel: en bok om steder og hus* (Oslo: Universitetsforlaget, 1978).

33.   Norberg-Schulz, "Frossen musikk," 43.

34.   "Musikken og arkitekturen både i sin opprinnelse og sine historiske manifestasjoner «speiler» hverandre. Når arkitekturen står musikken nærmere enn maleri og skulptur gjør, er det fordi vi i vårt forhold til begge kunstarter er «i» det som skjer. Vi står aldri *overfor* er musikkstykke, og vi er alltid omsluttet av den arkitektoniske helheten, selv når vi står «foran» en fasade. «Helhet» er nøkkelordet, og det innebar at musikk og arkitektur formilder en *hel* verden som vi altså er «i»". My translation, Ibid., 44.

35.   Ibid., 44.

36.   Norberg-Schulz. *Genius Loci,* 140–142.

37.   Ibid., 164.

38.   Ibid., 105.

39.   Ibid., 103.

40.   Ibid.

41.   Gernot Böhme, *Atmospheric Architectures: The Aesthetics of Felt Space,* edited and translated by A.-Chr. Engels-Schwarzpaul (London: Bloomsbury Press, 2017) 134.

42.   Elizabeth Norberg-Schulz (daughter of Christian Norberg-Schulz), interview and translation by Anna Ulrikke Andersen, place, June 2014.

03.

Setting the Tone in Early 20th-century North American Living Rooms: The Parlor Piano

Michael Windover and James Deaville

A 1913 photograph of a living room in Toronto provides at once an idiosyncratically decorated room and a representation of some of the complexities of early 20th-century modernity (Figure 1). The photograph was taken by the F.W. Micklethwaite's Studio for Consumers' Gas Company Ltd., ostensibly to illustrate the uses of natural gas at a time when hydro-electric power offered competing services for homes in the city. The living room in fact displays both forms of power. An electric lamp sitting next to an overstuffed sofa in front of a light-filled window complements gas-fueled illumination from a series of wall sconces and an inverted onion-domed ceiling fixture. The presence of a gas-fueled hot water radiator and gas radiant fire suggests the source of warmth required for the cozy atmosphere of this middle-class living room. The fire was no doubt meant to be the focus for Consumers' Gas Company. It presents a view of a negotiated modernity, one that references tradition in the form of the mantel-piece yet at the same time technological innovation.

Interestingly, the focal point of this modern living room is framed by music. The perspectival lines of the upright piano and bench direct the viewer's eye to the gas fire, which is accompanied on the left by a banjo that leans against the fireplace surround. On one hand, the presence of traditional musical instruments in this carefully staged room—alongside the arrangement of furniture, the prints and photographs hung on the wall and display of porcelain and small sculpture, not to mention the leopard skin rug—demonstrate the owners' artistic inclinations and desire to project a sense of worldliness.[1] On the other, the presence of the instruments suggests the importance of music to the spatial experience of the living room.

Like the gas- and electric-fueled fixtures in the room, the instruments point to an invisible source of energy in the still photograph: the presence of music in creating domestic atmosphere. And like the fixtures and modern utilities feeding them, the

Figure 1: Living room with gas radiant fire, hot water radiator, gas and electric lighting, leopard skin rug and piano. F.W. Micklethwaite's Studio, 1913. City of Toronto Archives, Fonds 1034, Item 887. Public Domain.

piano in the early 20th Century represented an important part of the modern parlor or living room. In the popular imagination, the parlor piano signified particular notions of domesticity associated with culturation and work ethic, tinged with Victorian moralism,[2] as well as emotional warmth. While these associations link the piano to the 19th Century, its wide availability amongst middle classes was a 20th-century phenomenon. Its mechanization in the form of player pianos and reproducing pianos was a development that altered the use and meaning of the instrument in North American homes.[3] As historian Peter Ward reminds us, "[a]s a symbol and physical object, the hearth and the piano reached the peak of their domestic influence during the first half of the twentieth century"[4] in Canada, despite the advent of central heating systems and availability of mechanically reproduced or broadcasted music. This is confirmed by the numbers of pianos manufactured: production reached a high point around the year 1909, with over 350,000 instruments made in the United States,[5] which followed continuous growth over the prior 50 years and mirrored a similar arc of rise and decline in production in Canada.[6] Given the similarity of these national trends in both the United States and Canada, we believe that general conclusions can be drawn across continent about the cultural discourse around the place and potency of the parlor piano, at least for English readers. Indeed, based on these statistics, in the early 20th Century, the piano was increasingly a visually and spatially structural element of many living rooms. It took pride of place as an expensive piece of furniture and showcase of owners' interests and sense of cultural taste, yet was an everyday object that had the power to change the mood of space (e.g., contemplative, boisterous, monotonous).

While media, design and architectural historians have begun to reconcile the acoustic, spatial, and decorative place of other 20th-century technologies—including the phonograph, the radio, the television and high-fidelity stereo system[7]—the piano's place in spatial practices of domesticity and its role in creating atmosphere in living rooms have been overlooked. This chapter redresses this omission by introducing the historical record and aesthetic context for the domestic piano in North America during the late Victorian and Edwardian Eras. In particular, we draw from texts, advertisements, and music published mainly in Eastern United States but circulating broadly across the continent. While regional and local variations and examples exist, our chapter offers observations based primarily on these widely available pieces. We understand the piano in the home as a site for the intersection of place, sound and people, occupying and animating a physical space for social interaction. Underscoring this confluence is the recognition that the piano serves as more than an inert furnishing; rather, it is an active agent in shaping the domestic space and the atmosphere of the parlor.

Our investigation first presents general considerations about how the instrument mediated atmosphere within the domestic space of the North American parlor (or living room) of the late 19th and early 20th Centuries.[8] We then turn to two contemporary interior design publications—separated by twenty years—that provided homeowners with advice regarding both the domestic piano's placement as an object of material culture and its role in creating social space within the home. To obtain a better understanding of the ambiences generated by the play of the domestic piano, we next consider the range of human emotions and spatial atmospheres the instrument evoked as represented in the era's popular novels and advertisements. Since it is music that produces the tone of the room where the piano resides, we explore in closing the repertoire and audience of so-called 'parlor music,' which (re-)creates the descriptive and affective world of its middle-class players. By exploring such wide-ranging sources, our chapter underlines the important place of the piano in middle-class culture generally. So affective was the piano in the early 20th Century, that its atmospheres extended beyond its spatial enclosure into the larger, cultural imagination.

The Presence of the Piano

The very presence of a piano in a middle-class parlor or living room affected the room's atmosphere. Like the fireplace, with its decorative mantle, the piano offered a site of cultural display and the potential to change the sensorial qualities of the room. Indeed, when arrayed with personal objects or open sheet music, the instrument could be a vehicle for the projection of personality. For some, the piano case itself was a site of artistic intervention, and its design or ornamental embellishments resonated visually with its room's *décor*.[9] However, for most middle-class piano owners the instrument—typically a less expensive upright model—was fitted into a living room. Given its scale (and expense), the piano commanded attention as a substantial piece of furniture and as an instrument, whose use could alter the character of the surrounding space. The room could become a place of cultural work or tedium (practicing, music lessons), a ritual site of family or community performance (as solo or accompaniment), or a space for informal entertainment (singalong, dancing).

Interior decoration advice literature, which blossomed in the early 20th Century alongside home economics movements and increased consumerism, provides some evidence of how the piano's presence was negotiated. Lillie Hamilton French's *Homes and their Decoration* (1903) reveals the tension between piano as aesthetic object and as instrument.[10] She notes that pianos have sometimes been used simply as stage props, left open with "a few sheets of music spread carelessly" to give the impression of activity and cultural work.[11] In opposition to this pretentious practice, she advises readers to design more around utility, outlining a balanced composition for a parlor. She proposes grouping furniture in front of the fireplace, with sofas in three of the room's corners to allow for other activities, such as reading, writing, and sewing, in addition to piano playing (Figure 2).[12] As is clear from the illustrations, her arrangements relied upon the rectilinear lines and compactness of the upright piano, as compared to the dominating size and curvilinear shape of the grand models that would have demanded a more central position and disrupted the room's harmony of compact zones of activity.

Later in the book, she discusses the practical and social reasons for situating a piano at right angles to a corner with keys concealed. In this way, the piano is provided with illumination from a window behind it, while the player is protected from view. She argues that in contrast to public performances of virtuosos, "in everyday houses and lives, music is for the entertainment of a family circle, and but small contributions to that entertainment are made by a view of a timid or embarrassed player."[13] She goes on to note that "there is always a little touch of mystery and sentiment lent to a player concealed behind the keys."[14] In this text, then, French offers evidence of how pianos were thought of in interior design schemes, points to distinct uses of domestic

Figure 2: Floor plan sketch, Lillie Hamilton French, *Homes and their Decoration* (New York: Dodd, Mead and Company, 1903), 197. Public Domain.

pianos (as opposed to public performances) and hints at how the instrument affects domestic atmosphere, adding an element "of mystery and sentiment."

Two decades later, pianos remained of interest to interior decorators. For instance, Emily Burbank calls for small groupings around the piano "to indicate that if some one is good enough to play, some one else is courteous enough to listen!"[15] In an explicit discussion of atmosphere, Burbank underlines the importance of the piano for music lovers: "If you are really a lover of music a piano is as much a part of your home as your desk is a natural feature in your sitting-room."[16] Rooms—including a living room with a piano—should express "the tastes of the family" and this "is how you make 'atmosphere.'" This approach to decorating and understanding consumer goods (including pianos) as expressive of personality, according to historian Karen Halttunen, supplanted the Victorian idea of rooms expressing character in the United States, and we are reminded of the power of the object itself to affect the mood of the room.[17] Later, Burbank evokes the creation of atmosphere for "A Room for the Amusement of Young People" (Figure 3):

> In thinking of this room one recalls an impression of space; a hardwood floor with rugs small enough to be easily taken up for the dancing; an open fire; a piano with songs on the rack; bright lights, plenty of them, with dainty pink shades […];

A ROOM FOR THE AMUSEMENT OF YOUNG PEOPLE IN A SMALL HOUSE

Figure 3: F. J. Kegel, "A Room for the Amusement of Young People in a Small House," Plate VII from Emily Burbank, *Be Your Own Decorator* (New York: Dodd, Mead and Company, 1923). Public Domain.

comfy chairs and one big sofa before the fire. […] Here [young people] could dance, sing, play bridge, or gather around the fire for story-telling, while some one toasted marshmallows. It was a young people's room to remember![18]

The piano joins the fireplace and easily moveable furniture to imbue a rather modest room with an air of playfulness and fun. Unlike the parlor upright with its concealed keyboard described by French, this instrument invites use, and casual performance. In both cases, however, the piano is cast as a performative agent in a room's design. Although the scenarios differ—timid performer for a familial audience to more energetic youth using the piano as a social as much as a musical instrument—they both indicate how the presence of the piano can encourage a sense of intimacy associated with domestic space.

'A Very Good Friend to this Family'

The evocation of intimacy and closeness cuts to the heart of music's function within the domestic parlor. As Lorraine Gorrell has argued, "the intimate setting of the middle-class home" served as the site (and inspiration) for music-making. This relied upon the piano,[19] both as an intermediary between performer and domestic listener and as a partner in close, "daily association." In an advertisement from 1916, the Steinway firm published the following description for the domestic use of their product:

> THINK of the dearest voice you know, lifted and carried on the Steinway's mellow tones… There is one to whom your gift of a Steinway would be a priceless possession. The Steinway means so much more than an ordinary piano. It has the power of creating a new world of happiness and in the closeness of daily association it gathers only added value with the years.[20]

The ad eroticizes the relationship of player and (Steinway) piano, anthropomorphizing the instrument and corporealizing the intimacy and pleasure from the experience.[21] It calls to mind a roughly contemporary promotional blurb for a "Symphonic Piano," which cites a testimonial identifying the instrument as a "very good friend to this family."[22] Sold by the mail-order Larkin Company for the stately sum of $450,[23] the player piano's "superior quality" is cited as the reason for why it secured such "an intimate place […] in that Massachusetts home to be called a 'friend.'" Far from a static object, the piano is granted the capacity to generate an atmosphere of familiarity; it even has the potential to bring the presence of another musician into the parlor or living room, when we consider the player piano's ability to play music recorded from perforated rolls. And not just any musician: as an article in *McBride's Magazine* of 1913 argues, "with the perfection of the player-piano each man becomes his own

Paderewski."[24] The trope of the piano as a precious member of a family recurs at moments of high sentiment in novels of the Edwardian Era. As author Marjorie Barkley McClure observes, the piano was supplanting the hearth as the domestic space where families assembled and felt at home, and that through the sounds it produced.

> In his home he loved song and piano because it had ever been the heart of the family life. Where another household would have gathered oftenest about the hearth, the Stevensons gathered about the piano. Such music was expressive of happiness, of merriment.[25]

For novelist John Love McKinnon, the piano again takes on the attributes of a human member of the family, primarily in its capacity to touch and lift their spirits.

> Miss Mary [...] a prodigy in music, was the owner of the beautiful piano in the home; she loved it as some dear friend, it was a solace to them in their lonely hours, and lightened and cheered their labors; she could make it talk cheer to them... It was the great comfort in the home for them all.[26]

The concept of the piano as a central site within the home for family bonding continued throughout the 19th into the early 20th Century, as attested by countless scenes in the literature, whether historical/biographical or fictional. Passages from novels of the first decade of the 20th Century by Agnes Russell Weekes[27] and the pre-eminent English writer John Galsworthy, for instance, reveal the role of the parlor piano as a site for the expression of extreme emotion. In her novel Weekes describes a scene where Premier Yarborough requests his childhood friend to play the piano for him as Yarborough himself reclines. In this case the instrument serves both as a performative agent of shared memory and as an intangible vehicle for transcending the present, while spatially communicating social bonds:

> Play to me, the way you used [to] at Chanston, when we were boys together. Do you remember those endless improvisations with the wind's voice wailing through their recurrent melodies? [...] I'll lie down here on the sofa and listen, and forget everything in the world except that I've got you back again.[28]

From Galsworthy's *The Patrician* of 1911, the following excerpt again reveals the piano functioning beyond the purely musical plane. Although in a British context, the affective dimension of the piano portrayed would resonate with North American readers. On the level of the surface, the piano fulfills the need for distraction; however, more deeply it embodies Audrey Noel's absent lover, whom she seeks elsewhere but whose spectral presence fills the space of the parlor.

[…] She sat down to her piano, resolutely, till tea came; playing on and on with a spirit only half present, the other half of her wandering in the Town, seeking for Miltoun. After tea she tried first to read, then to sew, and once more came back to her piano. The clock struck six; and as if its last stroke had broken the armour of her mind, she felt suddenly sick with anxiety.[29]

Musical Intimacy

We are not certain which compositions these fictional characters would have played, but such evocative parlor scenes draw upon a rich tradition of music performed in parlors to elevate one's mind and soul, to connect socially and romantically, to re-member (and forget), and to simply pass time. The solo music today's public most likely associates with the piano—Mozart, Beethoven, Chopin, Schumann, Liszt, Ra-chmaninov—could not have been played by the bourgeois owners of pianos because of its technical demands and emotional complexity. A more popular, more accessible style of composition arose to satisfy the requirements of the household that possessed a piano; known as "parlor music," the unpretentious genre fulfilling the needs of a burgeoning consumer public.[30] Descriptive and direct in expression, this household music was suitable both for the private performance of someone from the family and for social performance by two or more family members or guests, whether as four-hand music or accompanied song.

It is worth noting that the use of the 'duet bench' came into fashion in the 20th Century, acting as a material accomplice to intimate piano playing by pairs.[31] The piano bench also became something of a work bench, a site of labor for those families aspiring to membership in the cultivated class: it afforded not only a foundation for the tedious hours of practice, but also a platform for tutors' close surveillance over their charges. Such scrutiny was necessary to ensure the proper technical render-ing of the music on the piano stand, which in lessons could range from mechanical exercises like those by Hanon or Czerny to the parlor repertoire or canonic works by Bach, Mozart, or Beethoven. However, in contrast with the abstract musings of those three composers, parlor music excelled within the realm of the descriptive. It was filling the living room with the sounds of a mountain brook (Eduardo Poldini, "What the Forest Brook Babbles") or evoking in player and listener alike the passion of longing and desire (Carl Bohm, "Love's Greeting"). The expressive or descriptive titles of the pieces direct the performer to the mood or scene on display, which their auditor would comprehend through a well-established semiotics of affective musical gestures. This music's ability to create atmosphere quickly and easily helped to posi-tion the genre at the forefront of sheet music sales and, in turn, boosted the market for the piano. Whatever version of piano resided in the domestic space, however, its commanding presence and sound rendered it a focal point for personal expression and collective pleasure within the family.

Indeed, it would have been difficult for anyone in the house not to perceive the sounds emanating from the instrument in the parlor, faint as they might be for more distant rooms. As a result, the atmosphere created by the performance in the parlor could resonate however distantly throughout the home, diffusing the music's visceral references and emotional worlds to all who attended to its meanings. And the player, well aware of the dwelling's acoustics, might have taken into account such "peripheral listeners" and distributed affect when determining the pieces and their dynamic levels for domestic keyboard performance.

The audience for such parlor pianism could extend beyond the immediate family and individual friends of the player to guests invited to an afternoon tea, dinner party, or *soirée musicale*.[32] According to contemporary rules of etiquette, it would have been disingenuous for the host to perform at such domestic salons, which featured parlor music performed by family and guests. Etiquette also dictated set regimes of behavior at these events and even prescribed appropriate musical selections.[33] So the same instrument that served its owner(s) as a vehicle for self-expression and the entertainment of an intimate circle could also ironically become the site for the enactment of the stifling codes of manners that regulated socialized bodies (and ears) in the late Victorian and Edwardian eras.

Closing the Lid on the Parlor Piano

Like the radiant sunlight that strikes the open sheet music and keyboard with a brilliant, almost unnatural illumination in the photograph discussed at the outset, we have endeavored to draw attention to the often overlooked place of the piano in North American homes in the beginning of the 20th Century. Acoustically, socially, and visually, the instrument can be said to help set the tone for the expression of aspirations and/or an individual's (or family's) personality. Through our discussion of interior decorating literature, Edwardian middle-brow literature, advertisements, and parlor piano music, we have indicated the wide imprint of the piano across North American culture, particularly in how it affected domestic atmospheres. While the atmospheres could be quite formal, for the most part the piano occasioned a sense of intimacy. As a piece of furniture, it could display personal items (despite aesthetic and musical arguments against this practice!); and as a musical instrument, it changed the mood of the room, and rooms beyond, through its use. In this way, the piano was an active agent in the creation of social spaces and could sonically mark different rituals and activities in the day, week, or year.

Although it played a significant role in homes in the first third of the 20th Century, after a traumatic economic depression followed by a global conflict, the purchase of a piano became a true luxury. This, combined with improvements in record players, increasing affordability of radio receivers, and later, as the post-WWII economy recovered, the arrival of the television and hi-fi stereo, meant that piano lost its prominence in the organization and atmosphere of the typical middle-class North American living room. Playing the piano (or operating the player piano or reproducing piano) to entertain friends or provide music for a dance or singalong might have seemed like a nostalgic throwback to an earlier time. In the 1950s and 1960s, the television, the radio, or the hi-fi stereo would dominate the soundscape of the living room, continuing the evolution of intimate acoustic atmospheres at home.

Notes

1. See Judy Neiswander, *The Cosmopolitan Interior: Liberalism and the British Home, 1870–1914* (New Haven: Yale University Press for the Paul Mellon Centre for Studies in British Art, 2008). Although her study of interior decoration advice literature deals with the situation in Britain, the themes would have resonated as well in Canada, which was part of the British Empire and many of whose citizens were expressly Anglophilic.

2. Craig Roell, *The Piano in America, 1890–1940* (Chapel Hill: University of North Carolina Press, 1989), 3–12.

3. Initially, a unit called a 'piano player' was developed to be pushed up to any piano and to be played with mechanical fingers. This short-lived invention of the late 19th Century was superseded by the 'player piano,' which used a perforated-roll mechanism to play the piano and was pumped by an operator. Later, 'reproducing pianos' provided more accurate reproductions, driven by an internal electric motor and involving dampening or sustain pedals as well as keys for more dynamism. See Wayne Kelly, *Downright Upright: A History of the Canadian Piano Industry* (Toronto: Natural Heritage/Natural History Inc., 1991), 36–38.

4. Peter Ward, *A History of Domestic Space: Privacy and the Canadian Home* (Vancouver: UBC Press, 1999), 68.

5. *Biennial Census of Manufactures: 1921* (Washington, DC: Government Printing Office, 1924), 1153.

6. Roell notes that piano production grew faster than population growth in the first decade of the 20th Century by 6.2%, reaching a peak in 1909 (Roell, *The Piano in America*, 32). Statistics for Canadian piano manufacturing are more difficult to locate, yet a 1994 thesis does reveal estimated figures for the nation that illustrate a similar arc of rise and decline: from 10,000 in 1900 up to 32,000 in 1913 and back down to 24,762 in 1917.

See James Andrew Ross, "'Ye Olde Firme' Heintzman & Company, Ltd., 1885–1930: A Case Study in Canadian Piano Manufacturing" (M.A. Thesis, University of Western Ontario, 1994), 73.

7.   For examples, see Kyle Barnett, "Furniture Music: The Phonograph as Furniture, 1900–1930," *Journal of Popular Music Studies* 18, no. 3 (2006): 301–324; Michael Windover and Anne MacLennan, *Seeing, Selling, and Situating Radio in Canada, 1922–1956* (Halifax: Dalhousie Architectural Press, 2017); Lynn Spigel, *Make Room for TV: Television and the Family Ideal in Postwar America* (Chicago: University of Chicago Press, 1992); Dianne Harris, "A Tiny Orchestra in the Living Room: High-Fidelity Sound, Stereo Systems, and the Postwar House," in *Making Suburbia: New Histories of Everyday America*, eds. John Archer, Paul J. P. Sandul and Katherine Solomonson, (Minneapolis: University of Minnesota Press), 305–328.

8.   In this chapter we use the terms 'living room' and 'parlor' interchangeably. The term 'living room' largely replaces the 'parlor' in designating the more public-oriented gathering space of the home over the years under examination.

9.   Elsie de Wolfe cites examples of piano cases designed or ornamented by Sir Edward Burne-Jones, Sir Alma Tadema, Robert Lorimer, and Phoebe Anna Traquair in *The House in Good Taste* (New York: The Century Co., 1913), 187. (Available online through The Project Gutenberg eBook, #14715, January 17, 2005.) For other examples of Arts and Crafts contexts with reference to decorated pianos, see Ghenete Zelleke, "Harmonizing Form and Function: Mackay Hugh Baillie Scott and the Transformation of the Upright Piano," *Art Institute of Chicago Museum Studies* 19, no. 2 (1993): 160–173, 203–205; and Laurier Lacroix, "The Pursuit of Art and the Flourishing of Aestheticism Amidst the Everyday Affairs of Mankind," in *Artists, Architects & Artisans, Canadian Art 1890–1918*, ed. Charles C. Hill, (Ottawa: National Gallery of Canada, 2013), 20–55.

10. Lillie Hamilton French, *Homes and their Decoration* (New York: Dodd, Mead and Company, 1903).

11. Ibid, 19.

12. Ibid, 197.

13. Ibid, 374.

14. Ibid.

15. Emily Burbank, *Be Your Own Decorator* (New York: Dodd, Mead and Company, 1923), 8.

16. Ibid, 13.

17. Karen Halttunen, "From Parlor to Living Room: Domestic Space, Interior Decoration, and the Culture of Personality," in *Consuming visions: accumulation and display of goods in America 1880–1920*, ed. Simon J. Bronner, 157–189 (New York: Norton, 1989), 158.

18. Burbank, *Be Your Own*, 76.

19. Lorraine Gorrell, *The Nineteenth-Century German Lied* (Portland, OR: Amadeus, 1993), 172.

20. "Steinway: When Dreams Come True," *The Theatre* 34 (1916): 336. Steinway published the same advertisement in *Country Life, The American Review of Reviews, The Literary Digest, McLure's Magazine, The Etude, Women's Home Companion* and *Hearst's Magazine*, all in the December issue of 1916.

21. The most thorough study of the emotional world of pianism is Ivan Raykoff's *Dreams of Love: Playing the Romantic Pianist* (New York: Oxford University Press, 2014). He interprets 'romantic pianist' not in association with the historical Romantic Era, but rather as an affective practice. See also Arthur Loesser's classic text *Men, Women and Pianos: A Social History* (New York: Simon and Schuster, 1954); Therese Ellsworth and Susan Wollenberg, eds., *The Piano in Nineteenth-Century British Culture: Instruments, Performers and Repertoire* (Aldershot, UK: Ashgate, 2007); and Lise Karin Meling, "'The Lady at the Piano': From Innocent Pastime to Intimate Discourse," *Music & Practice* 5 (2018), at: https://www.musicandpractice.org/volume-5/the-lady-at-the-piano-from-innocent-pastime-to-intimate-discourse

22. Half-page advertisement for Larkin Co., *The Santa Fe Magazine* 9, no. 11 (November, 1915): 125.

23. $450 in 1915 would equate to approximately $11,448 USD in 2020 (See CPI Inflation Calculator, https://www.officialdata.org/). Calculating average annual income is challenging, given disparity in number of hours worked in a week. According to a study of 404,758 wage earners across 43 states and 28 industries from September 1918 to June 1919, the average annual earnings of a male worker were $1,332 (female workers earned approximately half this). See Paul H. Douglas, "Wages and Hours of Labor in 1919," *Journal of Political Economy* 29, no. 1 (Jan. 1921): 78–80.

24. "Player-Pianos for Piano-Players," *McBride's Magazine* 91 (1913): 249.

25. Marjorie Barkley McClure, *High Fires* (Boston: Little, Brown, and Company, 1924), 179.

26. John Love McKinnon, *History of Walton County* (Atlanta, GA: The Byrd Printing Co., 1911), 371.

27. H.R. Woudhuysen, "Some Women Editors of Shakespeare: A Preliminary Sketch," in *Women Making Shakespeare: Text, Reception and Performance*, Gordon McMullan, Lena Cowen Orlin, & Virginia Mason Vaughan, eds. (London: Bloomsbury, 2013), 84.

28. Weekes, *Yarborough the Premier* (New York: Harper & Brothers, 1904), 296.

29. John Galsworthy, *The Patrician* (New York: Scribners, 1911), 291.

30. About this style of music and the social practices that it represents, see above Wolfgang Fuhrmann, "The Intimate Art of Listening: Music in the Private Sphere During the Nineteenth Century," in *Oxford Handbook of Music Listening in the 19th & 20th Centuries*, eds. Christian Thorau and Hansjakob Ziemer, (New York: Oxford University Press, 2019), 277–311.

31. Alwyn T. Covell notes that piano benches were becoming more fashionable than piano stools for aesthetic and practical reasons in "Music in the Home: What Modern Furniture Offers to the Music Lover," *Style & Home Furnishing* (February 1916): 2.

32.   About salon performances on the piano see James Deaville, "The Well-Mannered Auditor: Zones of Attention and the Imposition of Silence in the Domestic Public Sphere of the 19th Century," in *Oxford Handbook of Music Listening in the 19th & 20th Centuries*, eds. Christian Thorau and Hansjakob Ziemer, (New York: Oxford University Press, 2019), 55–75.

33.   Thus the unnamed author of *"Etiquette for Ladies and Gentlemen* [1876] recommends the following: "For drawing-room pieces, some of Stephen Heller's compositions are admirably suited; they are short, *good*, graceful, and not too difficult. […] Beethoven's *sonatas*, and other long works of the great classical masters, should be reserved for other times." *Etiquette for Ladies and Gentlemen* (London: Frederick Warne and Co., 1876), 29.

04.

Playing to the Room: The Recording Studio as Instrument

Timothy Carey

In 1966, pianist Glenn Gould famously predicted the end of the live concert, and by extension that the institution of the concert hall itself would be "entirely taken over by electronic media."[1] Though usually framed as a pessimistic attitude towards the prospects of the live, public performance of music for a ticketed audience, Gould's staunchly polemical stance can just as easily be seen as an optimistic forecast for the prospects of recording and the respective technology's ability to rival the atmospheres of the concert hall experience. As he put it, "two generations ago, concertgoers preferred that their experience of music be fitted with an acoustic splendor, cavernously reverberant if possible, and pioneering recording ventures attempted to simulate the concert hall—the cathedral of the symphony."[2] Gould's pronouncement, then, alludes to the potential of the recording studio to replicate the sonic experience of a live concert, and supplant the concert hall as the primary architectural space of music production.

Curiously, the emergence of recorded music and the codification of concert hall acoustics occurred nearly concurrently. Boston Symphony Hall opened its doors in 1900 as the first concert hall whose acoustic character was derived from a numerical definition of how sound should behave in a concert hall.[3] Following closely on the heels of that milestone, the first commercially available recordings of music in the United States appeared in 1901, at which point recorded music gained the ability to compete with the concert hall experience by transferring the listening experience into the living room.[4] The intermediary to this sonic exchange, of course, was the recording studio—a space whose function and form was dictated not by program, aesthetics, or ritual as in the concert hall, but purely by sound and imitation. Parallel to the modern development of the concert hall, then, exists a history of recording studio architecture that was grounded in the mimicry of an acoustic character, atmosphere, and

Figure 1: Cellist Beatrice Harrison and composer Edward Elgar recording his Cello Concerto at HMV's studios, using the acoustic recording process. Public domain.

experience. One the one hand, the codification of concert hall acoustics beginning with Boston's Symphony Hall provided finality to a long-running thesis that there was a standardized acoustical atmosphere for performances in such spaces. The less studied and corollary phenomenon, however, is the role that replicating that acoustic experience truthfully and realistically played in the development of the recording studio as a typology. These spaces, sequestered away from a live audience, became environments that allowed the relationships between room, acoustic atmosphere and performance to further complicate and unravel.

From the Top: Early Recording Techniques and Room Sound

The relationship between recording technology and the recording studio largely consisted of continually evolving ad hoc solutions from the technology's infancy. Early acoustical recording techniques used from Thomas Edison's invention of the phonograph in 1877 until roughly 1925 relied on the ability of the sound to quite literally imprint itself on the recording cylinder via vibrations sent through a recording horn. Consequently, all musicians had to be contained within a small room and be as close to the horn as possible to register on the recording (Figure 1).[5] Ensemble configurations that would now be considered highly unconventional abounded, from singers being required to insert their entire head into the recording horn,[6] to pianos being raised on platforms with fronts and backs removed.[7] Needless to say, these recordings had little acoustic sensitivity to the sound of the room, so were often produced in "any convenient location" at first, or later in purpose-built recording rooms that at least provided a quiet location.[8] Little thought was put into the acoustic atmosphere of the room, however, as it had little bearing on the artifact of the performance that would be heard on the recording.[9]

Figure 2: Paul Weston and Jo Stafford in the recording studio. Public domain.

With the arrival of electrical recording in the mid-1920s, the acoustic space of the recording studio was finally awakened. Condenser and omnidirectional microphones used with electrical processes listened "in all directions at once" and were finally sensitive enough to pick up the sounds of room reverberation rather than simply direct sound (Figure 2).[10] This more advanced technology used in electrical recording, then, was able to capture the reverberation of the room in a way that acoustic recording horns could not,[11] allowed performers much greater freedom to move about the space,[12] and was also seen as requiring more "control" of the room's acoustic qualities.[13] The acoustic atmosphere of the recording room itself thus quickly entered into the discourse surrounding the emerging technology, as the connection between the acoustic qualities of the room and the sound on the other side of the microphone became clear.

Consequently, there arose a debate as to whether electrical recording's ability to capture the room's acoustic atmosphere and reverberatory qualities provided information that was beneficial or extraneous. On one side of the argument, Edison and others working in his field "wanted to capture just the music and edit out the world around it."[14] Electrical recording was criticized by this camp for capturing "a whole lot more" than simply the music itself[15] and the resulting recordings were criticized as a "specious and spurious kind of reproduction."[16] On the other side of the argument, proponents of room sound on a recording perceived it as a "move toward greater realism and fidelity" as it more closely mimicked the sound heard in a hall at a live performance.[17] An important theoretical underpinning, then, was established in these early spaces: the notion that there was a relationship between reverberation on a recording and an attitude towards what "realism" or "truthfulness" in the recording process represented.

What is often overlooked, however, is the fact that these two philosophies towards reverberation in recording correlated directly with two attitudes towards the architecture of the ideal recording studio. In the first, purpose-built recording studios were constructed with little reverberation in the tradition of Edison, though over time efforts to bring reverberation into those spaces led to the use of nearby auxiliary rooms and reverberation chambers. In the second, existing rooms with impressive reverberation levels, typically church sanctuaries or the auditoria of abandoned theaters, were converted into recording studios despite the difficulties of rendering such high levels of reverberation to disc. The prevailing distinction between recording studio types, then, was between rooms with little acoustic character that were gradually augmented to add reverberation, and highly reverberant rooms that were "tuned" through architectural intervention and engineering prowess to suit the purposes of recording. In each case, then, the studio room itself was instrumentalized in conjunction with a differing stance towards the relationship between realism, reverberation, and recording practice.

Take 1: Early Studios and the Introduction of Reverberation

Most early studios in the first decades of electrical recording sided with Edison, and the initial approach for all recording studios involved low reverberation levels largely for two reasons. First, the complexities of reverberation initially escaped early understanding of the recording process, so the problem was solved by working to eliminate reverberation rather than contend with it.[18] Second, there was a general notion that reverberation needed to be deadened in order to avoid overwhelming the new, more sensitive microphones during the recording process.[19] Consequently, even engineers who argued for the presence of reverberation on recordings initially advocated for amounts far below those heard in the concert hall, while those who argued against reverberation on a recording pointed to the problematic layering of acoustic spaces when a track was played into a living room with a room sound of its own.[20] For the most part, these smaller studios were built in the tradition and philosophy of the broadcast radio studios of the 1930s, which was the more profitable, established, and expansive enterprise, and required low reverberation times to better accommodate the recording of speech.[21]

Yet as the industry surrounding recorded music expanded and experimentation in the studio sought to meet the varied demands of recording artists, efforts were gradually made to introduce reverberation into these spaces. These rooms had been designed to produce records without room sound and thus, architecturally, did not have the means to produce it naturally.[22] While there was some possibility of achieving this goal in post-production,[23] for the most part early attempts were rooted in ad hoc architectural solutions to make use of the reverberant qualities of nearby spaces. In perhaps the earliest case of this strategy, bandleader Raymond Scott placed additional microphones in a hallway and men's room outside of the recording studio in a 1937 session to gain reverberation from the acoustic reflectivity of the ceramic tiles.[24] Over several decades, this became a tried-and-true tradition, even among the most well-regarded and prestigious labels—Columbia Record's Seventh Avenue Studio used the same technique in the building's ten-story stairwell in the 1950s.[25] Later in the 1960s, Motown's Detroit studios frequently used restrooms and attic spaces to render additional reverberation onto tracks,[26] and Mira Sound's use of Associated Studios included the use of the fire escape stairwell.[27]

Over time, these spaces became codified into purpose-built reverberation chambers, constructed adjacent to the recording studio. Generally, an existing track recorded in the main studio room would be played into the chamber, where another microphone would pick up the more reverberant version of the original.[28] Typically ten to fifteen feet long and with a low ceiling, the chambers sought to replicate the effects of the restrooms and stairwells used previously—in fact, many of these spaces were finished with ceramic tile in order to best mimic the restrooms that were their predecessors.[29] The chambers and the atmosphere they could create also became a part of certain studios' sonic signatures—Gold Star Studios in Los Angeles, for example, acquired a reputation for its reverberation chambers after their use by producer Phil Spector in the 1960s,[30] while Sunset Sounds' reverberation chambers became known for their associations with Brian Wilson, the Beach Boys and the Doors.[31] Beginning in the late 1950s, reverberation chambers could even be ordered "off the shelf" and attached to existing recording studios.[32] The acoustic atmosphere that was desired for a track, then, led to a more mutable relationship between the acoustic atmosphere that existed in the room and the version of that atmosphere that was layered onto the recording.

As reverberation chambers became increasingly common, the acoustically dry studios they were associated with became grounds for significant experimentation in the sonic atmospheres they could create. From clotheslines being inserted into reverberation chambers to allow remote control of microphone placement,[33] to percussion instruments and vocalists being placed directly into the chamber,[34] these studios began to move further away from the goal of faithfully reproducing the live concert experience. As audio engineer Philip Erhorn put it at the time, producers and musicians using these studios in these ways began to seek out and demand "all kinds of exaggerated sounds [involving] the use of echo chambers, program equalizers, sound effects, and sound effects filters."[35] So while reverberation chambers were initially designed simply to bring minimal reverberatory qualities into acoustically dry studios, these studios became the sites of significant experimentation into what types of sounds could be committed to disc, and what the sonic artifact of a performance might entail.

Producers and artists who manipulated the studios in these ways abounded throughout genres like rock and pop from the 1960s onward, using the echo chambers to create tracks that had "no connection to real world sound,"[36] or that were rooted in a "pseudo-reality, created in synthetic space."[37] Spector, for example, made use of the reverberation chambers to pioneer his "Wall of Sound" aesthetic with artists like the Righteous Brothers and the Ronettes in which "oceans of echo and reverb" precluded one instrument from being distinguished from another.[38] Tellingly, because the Wall of Sound was built up via so many layers of reverberation and the echo chambers were used "full crank,"[39] it was not palpable in the recording studio itself. As one engineer put it, "you wouldn't have heard it if you walked in while we were recording it."[40] Wilson, on the other hand, frequently layered different acoustical atmospheres on top of each other, and the recordings he produced move swiftly between tracks with different levels of reverberation, and gave the impression that they were recorded in different rooms. Consequently, tracks produced by Wilson often take the listener "into new sonic realms every 30 seconds or so."[41] Room sound presence on these tracks ran the gamut from electric guitars being connected directly to the recording equipment and bypassing the room altogether, to significant use of echo chambers to achieve high levels of reverberation that did not exist in the studio proper.[42]

In many ways, then, the initial lack of reverberation in these spaces opened the opportunity for an instrumentalization of the studio in which reverberation chambers and auxiliary spaces were used to render tracks with acoustic atmospheres quite different from those found in the studio room itself. Ironically, the acoustic dryness of these studios had direct ties to concerns about layering of acoustic atmospheres between the space of recording and the space of playback. Yet it was these rooms that gave rise to recording styles so complex in their layering of acoustic atmospheres that the many of the tracks produced in them could never be reproduced acoustically in a single room, much less the one they were initially recorded in. The interplay between the room, its acoustic atmosphere, and the sonic qualities that it could render onto a recording, then, reached a dynamism through these ad hoc interventions that continued to complicate and expand those relationships.

Take 2: Found Spaces and the Tuning of the Reverberant Room

Yet on the other side of Edison's argument, rooms for recording that privileged reverberation developed their own relationship between room sound, reverberation, and realism. This alternate tradition of seeking out existing spaces with exemplary acoustics to retrofit into recording studios largely began in 1927 with Victor and Columbia Records' use of Liederkranz Hall, a former German beer hall on East Fifty-eighth Street in New York City.[43] A room prized for its "concert hall ambience" and nearly

100 feet long by 60 feet wide,[44] Liederkranz's sound won a respect among its users that established a reverence and vocabulary for these spaces that continued throughout the following decades. Perhaps the most famous of these rooms, Columbia Records' legendary "Temple of Sound" at Thirtieth Street in New York City, was the sanctuary of a former Greek Orthodox Church and possessed "something you don't find in today's studios—it had an identifying sound."[45] Meanwhile Webster Hall, RCA's conversion of an early 20th Century meeting room on East Eleventh Street in New York City, was similarly described as a "perfect" room,[46] while Decca's Pythian Temple in the same city, also a former church sanctuary, was described as a room that "rocked."[47]

The narrative, then, was nearly always that of discovery and excavation—not of creating music within an established acoustic atmosphere as in the concert hall, but of discovering spaces with the ideal atmosphere for a specific track or genre. The process of discovering the "Temple of Sound" at Thirtieth Street, for example, was described as a "hunt"[48] while the Capitol Theater auditorium in Memphis that would become Stax Studios was "found."[49] So while these rooms had already been built for other purposes, the intentionality with which existing spaces were chosen to be exalted as exemplary recording studios indicates the degree to which the success of transferring that acoustic atmosphere to disc determined the suitability of the space.

Yet at the same time, the strategy of utilizing existing rooms with substantial reverberant qualities required a combination of preservation and instrumentalization—a balance between maintaining the acoustic atmosphere as it was found, while taming it to sound its best on disc. At Thirtieth Street, for example, senior engineer Harold Chapman insisted that the church be left largely untouched, for fear of such minor alterations as painting and sanding affecting the acoustics.[50] Furthermore, during certain periods, washing the floors was strictly forbidden.[51] Similarly, Mediasound, one of New York City's most popular studios of the 1970s and also a former church sanctuary, "left things pretty much intact from the church days" with "old wooden floors with no finish whatsoever."[52] Dimensions were also sacrosanct, with the preservation of existing ceiling heights having been cited at Stax Studios[53] and Mediasound[54] as contributing to their sonic character.

Though while much of the broader narrative surrounding these rooms revolved around their "perfect" acoustics, the circumstances of the recording process reveal a great degree of engineering innovation in the space. Despite the reverence that was applied to these studios, an almost equal reverence was applied to the engineers with the skill to navigate the complexities of recording in such a reverberant environment—those who "knew the room."[55] As David Simons put it in his survey of New York City recording studios,

> …harnessing the enormous ambience of these rooms was not for the faint of heart. But in those heady times, the early 1950s, there emerged a select group of studio

craftsmen whose ability to capture…the excitement of a live performance within a large studio setting – using few gadgets but endless ingenuity – made them the acknowledged masters of their trade.[56]

Indeed, Fred Laico, one of the principal engineers working in these studios, described an engineer's rule book used at Thirtieth Street that established a framework for using the studio and allowing all of the sessions to "[sound] very similar."[57] One of these time-honored tricks, for example, involved manipulating the reverberation of the room itself, recording it back onto the track through a tape machine to "take the edge off the echo."[58] Maintaining the studio's reputation for the "class and quality" of its sound and the engineer's wishes to create as "transparent" a sound as possible,[59] then, involved a great degree of engineering prowess and instrumentalization of the space. So while much of what was prized about the studio's sound was its consistency, the commitment of that sound to disc was not merely the result of the acoustics of the room but also carefully considered efforts to capture that sound effectively.

And despite the fact that the consistent sound of these spaces was prized, nearly all of these refurbished rooms were equipped with architectural means to alter the reverberation of the space. A "cavernous, hockey rink of a studio" like Webster Hall had a large curtain that was deployed to varying degrees to suit the ensemble in the studio that day,[60] while the renovation of Stax Studios from a theater auditorium included the design of hanging acoustical drapes, and a series of baffles.[61] The "Temple of Sound" at Thirtieth Street also made use of moving baffles and curtains, many extant from the studio's days as a church sanctuary,[62] and tricks of the trade abounded related to these interventions. Indeed, Laico recalled using a unique configuration of microphones and moving partitions specifically for French Horn players to focus a small amount of reverberation on that particular instrument.[63] And while the "Temple of Sound" was praised for the consistency of its acoustic atmosphere, photos of the space in use reveal quite the opposite—Simon and Garfunkel are repeatedly photographed close to baffles in the middle of the room,[64] while some photographs of Miles Davis recording in the room show a setup in a corner of the room with fewer of the acoustic treatments deployed,[65] and written accounts of Glenn Gould recording in the space recall the temporary introduction of carpet.[66]

The recording studios of this era that aligned with the stance that associated reverberation with realism, then, prized themselves on their inherent sonic qualities but simultaneously required significant manipulation and "tuning". The instrumentalization of these studios was largely in pursuit of consistently relaying the experience of hearing a performance in that space, room sound and all—from the variety of architectural interventions used to tune the room, to the level of engineering expertise needed to tame the sound. Compared to the smaller rooms that relied on reverberation chambers, then, these rooms and the recordings associated with them had an arguably tighter relationship between the room, its acoustic atmosphere, and the presence of that atmosphere on disc. These spaces and the tracks produced in them, however, also represented the culmination of a narrative that had previously criticized such recordings as artificial and suspect.

Mixing and Mastering: Instrumentalization, Reverberation, and Realism

In many ways, then, these advancements toward the faithful reproduction of a sonic experience and the two conflicting stances on what that entailed led to two divergent recording studio typologies that were each instrumentalized to different ends. Both were synthetic to a degree, yet also complicated and enriched earlier notions of what "realism" and "truthfulness" in a recording represented. While smaller, acoustically drier studios were initially aligned with Thomas Edison's conceptualization of the most realistic method of rendering an artifact of a sonic experience, the lineage of those spaces and the way that they were instrumentalized led to a proliferation of recordings with acoustic atmospheres that could never be reproduced in a live concert setting or in a single room. That initial lack of reverberation and the codification of means to introduce it, then, led to sites of production for tracks that moved increasingly further from Edison's idea of realism in a recording to the point of flouting it altogether.

Found spaces like church sanctuaries, meeting rooms, and theater auditoria, on the other hand, provided more realistic accounts of a performance according to those on the other side of the argument, yet considerable skill from the engineers and a variety of interventions in the space were required to bring that sound to fruition. The variety of architectural interventions made in these spaces point to this perhaps most fully—that providing a consistent acoustic atmosphere and reverberation level on disc in many instances required continued manipulation of the elements of the room itself. Though earlier proponents of deadening reverberation in studios had pointed to the inclusion of room sound as an "illusion,"[67] the camp that took the opposite stance instrumentalized the studio space to great degree in order to replicate that reverberation on disc as faithfully as possible. So while the recently codified acoustic atmosphere of the concert hall implied that sounds within it should conform to a certain character, the recording studio and the variety of interventions happening within the typology implied a more nuanced interpretation of whether the nature of the space shapes the sound within it, or vice versa. In any case, the initial effort to mimic the live concert experience in the recording studio further developed and complicated the relationships between realism, room sound, and acoustic atmosphere in the experience of music.

Gould was evidently prescient, then, in emphasizing the transformative power of recording and the eventual influence of the recording studio, adding that "for better or worse, recording will forever alter our notions about what is appropriate to the performance of music."[68] Writing in 1966, many of the aforementioned innovations were underway, but in 1982 Gould's second recording of Bach's Goldberg Variations became the last session recorded in Columbia's "Temple of Sound" at Thirtieth Street before it was demolished.[69] Like many musicians and producers working in these studios, the relationship between room reverberation, recording, and realism continued to be mutable in his ears, and fully in the service of the performance itself. So while Gould had previously claimed that the listening public's preference might be towards "cavernously reverberant"[70] recordings in the essay that opened this text, he famously exclaimed the opposite in one recording session: "You're aware that my style of performance in the Bach involves using a very staccato articulation…Please, after all my effort, don't undo that for me by tying all my notes together with reverberation!"[71]

Notes

1.   Tim Page, *The Glenn Gould Reader* (New York: Random House, 1984), 331.
2.   Ibid, 333.
3.   Emily Thompson, *The Soundscape of Modernity: Architectural Acoustics and the Culture of Listening in America, 1900–1933* (Cambridge: The MIT Press, 2002), 44.
4.   Greg Milner, *Perfecting Sound Forever: An Aural History of Recorded Music* (New York: Farrar, Straus & Giroux, 2009), 37.
5.   Robert Philip, *Performing Music in the Age of Recording* (New Haven: Yale University Press, 2014), 27.
6.   Timothy Day, *A Century of Recorded Music: Listening to Musical History* (New Haven: Yale University Press, 2000), 9.
7.   Susan Schmidt Horning, *Chasing Sound: Technology, Culture & the Art of Studio Recording from Edison to the LP* (Baltimore: Johns Hopkins University Press, 2013), 19.
8.   Michael Chanan, *Repeated Takes: A Short History of Recording and Its Effects on Music* (New York: Verso, 1995), 31.
9.   Ibid.
10. Thompson, *The Soundscape of Modernity*, 264.
11. Ibid.
12. Schmidt Horning, *Chasing Sound*, 33.
13. Ibid, 42.
14. Milner, *Perfecting Sound Forever*, 55.
15. Ibid.

16. Oliver Read and Walter T. Welch, *From Tin Foil to Stereo: Evolution of the Phonograph* (Howard W. Sams: New York, 1976), 238.
17. Thompson, *The Soundscape of Modernity*, 264.
18. Schmidt Horning, *Chasing Sound*, 78.
19. Thompson, *The Soundscape of Modernity*, 266.
20. Milner, *Perfecting Sound Forever*, 37.
21. Schmidt Horning, *Chasing Sound*, 80.
22. Ibid., 92.
23. Thompson, *The Soundscape of Modernity*, 282.
24. Schmidt Horning, *Chasing Sound*, 93.
25. Jim Cogan and William Clark, *Temples of Sound: Inside the Great Recording Studios* (San Francisco: Chronicle Books, 2003), 188.
26. Cogan and Clark, *Temples of Sound*, 146.
27. David Simons, *Studio Stories: How the Great New York Records Were Made: From Miles to Madonna, Sinatra to the Ramones* (San Francisco: Backbeat Books, 2004), 54.
28. Thompson, *The Soundscape of Modernity*, 281.
29. Schmidt Horning, *Chasing Sound*, 93.
30. Buskin, Richard, "Classic Tracks: The Ronettes 'Be My Baby'", *Sound on Sound* 22, no. 6 (2007): 104.
31. Cogan and Clark, *Temples of Sound*, 45.
32. Schmidt Horning, *Chasing Sound*, 94.
33. Simons, *Studio Stories*, 54.
34. Ibid., 133.
35. Philip C. Erhorn, "Audio Console Design Notes," *Journal of the Audio Engineering Society* 4 (Apr. 1956): 65.
36. Milner, *Perfecting Sound Forever*, 151.
37. Virgil Moorefield, *The Producer as Composer: Shaping the Sounds of Popular Music* (Cambridge: The MIT Press, 2010), xv.
38. Milner, *Perfecting Sound Forever*, 151.
39. Mark Ribowsky, *He's a Rebel: The Truth About Phil Spector – Rock and Roll's Legendary Madman* (New York: E.P. Dutton, 1989), 221.
40. Buskin, "Classic Tracks", 113.
41. Moorefield, *The Producer as Composer*, 21.
42. Charles Granata, *Wouldn't It Be Nice: Brian Wilson and the Making of the Beach Boys' Pet Sounds* (Chicago: Chicago Review Press, 2016), 126.
43. Gary Marmorstein, *The Label: The Story of Columbia Records* (New York: Avalon, 2007), 168.
44. Simons, *Studio Stories*, 24.
45. Kahn, Ashley, *Kind of Blue: The Making of the Miles Davis Masterpiece* (Cambridge: Da Capo Press, 2000), 76.

46. Simons, *Studio Stories*, 173.
47. Simons, *Studio Stories*, 170.
48. Marmorstein, *The Label*, 51.
49. Cogan and Clark, *Temples of Sound*, 66.
50. Robin D.G Kelley, *Thelonius Monk: The Life and Times of an American Original* (New York: Simon & Schuster, 2009), 327.
51. Simons, *Studio Stories*, 35.
52. Ibid., 142.
53. Cogan and Clark, *Temples of Sound*, 66.
54. Simons, *Studio Stories*, 145.
55. Kahn, *Kind of Blue*, 77.
56. Simons, *Studio Stories*, 14.
57. Cogan and Clark, *Temples of Sound*, 185.
58. Ibid.
59. Milner, *Perfecting Sound Forever*, 149.
60. Simons, *Studio Stories*, 172.
61. Rob Bowman, *Soulsville U.S.A.: The Story of Stax Records* (New York: Schirmer, 1997), 8.
62. Simons, *Studio Stories*, 13.
63. Cogan and Clark, *Temples of Sound*, 32.
64. Ibid., 187.
65. Kahn, *Kind of Blue*, 89.
66. Paul Elie, "30 Variations and a Microphone" at *The New York Times*, September 7th, 2012, 2.
67. Chanan, *Repeated Takes*, 59.
68. Page, *The Glenn Gould Reader*, 337.
69. Elie, "30 Variations and a Microphone", 3.
70. Page, *The Glenn Gould Reader*, 333.
71. Andrew Kazdin. *Glenn Gould at Work: Creative Lying* (New York, E.P. Dutton, 1989), 116.

05.

Vibe, c. 1969: The Technicity of Operative Ambience in Jimi Hendrix's Electric Lady Studios

Clemens Finkelstein

Like fear, vibe is a cultural construct. The neutrality of the environment is a myth. Every place—knowable only through our reading of it—produces a vibe—what used to be called a *genius loci*. […] And this is why monuments and architecture are so important to vibe: they fix our desires where everyone can see.[1]

— Michael Sorkin

"Have you ever been to Electric Ladyland […] the magic carpet place, for you […] I want to show you different emotions […] I want to run to the sounds and motions […] so it's time to take a ride […] soon you'll understand," serenades the disembodied voice of Jimi Hendrix auspiciously.[2] Accompanied by mellow guitar riffs, slow drum beat, and hypnotically echoed chorus, its high pitch and soft timbre immerses listeners in the diegetic acoustics of his final studio record *Electric Ladyland* (1968). Soon after its release, in early 1969, Hendrix commissioned a twenty-two-year-old graduate from Princeton University's School of Architecture, John Storyk, with the design for a club in Greenwich Village, to be named after the successful third Jimi Hendrix Experience record. The desired design parameters for the club, which was soon transformed into a personal recording studio, were sourced from Hendrix's and Storyk's experiences in the creativity conducing ambience of the nightclubs and happenings that punctuated New York's arts and music scene in the late 1960s.

The same experimental spaces served designers as perceptual laboratories for the new mediatechnological condition that permeated environmental design and architectural practice across Europe, Japan, and the US since the 1950s. Affordable, mobile technologies (i.e., video projectors, high-fidelity stereo systems) triggered imaginations and swiftly transposed the modernist dictum of a romanticized aesthetic of technology to an amorous entanglement with the aesthetics of *technicity*. Shifting their focus from formal analysis to anthropological synthesis, architects were captivated by the possibility of a systemic alliance between design and media technologies. Designers, building on the modernist ideal of the machines-for-living-in, extended their desired efficacy to encompass an infinitely modifiable *operative ambience*. "After instant food, instant sleep, and instant dreams now turned-on environments are a product of our instant age. Why not?" the architectural critic C. Ray Smith considered in 1967, welcoming the possibility to "change a room simply by flicking a button on a new projected transparency."[3] While professionally preoccupied with constructing stable entities, this "turned-on-décor" offered architects innovative modes to engage with the human element that came into contact with their designs, leading them to recalibrate their classical, primary concern with static space towards the performance of dynamic spatiotemporal events.[4]

Implicating its dwellers in this radical adjustment, human beings were accordingly conceived of as a system of phases, "a relation of equilibrium and of reciprocal tensions."[5] Rather than acting upon a fixed individual, this process of *individuation* adhered to what the French mechanologist Gilbert Simondon distinguished in the 1950s as eternal becoming, where "the individual is not a being but an act."[6] The key determinant, argued Simondon, is the individual's *associated milieu*: an ensemble of environmental modalities and constitutive elements, which the individual continuously integrates into its functioning.[7] The inquiry that follows pays close attention to the modifications made in one such specific conditioning environment, Hendrix's Electric Lady Studios (ELS). It analyzes the architectural interventions and theoretical approaches that sought to assemble percepts and affects in the explicit pursuit to transform dwellers—across mediatechnological and sociotechnical networks—into *technical ensembles*. Akin to contemporaneous media theory, especially Marshall McLuhan's *Medium is the Massage* (1967), this demanded both a futuristic outlook and an instinctual recalibration of the human sensorium—humanity's return to "acoustic space."[8] Architects and environmental designers correspondingly sought a new mode of transmission between static architectural envelopes and dynamic (bio)technical ensembles. They envisioned a substance that could capture or synthesize percepts and affects in space and time. An operative ambience that would, as Steve Goodman contended, "simultaneously draw in the physics of its environment (its vibrations) and the moods of its populace (its vibes)," to further create, react, and transmit one and the other.[9]

An Abstract Universal Language

Commissioned by Hendrix as an 'architecture of vibe,' ELS affords unique insights into the complex entanglement of physical vibrations and metaphysical vibes at the field's turn towards dynamic, spatiotemporal performance and architectural technicity. It further takes as its point of origin one of the experimental nightclubs in 1960s New York—SoHo's short-lived Cerebrum—in the creativity-conducing ambience of which Hendrix would often recharge.[10]

"Cerebrum: Club Seeking to Soothe the Mind" announced *The New York Times* on Saturday, November 23, 1968, after its opening.[11] Focused on providing a space and time for altered sensory perception, Cerebrum was "not so much a disco as a public happening."[12] Synthesizing visual, sonic, haptic, olfactic, gustatory, and proprioceptive sensations through scripted theatrical processes, the avant-garde club aimed at an all-enveloping and all-permeating vibe. This operative ambience was bounded to its component frequencies: the architectural elements, mediatechnological devices, and the anthropoid dwellers it sought to affect. Participants became both audience and performer within the spatial and temporal confines of the three-hour-long happening.

Hailed by its twenty-four-year-old leader Ruffin Cooper Jr.[13] as a "new form of communication," Cerebrum was realized by the playful architectural interventions of recent Princeton graduate John Storyk.[14] The "'pot architecture' of this Nirvana," as Smith reviewed Storyk's design in *Supermannerism* (1977), merged resonant chambers for transsensorial stimulation and non-verbal communication in a performative architecture of vibe.[15] Featured on its cover, *Life* magazine from April 4, 1969, emphasized Cerebrum's tenet: "a teetotal nightclub where personal experience is all."[16] Hand cream was squirted into the tangle of fingers, cooling menthol-ice smeared on participants' lips, or other skin-tingling substances exchanged—all that had "an ethereal, gentle, transcendental effect," recalled media theorist Gene Youngblood in *Expanded Cinema* (1970).[17] "An evening at Cerebrum follow[ed] from Form to Structure to Place," he deduced.[18] On the *form* level, participants transitioned "from a dark closet [orientation room] to a larger room, down a narrow hallway to an open space."[19] Once inside the large, white rectangular space, the *structural* experience was enforced by seven seemingly floating platforms that were raised about three feet from the floor. The carpeted, geometric islands—each holding four to six participants that switched between them every twenty minutes—were connected by a catwalk, creating various mini-environments. Modifiable via inset electronic control panels, they contained either headphones for personal sonic immersion or percussive instruments and handheld projectors that allowed participants to inflect their own vibe as part of this technical ensemble.[20] The combined elements of formal transition and structural variance culminated in the experience of *place*—its transmissible vibe. Captivated by the unique vibe of Storyk's architectural entities, Hendrix sought out the designer to transform a property that he and his manager, Michael Jeffrey, had recently leased on 8th Street and which still housed the blues club Generation[21] (52 West 8 St) in the basement of Frederick Kiesler's 1929 designed Film Arts Guild Cinema.

What is this pervasive "vibe" that led Hendrix to hire a novice[22] with no expertise in architectural acoustics to design a nightclub/recording studio? Frequently reduced to its metaphorical dimension—immaterial, invisible, purely qualitative, metaphysical—vibe's mediatechnological nature is rooted in the physics of vibration, the physical disturbance of a prior state of equilibrium.[23] The modification of vibration to vibe is grounded in the former's connotations of metaphysical kinetics and affective emotions, which entered art and architectural space theories of the 1890s through the psychological aesthetics of *Einfühlung* ["in-feeling," empathy] and the work of 19th-century German psychophysicists like Weber, Fechner, Helmholtz, and Wundt.[24] Formulating architecture as *Raumgestalterin* [creatress of space] and *tectonics* as its synthetic science, German-writing historians of art and architecture like Hildebrand, Riegl, Schmarsow, Vischer, and Wölfflin posited *Raumbildung* [space formation] to be elemental in the formulation of modern identity. It, they argued, was conditioned by the human organism's alliance with the *Schwingungen* [vibrations] of physical and metaphysical dimensions, mediated by architecture as a growing *Lebewesen* [living being] that ought to tune the subject symbiotically to its changing environment.[25]

The earliest registration of vibe as a colloquialism for the musical instrument vibraphone appeared in the 1940s and 1950s in relation to swing or jazz publications and remained strongly tied to the physical notion of acoustics and sonic vibrations.[26] Detaching itself little by little from the purely musical association, the notion went through a notable semantic transformation in the decades that followed. A *Sunday Times* article from October 1, 1967, announced, "we're not getting the right vibes," and on March 24, 1968, the *Los Angeles Times* reported on the correct "vibing" that had occurred at the nightclub Troubadour. "To vibe" meant to either "transmit or express (a feeling, attitude, etc.) to others in the form of intuitive signals or 'vibes'" or "to perceive on the basis of such signals."[27] Eugene E. Landy's 1971 *The Underground Dictionary* furthermore colored vibe adjectively and qualitatively: "*He bad vibed me.*"[28] The increased linking of architectural space to vibe quickly transitioned from a descriptor of *placeness*—the quality of occupying a particular locality—to being densified into an exportable substance, an engineered affect. Produced by a systemic alliance of mediatechnological devices and architectural design, vibe could be performed and adapted in various locations, depending solely on space, time, and the adequate elements of the technical ensemble. "What gives a vibe 'authenticity,'" argues literary theorist Peli Grietzer, "is its ability to evoke—using a small number of disparate elements—a certain time, place and milieu; [...] a systemic, structural gestalt representation of a worldly set whose vibe it idealizes."[29] This mode of remodeling elucidates the synthetic properties of vibe, emphasizing its proximity to architecture in world-making.

R. Buckminster Fuller provides a potent link between these popular techno-eco-logical synergies and the re/modeling of worlds c. 1969. In his introduction to Young-blood's *Expanded Cinema*, he envisioned a substance of cosmic transmission termed "intuitive thought" that would provide "worldaround man with the most effective communication techniques for speaking universal language to universal man."[30] His reasoning relied on a radical breakdown of the human body into frequencies:

> Because humans consist of a myriad of atoms and because atoms are themselves electro-magnetic frequency event phenomena—not things—it is theoretically pos-sible that the complex frequencies of which humans are constituted, together with their angular interpositioning, could be scanningly unraveled and transmitted.[31]

Deducing that humans may be linked to each other sub-atomically, it would thus be possible, Fuller mused, that the "electro-magnetic wave pattern oscillations" that indicate someone's brain function may be picked up by others intuitively.[32] Echoing the contemporaneous concretization of vibe as a cybernetic element, these signals enabled the exchange of information and feelings through an interconnected mesh of frequencies and across apparent linguistic or cultural divides. Hendrix was similarly obsessed with discovering a new "abstract universal language" (musical in essence) and tasked Storyk to design a space where he could realize and record it.[33] Yet, if architecture accumulates positive or negative vibes—by tracing the meta-history of events, being universal as well as subjective, internal and external, engendered natu-rally or artificially produced—"[h]ow," the urbanist Michael Sorkin fittingly queried in "Notes on Vibe" (1998), "does architecture reinforce the good vibe?"[34]

Between the Engendered and the Produced

Implementing many of the architectural and media-environmental aspects developed for Cerebrum, Storyk initially designed ELS as a nightclub that was dominated by geometric shapes and bowed edges: a central rectangular space; a spiral-like stage for live acts to the left; an adjacent dance floor marked by a curved back wall; a triangu-lar bar in the upper center; a detached control room at the right outer limit; and an upper seating area. Arguing for a critically needed personal recording studio instead, Hendrix's venue manager, Jim Marron, and sound engineer, Eddie Kramer, soon convinced the musician to have Storyk transform the design mid-way (Figure 1). As Kramer recalled: "We wanted to create a vibe, a place for Jimi to come in and feel comfortable playing day or night."[35]

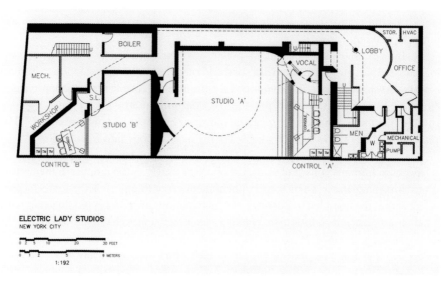

Figure 1: Electric Lady Studios, floor plan (redrawn), May 1969. Design by John Storyk. Courtesy of John Storyk.

Entwining acoustical programming with the adaptable soothing atmosphere of sinuous elements and white projectable surfaces, ELS's interior architecture adhered to Kramer's acoustic demands and Hendrix's explicit desire for a techno-organic spaceship vibe. The prominent mural by Lance Jost, requested by Hendrix to 'create space' painterly and featuring two blonde spaceship operators in their approach of an Earth-like planet, attests to the musician's Afrofuturistic conception of the recording studio as a cosmic vehicle disseminating a new abstract language. Grounding Hendrix's desires for metacommunication, ELS sought to transform the technologically complex environment of its special typology—exemplified by London's Olympic Sound and Abbey Road—from a sterile machinic environment, the live room, to a dynamic 'living' room. Rather than stunting recording artists by having to rent uninspired and expensive studio space, the atmosphere of Hendrix's lair was meant to stimulate and liberate everyone that came in touch with its engendered or produced vibes. Pioneering a new type, the artist-studio shifted ownership from the purely economically driven record companies back to the artistic community. ELS opened on August 26, 1970, following one million US dollars of investment and a year of construction. Hendrix soon thereafter succumbed to a chemical cocktail of alcohol and barbiturates, asphyxiating on his vomit in a London Notting Hill apartment on September 18, 1970. He would not see his Electric Lady emerge as one of the most iconic and successful recording studios to date.

Figure 2: Electric Lady Studios, entrance on 52 West 8th Street, New York, 1970.
Photography by John Veltri, Courtesy of Authentic Hendrix, L.L.C.

The sinuous demands of acoustic space eventually manifested in an overarching semicircular geometry that can be observed in Storyk's interior and exterior architectural interventions. Sharply contrasting with the rectangular architecture of Kiesler's former Film Arts Guild Cinema, Storyk deconstructed the preexistent structure on the first-floor level and inserted a curved exterior façade whose convex mass of dark brick bowed towards the sidewalk (Figure 2). Containing the main entrance, this element served symbolically and formally as a transitional zone between the fractious urban noise outside and the controllable operative ambience inside. Advancing downstairs and along a narrow corridor, visitors arrived in a semicircular lobby illuminated by theatrical lighting (Figure 3). Moving counterclockwise around the lobby's central column and along a narrow corridor to the left, they turned left once more to transition between two doors with round porthole windows, after which they reached a curved wall on the right that opened onto a spacious rectangular studio space to the left.

Figure 3: Electric Lady Studios, reception area with spaceship mural by Lance Jost, c. 1970. Photography by John Veltri, Courtesy of Authentic Hendrix, L.L.C.

Studio A—the only one completed before Hendrix's untimely death—was modeled after New York's A&R Studios (Figure 4). To provide a spacious, resonant field that would be needed, argued Kramer, to unfold the entire range of sonic vibrations emitted by the drums, the basement was excavated until reaching the water table. Without prior experience in acoustical design, Storyk was fortunate to enlist the help of the industrial acoustician Bob Hansen. He taught the novice to shelter the "good" musical vibrations while working on soundproofing the space, isolating "bad" vibrations or noise, such as machinic humming or disruptive pulsations from the street or the flowing stream beneath the studio. Transposing the sinuous modes formally inscribed in the preceding façade and antechamber, the geometric leitmotif culminated in a twisting, seemingly floating ceiling element that controlled the versatile trans-

Figure 4: Electric Lady Studios, Studio A, interior with acoustic "propeller" and polychromous light system. Photography by John Veltri, Courtesy of Authentic Hendrix, L.L.C.

sensorial atmosphere of Studio A. Christened "the propeller" by Storyk, its curvy form grew out of the adjacent studio wall, spreading deep into the center where it was supported by a smooth column. Both a highly technological and technical architectural entity, it contained necessary air vents, high-fidelity recording equipment, polychromatic lights, and additional outlets to mount equipment. Storyk had installed the architectural element on the flattened ceiling to act as a giant frequency membrane absorber—low frequencies were absorbed more efficiently than high frequencies, decreasing reverb time simultaneously at high frequencies, which enabled the studio technicians to produce clearer recordings at high volume. Made of air-entrained plaster, the acoustic propeller's half-scattering, half-absorbing surface produced a unique sonic environment in which the entire live room and its architectural envelope became instrumentalized.[36] On the level of technicity, it also served to modulate the space through distinct climatic and chromatic atmospheres whose totalizing vibe was aimed towards enhancing Hendrix's creative experience—"we were mixing light like colors with those dichromatic bulbs," Storyk recalled.[37] Hovering anticipatingly in space, the propeller tied together the architectural and mediatechnological elements of the studio into a technical ensemble.

Half-wooden and half-carpeted floors, white carpeted walls, and Bohemian fabrics added simultaneously to the overall aesthetic style and atmosphere of the place, complicating the geometric wave proportions and frequency reflection anomalies of the 1500 sq. ft resonant space. In order to produce a more authentic vibe, these objects were instrumentalized to break, absorb, or alter the sonic vibrations emitted by musical instruments, human voices, and their electrically enhanced reverberations. The acoustic atmosphere of Studio A was warm and balanced. Crucially, however, its conducive vibe remained adaptable to various moods and musical genres. Together, the prop-like furniture, the floating media-apparatus, instruments, technical equipment, reflex baffles, and standing acoustic panels enforced a transductive theatricality of operative ambience for its recording artists. ELS had finally departed from the aesthetic neutrality of recording studios elsewhere towards architecture as event.

The studio was installed with state-of-the-art sound recording and engineering equipment and contained a vast archive of tapes and recordings Hendrix had amassed touring and jamming. This vibe defining set of objects was carefully regulated by technicians and sound engineers, who operated at a level of *just noticeable difference* (JND[38]) and from the isolation of a studio-adjacent control room that was connected visually via a soundproof glass window and sonically through the recording and replay of electrified signals. The sound engineers' role had shifted in accordance with ELS's typological transformation. Whereas they previously only recorded and edited sonic matter, they were now additionally tasked with elaborately customizing the architectural space through mediatechnological devices and turned-on décor. As novel technicians of vibe, they were crucial in the quotidian operation of the studio once the architect and architectural acoustician had left. It was up to them to yield the potential of the architecture-system Storyk had designed. ELS, therefore, coupled sound engineers and artists in a secondary environment that synthesized the correct vibe out of sound recordings, architectural space, post-production, and the comprehensive presence of the artist throughout this process. This technical ensemble was crucial in realizing the full spectrum of vibe as an operative ambience. Conceived as an engineered affect, vibe could be engendered by the architectural components, registered by sensors, encapsulated by hi-fi recording equipment, then processed in post-production and disseminated to simulate the same vibes in clubs, through radio stations, and in homes across the globe. There it would initiate, for its audience, an individuating process, closing the loop from producing to engendering vibe.

Operative Ambience as a Form of Capacitation

An intimate entanglement of spatial performance and temporal criticality defines the technicity of operative ambience in ELS. Vibe, as Grietzer stressed, thereby sustains its very own set of internal logic, mediating between *dense vibe* (imaginary world) and *loose vibe* (real world)—the former replicating and intensifying the structural composition of the latter.[39] What may seem like a virtuous relationship carries an inherent precarity. Due to the instability and frequent decay of dense vibe, operative ambience requires constant regulation. ELS this way exploited what Smith, citing Vincent Scully, called the "permissiveness" of environment and bodies, a "'softness,'" or "architectural looseness […] based on a rigorous pluralism and a willingness to face the complexity that surrounds us."[40] This permissive technicity was mediated by the studio's distinct architectural processes of buffering (e.g., acoustic or sociopolitical noise), isolating (e.g., conducive atmospheres), and (re)connecting partitioned zones. Densified vibe transmits its inherent instability through insulated channels to secondary receivers, who seek a similar de-coupling from their tumultuous reality, even if temporary. This process of *capacitation* on the side of the individual—whether Hendrix in the studio or secondary consumers at home—hinges on the characteristic instability of vibe. It mirrors what musicologist Marie Thompson describes as the "shared and collective registers of the experiential" in affect, being "both a-objective and a-subjective, a-signifying and a-representational, existing as part of, but never being fully captured by, subjects, objects or signifiers."[41] Internalizing individualized capacitation as its driving force, vibe c. 1969 distinguished itself markedly from the homogenizing process that Sorkin had ascribed to early architectural modernism, which "sought to harmonize vibe" in an effort to conceive of "the global environment as uniform as possible […] celebrating a uniform idea of subjectivity."[42] Architecture, after all, is always a form of mind control," Sorkin stressed.[43] Whether loose or dense, good or bad, vibe thus demands careful attention as it may shift from conducive to restrictive at any moment.

For Hendrix, ELS was a safe haven, a space where he could escape the ethnic and social categorizations that haunted him and constantly threatened to undermine his identity as a musician. African American audiences critiqued him as a Black man playing the white man's music. Caucasian audiences seemingly tended to ignore his Blackness or projected negative stereotypes of the mysterious, oversexualized drug user. Many musicologists and scholars of African American Studies have worked on carefully reconstructing the racial meditations that played an important role in the musician's life, exploring his image from both perspectives.[44] Hendrix himself aimed to diffuse these binary categories and "would later rationalize his ambivalence towards both blackness and America through the nomadic ideology of the gypsy," remarked the historian Paul Gilroy.[45] The spaceship vibe of ELS is closely connected to these nomadic desires.[46] Engaged in realizing Hendrix's philosophical approach, ELS was "like a black and white photograph," Storyk fittingly recalled, "you have to color and paint it yourself in your mind."[47]

The developing parallels between Hendrix and vibe are important aspects of this inquiry and crucially highlight the undifferentiated cultural appropriation that is embedded in the concept. Vibe emerged from a Black music context to be adapted across pre-conceived sociocultural and ethnic boundaries. Exemplifying obscene appropriation and coevolutionary coupling, Hendrix befell a posthumous transformation worthy of what Simondon called an *infra-individual technical object*—distinct from "true individuals" in having no associated milieu, thus, able to plug into any system.[48] Cultural science theorist Bruce Clark fittingly remarked on Hendrix's frequent coupling of "the electric guitar and its amplification and sound-processing technologies *to* the body *in* performance" as "communicating his own cybernetic fusion to his actual live and virtual mediated audiences."[49] This synthesis found its ultimate culmination in a foot-pedal-operated phase shifter designed by audio engineer Fumio Mieda for the Japanese company Shin-ei in 1968, distributed by Univox in North America, and aptly titled Uni-Vibe. This effects unit, a square aluminum box covering "a pulsing light bulb, [...] surrounded by four light sensors that control the four stages of phasing," encapsulated the "throbbing, hypnotic pulse and lo-fi sweep" that would become synonymous with one of its most devoted users, Jimi Hendrix.[50] Jimi Hendrix™ Uni-Vibe® is now a registered trademark of Dunlop Manufacturing, Inc., available as Chorus/Vibrato or Jimi Hendrix™ Fuzz Face® Distortion, Jimi Hendrix™ Octavio® Fuzz, and Jimi Hendrix™ Gypsy® Fuzz. "Authentic Hendrix" reassures a logotype printed on the backside of the effects unit. Once plugged into both guitar and amplifier, it is able to (re)produce the authentic vibe of the artist in any space and for any user—so the promise of Dunlop Manufacturing, Inc.

The Uni-Vibe phase-shifter dramatically hyperbolizes the role ELS assumed within the emergent ecology and economy of vibe c. 1969. Whereas vibe-inducing artifacts—e.g., technological equipment, sound, or drugs—were heavily commodified and easily consumed, they remained ultimately limited to densifying vibe temporarily. What was being engendered and produced at ELS, however, was more than one of these elements—sound—and its relational capacity but the traced architecture and its encapsulated space. Architecture gained instrumentality as the synchronization of these disparate elements and as the analogic display for the capture of acoustic vibrations and the staging of atmospheres. It reacted to the modulation techniques of vibes and vibrations and translated the architectural space and ambience from which they emanate.

Acknowledgments

In memoriam: Michael Sorkin (1948-2020). This paper is dedicated to the life and work of the esteemed architect, critic, educator, and urbanist for whom architecture was as vibrant as life itself and who realized the gravity of vibe (sign-signifier) in co-constitutively entangling the human and the environment in a perpetual process of exteriorization and individuation. I owe a debt of gratitude to John Storyk for opening the doors to his private archive and for sharing a part of his formative history with me, ever kind, modest, and interested. Sylvia Lavin and Spyros Papapetros deserve profound recognition for their critical instruction in the initial stages of this project and my abiding thanks for their continuous intellectual guidance.

Notes

1. Michael Sorkin, "Notes on Vibe" (1998), in *Some Assembly Required* (Minneapolis: University of Minnesota Press, 2001), 70–77 (77).

2. The Jimi Hendrix Experience, "Have You Ever Been (To Electric Ladyland)," *Electric Ladyland,* Reprise Records 2RS6307, 1968, 2 x Vinyl LP.

3. C. Ray Smith, "Instant Interiors," *Progressive Architecture* 48, no. 6 (June 1967): 176–181 (176–177, 178–179); C. Ray Smith, "Projection: The New Turned-On Décor," *House Beautiful* 109, no. 9 (1967): 130–132; C. Ray Smith, "The New Interiors: Fad or Fact?," *Progressive Architecture* (October 1968): 150–159.

4. Sylvia Lavin has likewise described this symptomatic shift across cultural and counter-cultural streams as "architecture's move in the postwar period from space to event."—Sylvia Lavin, "The Turn-On," in *Flash in the Pan* (London: Architectural Association, 2014), 138–155 (144–145).

5. Gilbert Simondon, *Du mode d'existence des objets techniques* [On the Mode of Existence of Technical Objects] (Paris: Aubier, 1958) (Simondon's secondary thesis for the *Doctorat d'Etat*, written between 1954 and 1958), 159—cit. in Gilbert Simondon, *On the Mode of Existence of Technical Objects*, trans. Cecile Malaspina and John Rogove (Minneapolis: Univocal, 2017), 173.

6. Gilbert Simondon, *L'individuation à la lumière des notions de forme et d'information* (Grenoble: Jérôme Millon, 2005), 191—cit. in Jean-Hugues Barthélémy, "Fifty Key Terms in the Work of Gilbert Simondon," trans. Arne De Boever, in *Gilbert Simondon: Being and Technology*, eds. Arne De Boever, Alex Murray, Jon Roffe, and Ashley Woodward (Edinburgh: Edinburgh University Press, 2012), 203–231 (213).

7.   Simondon, *Du mode d'existence des objets techniques*, 65; *On the Mode of Existence of Technical Objects*, 67.

8.   Marshall McLuhan, *The Medium is the Massage* (New York: Penguin Books, 1967), 63; Marshall McLuhan, "Living in an Acoustic World," lecture at University of South Florida 1970.

9.   Steve Goodman, *Sonic Warfare: Sound, Affect, and the Ecology of Fear* (Cambridge, MA: The MIT Press, 2010), 76.

10. Cerebrum existed for less than a year (November 1968 – Summer 1969) at 429 Broome St and Crosby St. Radio Advertisements on programs such as WNEW-FW called it an "electric studio of participation," a "super, electric, turned on, far-out fantasy land," that offered two three-hour sessions nightly (8-11pm, 11:30pm-2:30am), and only with reservations made telephonically under "966–4031."

11. Dan Sullivan, "Cerebrum: Club Seeking to Soothe the Mind—'Studio' Offers Trip for 'New Form of Communication,'" at *The New York Times*, November 23, 1968, 63.

12. Dorothy Kalins, "Here's Looking at You: Voyeurism in New York," at *New York Magazine*, March 3, 1969, 39–40 (40).

13. Ruffin Cooper Jr., son of a Texan banker, later achieved modest fame for his architectural and abstract photography characterized by extreme close-ups—most evident in the "Taos Church" (1979) and "Sky" (1980) series that negotiate architectural mass and negative space as geometric assemblies.

14. Sullivan, "Cerebrum: Club Seeking to Soothe the Mind—'Studio' Offers Trip for 'New Form of Communication,'" 62.

15. C. Ray Smith, *Supermannerism: New Attitudes in Post-Modern Architecture* (New York: Dutton, 1977), 302.

16. "A Teetotal Nightclub Where Personal Experience is All," in *Life*, April 4, 1969, 28–29 (29).

17. Gene Youngblood, *Expanded Cinema* (New York: P. Dutton & Co., Inc., 1970), 362.

18. Ibid., 360.

19. Ibid.

20. See the recollections of Richard Currie, one of the collaborators that conceived of Cerebrum, in David Kaufman, *Ridiculous! The Theatrical Life and Times of Charles Ludlam* (New York: Applause Theatre & Cinema Books, 2002), 167–168.

21. Storyk, himself a musician (guitar) in a twelve-piece Blues band while at Princeton, would often come to the Generation club for the musical performances that featured such greats as B. B. King, Paul Butterfield, and Jimi Hendrix. — John Storyk, "Jimi's Vibe Infused in the Architecture of Electric Lady Studios," interview with the author, March 31, 2019.

22. Freshly graduated from an undergraduate program, Storyk was unlicensed. All plans filed with the NY authorities had to be signed and stamped by registered architect Robert Cabrera (Brooklyn, NY).

23.   See A. B. Pippard, *The Physics of Vibration* (Cambridge: Cambridge University Press, 1989); Philip M. Morse, *Vibration and Sound* (New York and London: McGraw-Hill, 1936); Philip M. Morse and K. Uno Ingard, *Theoretical Acoustics* (New York and London: McGraw-Hill, 1968).

24.   See Ernst Heinrich Weber, *De Tactu (De Pulsu, Resorptione, Auditu et Tactu)* (Leipzig: C. F. Koehler, 1834); Hermann von Helmholtz, *Die Lehre von den Tonempfindungen als physiologische Grundlage für die Theorie der Musik* (Heidelberg, 1863); Gustav Theodor Fechner, *Elemente der Psychophysik* (Leipzig: Breitkopf & Härtel, 1860); Wilhelm Maximilian Wundt, *Beiträge zur Theorie der Sinneswahrnehmung* (Leipzig: Winter, 1862); Wilhelm Maximilian Wundt, "Selbstbeobachtung und innere Wahrnehmung." *Philosophische Studien*, vol. 1 (1888): 615–617.

25.   See esp. August Schmarsow, *Das Wesen der architektonischen Schöpfung.* (inaugural lecture at K. Universität Leipzig, November 8, 1893) (Leipzig: Karl W. Hiersemann, 1894), August Schmarsow. "Über den Werth der Dimensionen im menschlichen Raumgebilde," in: *Berichte über die Verhandlungen der Königlich Sächsischen Gesellschaft der Wissenschaften zu Leipzig, Philologisch-Historische Klasse*, vol. 48 (1896): 44–61; Robert Vischer, *Über das optische Formgefühl: Ein Beitrag zu Ästhetik* (Leipzig: Hermann Credner, 1873); Heinrich Wölfflin, *Prolegomena zu einer Psychologie der Architektur* (Munich: 1886).

26.   See Leonard Feather, *Encyclopedia of Jazz* (New York: Horizon, 1960).

27.   Oxford English Dictionary, s.v. "vibe"; Eugene E. Landy, *The Underground Dictionary* (New York: Simon and Schuster, 1971), 193.

28.   Landy, *The Underground Dictionary*, 193.

29.   Peli Grietzer, "Ambient Meaning: Mood, Vibe, System," Ph.D. diss., Harvard University, Cambridge, MA, 2018, 63; see Peli Grietzer, "A Theory of Vibe," *Glass–Bead Journal, Site 1: Logic Gate, the Politics of the Artifactual Mind* (2017).

30.   R. Buckminster Fuller, "Introduction," in Gene Youngblood, *Expanded Cinema* (New York: P. Dutton & Co., Inc., 1970), 15–35 (33–34).

31.   Ibid., 30.

32.   Ibid., 28.

33.   Patti Smith, *Just Kids* (New York and London: Bloomsbury, 2010), 169.

34.   Sorkin, "Notes on Vibe", 70.

35.   Eddie Kramer, Electric Lady Studios, "At Guitar Center," interview, YouTube; https://www.youtube.com/watch?time_continue=127&v=MtOuQviX-UY; accessed May 10, 2018.

36.   Jeff Touzeau, "Professional Sound: Electric Lady Studios—Historic Design, Modern Methodology, WSDG (Walters-Storyk Design Group website: https://wsdg.com/professional-sound-electric-lady-studios-historic-design-modern-methodology; accessed May 10, 2018.

37.   John Storyk, "Cerebrum, ELS, and the Acoustic Architecture of Vibe," interview with the author, May 24, 2019.

38.   *The Sonification Handbook*, eds. Thomas Hermann, Andy Hunt, John G. Neuhoff (Berlin: Logos, 2011), 255.

39.   Grietzer, "A Theory of Vibe," n.p.

40.   Vincent Scully cit. in C. Ray Smith, "The Permissiveness of Supermannerism," *Progressive Architecture* 48, no. 10 (October 1967): 169–173; Smith, "Instant Interiors" (1967), 179.

41.   Marie Thompson, *Beyond Unwanted Sound Noise, Affect and Aesthetic Moralism* (New York and London: Bloomsbury, 2017), 11.

42.   Sorkin, "Notes on Vibe", 75.

43.   Ibid.

44.   See Greg Tate, *Midnight Lightning: Jimi Hendrix and the Black Experience* (Chicago: Chicago Review Press, 2003).

45.   Paul Gilroy, *The Black Atlantic: Modernity and Double Consciousness* (Cambridge, MA: Harvard University Press, 1993), 94.

46.   See Jeremy Wells, "Blackness 'Scuzed: Jimi Hendrix's (In)Visible Legacy in Heavy Metal," in *Race Consciousness: African-American Studies for the New Century*, ed. Judith Jackson Fossett and Jeffrey A. Tucker (New York: New York University Press, 1997), 56.

47.   Storyk, "Cerebrum, ELS, and the Acoustic Architecture of Vibe".

48.   Simondon, *On the Mode of Existence of Technical Objects*, 66.

49.   Bruce Clark, *Neocybernetics and Narrative* (Minneapolis: University of Minnesota Press, 2014), 81—emphasis in original.

50.   Michael Heatley, *Jimi Hendrix Gear: The Guitars, Amps & Effects that Revolutionized Rock 'n' Roll* (Minneapolis: Voyageur Press, 2009), 120.

06.

Resonant Rooms as Tuning Forks: Architectural Implications of Sound Art

Ross K. Elfline

The literature on sound art is seemingly preoccupied with space—from buildings to walls to floors—a preoccupation so significant that one may be tempted to say that the literature suffers from an "architectural complex."[1] Unlike the rootedness and placebound identity of art, so critics argue, sound is slippery and mobile. It cannot be contained, to the point where authors continually make the point that sound can maneuver around corners in its relentless, oozing progress.[2] As such, sound art works challenge the architectural frame in which they are installed. Sound art can therefore be lumped together with other neo-avant-garde attempts to question the institutional parameters of art. Its claims to critique are only amplified once sound works leave the gallery or museum in the form of the itinerant recorded object: an LP, compact disc, flash drive or MP3 file can easily be duplicated and sent around the world in a moment's notice, ending up in thousands, even millions of ears, thus circumventing the normal distribution apparatus of art.[3]

Though to wish away the materiality of sound—and the architectural surround into which it is amplified or broadcasted—neglects to consider the unique formal properties inherent to the medium of sound art itself. After all, while sound can travel around a doorframe, it also shakes that frame, as well as the floor joists and roof beams. Sound's impact is indeed manifestly physical and palpable, rooted in places, buildings, and bodies. It is to be found within rooms, sometimes concentrating the feeling of interiority. "Feeling" is the operative word here, for sound, despite its materiality as an objective fact, adds sensuousness and delight to its spaces of performance, and this delight is experienced within individual bodies both as facts and as subjective encounters with space. As such, sound has the power to subtly alter both our immediate perception of architecture and, as we will see, the architectural program of a given space.

I will linger over a particular moment in the development of sound art to demonstrate the manner in which sound is intimately tied to place, and more specifically to the intimate interior space of its transmission and the bodies that populate those very rooms. The case studies I have chosen are well-known: La Monte Young's *Dream House* installation works from the 1960s and 70s and Alvin Lucier's *I am sitting in a room* from 1969. Both works utilize the architectural surround as sounding medium and catalyze the bodies populating the spaces as active agents in the performance setting. Sound, as an event literally taking place, alters the ways in which we perceive architecture, and thus shifts the way we interact with place.

The claim that sound is determined largely by its site of performance is by no means radical. As Christoph Cox has noted, the field of sound art studies uses spatial metaphors to an overwhelming extent.[4] But rather than looking at what sound does to the discipline of art, my curiosity is in what sound can do to our perception of architecture and its atmospheric aspects. What do we notice about space when our aural senses are heightened, and how do we then proceed to navigate the resulting space? This leads to the ultimate question: How might sound alter the architectural program of a given space? It is my claim that Young and Lucier both encourage us to experience architecture differently, but also that their works have other architectural implications—they *create* architecture via non-tectonic means, specifically by engaging bodies as activating agents.

La Monte Young's *Dream House* and the Itinerant Beholder

As an initial case study, I would like to consider the American composer La Monte Young's series of sound installations from the mid-1960s through the present day that he and his wife and collaborator Marianne Zazeela present under the title *Dream House*. These installations derive from Young's signature, pared-down compositions, which emerged in the late 1950s. These feature long, sustained notes, as epitomized in his work "Composition 1960 #7," which featured a perfect fifth "to be held," in Young's words, "for a very long time." This would prove the beginning of a long investigation into the psychoacoustic properties of sustained tones, or drones. When held for extremely long periods of time, and played at intense volume levels, these tones provoke the sensation of hearing overtones that are not, in fact, physically present in the room. As authors like Brandon LaBelle and others have wisely pointed out, these works of such bone-rattling intensity present themselves to the listener as a physical force.[5] However, since they lack any sense of rhythm and dynamic markings, and thus do not mark out time, they allow the listener to settle into a sound. Stripped of any sense of progression or resolution, the listener is presented with simply the thing itself, a pure musical vibration, and deeper knowledge of this sonic material comes only after extended absorption.

Young soon became increasingly sensitive to the environmental aspects of his works. One of the reasons he employed single tones or perfect fifths in contained environments was to capture the unique sonic properties of the room. When a sine wave would reflect off a surface and meet with a wave of the same frequency back in the space of the performance, they would become superimposed one atop the other, creating a node of especially intense sound. Furthermore, when two sine waves were amplified into a given space, a complex network of sounds were produced. See Young's description of such a spatial situation: "As the phase relationship between the two sine waves alters, due to the change of air pressure within a space, both pitch and volume vary according to one's location within the room; this 'allows the listener to actually experience sound structures in the natural course of exploring the space'."[6] The result was the creation of unique sites within the room, with more or less discrete contours or edges, that listeners would discover only once they traversed the space.

Due to the spatialized aspects of his performances, the language of three-dimensional form dominates the literature on Young, with critics discussing the manner in which the composer "sculpts" sound in space, and how his tones strike the listener almost like a blunt object.[7] Or, if not struck by sound, the audience is suffused into a murky liquid that fills the space of the performance. Whatever physical metaphor one chooses, it is clear that the sound itself would seem to take on a palpably tactile dimension. It is literally and physically felt, but the immediacy of touch and sound on the body leads the perceiver to sense the room both intuitively and emotionally.

If sound was presented as almost physical in nature in Young's performance venues, further questions emerge around their reception: What were their atmospheric properties, and how were beholders meant to approach these sound-objects? Were they imposing and constricting, or were they welcoming, allowing for careful scrutiny? In discussing the experiences of the loft performances that led to the *Dream House* concerts, art historian Branden W. Joseph determines that the room becomes one of crushing compression: "Young's listener and sound were engaged in a type of struggle, the phenomenological particularities of hearing in 'one's own terms' struggling for autonomy against the nearly overwhelming pressure of the sound."[8] For LaBelle, however, the listener is granted much more agency in co-creating the aesthetic encounter: "Young emphasizes the movements of the individual to generate spatiality. In this regard, auditory experience is determined through the bodily flow of an individual whose decisions as to where to be constructs the composition and the subsequent articulation of space."[9] Whether oppressive and domineering or open and welcoming, the sustained tones of Young's performances imbued the rooms with distinct feelings, and in so doing affected the movement of bodies through space.

Figure 1: La Monte Young and Marian Zazeela, Re-Creation of *Dream House*, Church Street, New York City, 2015. Photgraph: Marian Zazeela. Public Domain. (Plate 1, p. 289)

Without adjudicating the debate between Joseph or LaBelle, it is important to note that Young's sonic environment becomes a space wherein the intense reverberations off the walls concentrate the play of power between the listener and the object perceived. The room becomes a place of spatial negotiation. Young's works do liberate beholders from a fixed point of apprehension (such as one might find within a standard concert situation), but they are still guided toward spatialized points in the room. However, these points in the room may differ from those dictated by the built architecture. If a new architecture is produced, it is an agonistic one established by the confluence of tectonic space, amplified sound, and itinerant bodies.[10] In describing the performance situation as agonistic, I mean that the sheer sustained volume of the tones amplified in space established a lasting tension between them and the beholder. However, instead of viewing the situation as one in which the beholder is made wholly subservient to the oppressive sonic dictates of the space, one might rather posit the beholder as a co-creator of the aesthetic experience. The result is not an overtly antagonistic relationship between sonic space and the beholder, but one in which a productive tension is sustained through interactivity.

The appearance of the newly itinerant listener, alternately seeking out or repelled by the nodes of sonic intensity within the room of the performance, reveals the ways in which the architectural programs of such performance spaces are altered by the insertion of Young's tones. The contours of the resulting environment both depend on, and yet depart from, the geometry of the room in which the performance takes place. Crucially, the invisibility of the sound waves makes it necessary for the listeners' bodies to discover the form for themselves. If the architectural surround had assumed one form of organization of users in space, Young's sonic environment produces another one entirely. The spatialized event counters the parameters of the room while propelling the listeners into space as co-creators of the environment.

The apogee of Young and Zazeela's research into the architectural qualities of sound and light came in 1979 when the Dia Art Foundation funded the creation of a permanent large-scale installation work titled *Dream House* in the former Mercantile Exchange Building in Lower Manhattan (Figure 1). Each room in the structure was taken over by a set of electronic tone frequencies derived from Young's piece *Well Tuned Piano*. Zazeela installed her work *Magenta Lights* to accompany the unique frequencies within each space. What the visitor encountered, then, was a sequence of different rooms, each with unique sonic qualities. She could wander through the building freely, contemplating the sounds and the resulting overtones that would occur. Rather than sitting for a unique performance of the work, in which each chord would be performed in a set sequence (as one normally would for the exceedingly long performances of *Well Tuned Piano*), the visitor to the *Dream House* would effectively be a co-creator in the score. Since there was no set progression or sequence in which one should walk through the rooms, there was a degree of improvisation that Young and Zazeela allowed for. As LaBelle summarizes, "By moving through the different rooms, a visitor would create the composition: spending time in one room, sleeping in another, avoiding others, acted as a form of improvisation, a kind of performance in which sound, space, and the individual unite."[11]

One important conclusion from this description is that the rooms themselves served as active forces rather than as neutral repositories or frames for the musical work. LaBelle points to this aspect of the *Dream House* by stating that, "Young works with the given space as an extended instrument through acoustically conversing with it."[12] Walls, floor joists, roof beams all shook in accord with the tones amplified in the various spaces, effectively turning each room into a large tuning fork.

However, these ambiences created within the work changed—both within a given room and from room to room—as the listener traversed the space. As LaBelle's description above indicates, some rooms were suffused with a more relaxing, even soporific atmosphere. Others one would have evaded entirely. The point is that our perception of different sounds, as spatially distributed in space, affects how we navigate space, but just as important is the ineffable perception of architectural atmospheres that are thus created by the presence of different sounds as well. The sounds of Young and Zazeela's *Dream House* may subtly direct our bodies, but what we do there and how we act are, to some extent, dependent on how the sounds make us feel. Are we liable to fall asleep, duck around anxiously in avoidance of a discordant sound, or linger inquisitively? How we feel with respect to the broader character of the environment is tied to a multitude of sensory properties of the space, including sound. As Gernot Böhme has noted, the atmosphere of a given room is something "quasi-objective," in that it is both something unique to a given environment, and yet it is dependent upon the receiver assembling and responding to all the various sensory cues within the space.[13] *Dream House* is space completed by the listener; however, the listener acts in an agonistic situation established among the palpably physical architectural surround, the aggressively loud "shape" amplified within it, and his or her own body physically traversing the space. The individual response to that scenario is caught, then, in the quasi-objective condition of the architectural atmosphere of the *Dream House* and how one chooses to engage its varying moods. Through the addition of sound, the room becomes a place of active and sustained tension between built form, ambient sound, and perceiving bodies.

Alvin Lucier's *I am sitting in a room* and Sympathetic Vibrations

The architectural surround as a resonant sounding device also features in American composer Alvin Lucier's best-known work *I am sitting in a room* from 1969, a work that foregrounds the material process of sound production (Figure 2). For this piece, Lucier set up a recursive process by which the recitation of a text was recorded, played back, re-recorded, and again played back repeatedly until all that was left was a droning hum punctuated occasionally by rhythmic thrums of speech. The suggested text for the work, written by Lucier, explains its process as well as its motivation:

> I am sitting in a room different from the one you are in now. I am recording the
> sound of my speaking voice and I am going to play it back into the room again
> and again until the resonant frequencies of the room reinforce themselves so that
> any semblance of my speech, with perhaps the exception of rhythm, is destroyed.
> What you will hear, then, are the natural resonant frequencies of the room articu
> lated by speech. I regard this activity not so much as a demonstration of a physical
> fact, but more as a way to smooth out any irregularities my speech may have.[14]

Importantly, *I am sitting in a room* once again uses the architectural frame as a sounding device. As Lucier describes it, the piece is one of several intended to "explore the natural properties of sound and the acoustic characteristics of architectural spaces as musical objectives."[15] It does so by using the sound itself as a catalyst: sound waves travel through the room and cause the room itself—its walls, floors, decorative details and the like—to vibrate in kind with the frequency. However, in successive recordings of the sound, the specificities of speech recede into the background, leaving only the unique resonant frequency itself, as if the room itself is a tuning fork being gently, though steadily, struck.

The listener now does not traverse the space of the resulting sonic environment, but merely hears the indexical trace of another absent room. That record of the absent space is acoustically mapped by the sound of the artist's voice, tripping off the

Figure 2: Alvin Lucier performing *I am sitting in a room* in 2010. Public Domain. (Plate 2, p. 289)

sounding of the architectural space.[16] It is a room defined, and made perceptible by, the individual voice that triggers the space into sympathetic reverberation. Once again, our perception of the architectural space and its atmosphere is informed by—indeed, contingent upon—bodies, or rather the singular body of the lone composer marking his presence in space. Gradually, as the smooth hum of the recording takes over, all the static and sonic outliers fade away, and the listener is left with a consonance between the performer's voice and the site-specific sound of the performance space itself. Indeed, what Lucier had hoped to achieve is an awareness of space that one could not achieve through sight alone. The unique sonic property of a room—the resonant whirr that would result if one were able to strike the room itself—is not usually revealed to us. However, by re-orienting the room's program—now as a sounding device—such properties can be perceived, felt, and even studied and compared to other spaces. Architecture provides us with a different sort of pleasure. As architectural historian and critic Sylvia Lavin argued in *Kissing Architecture,* buildings— specifically their surfaces—offer the potential for feeling and pleasure that exist quite apart from any ostensible program inherent in their form.[17] So too with Lucier's performance: the sound reflected off the resonant surface of the wall serves no further function than to delight us with its soft and warm wave.

The relationship between architectural envelope, sound, and the body is not one of agonism here but rather of sympathy. The voice exits the body, encourages the sympathetic vibration of the surrounding space and comes back as reflected sound. The process is repeated until the voice, in all its quirks and variations, recedes, and we are left with the room's hum. To perceive the room, it needed to be activated by a voice, a voice that began its recitation with a simple statement of obstinate presence: "I am sitting in a room." The voice then merges with the echo of the room, and we are left with a feeling of consonance. We, the absent listeners, perceive the room and its occupant in a uniquely intimate fashion via the sound waves emitted by a body's vocal cords that ping the walls of a room in sympathetic vibration and enter our own ear canal. We are connected and yet forever absent from the activated room, and yet through the imminence of sound we understand something of its character, as well as the character of Lucier.

Acoustic Atmospheres and Bodily Subjectivity

With these two examples in place, we can see how architecture is thematized in the works and the literature of sound art. These two works are, in fact, the primary reasons for historian Brandon LaBelle's argument that the shift from "music" to "sound art" is epitomized by the shift in emphasis from time to space. Leaving aside the fact that neither Young nor Lucier define themselves as sound artists, it is important to consider what these works have to say about "space" itself. Undoubtedly, these works are spatially rooted, or, "site-specific," meaning that their very form is contingent upon the site of their installation or performance.[18] To repeat the work in another locale is to behold a fundamentally different work in both form and atmosphere. While the entire industry of acoustical engineering has been built on the attempt to mitigate against the differences from one space to the next, the very existence of this field is testament to the fact that the specificity of space and rooms matters.[19]

More than asserting the specifics of a particular place, or foregrounding the *genius loci* of rooms, the importance of these case studies lies in their capacities to draw our attention to the alternate architectures that exist within rooms, alternatives that are the result of a relationship—alternately conflictual or sympathetic—between the architectural envelope, the amplified sound within it, and the body or bodies present in the room as co-creators of the space.[20] By using architecture itself as a vibrating, resonating object or instrument, our attention is drawn to the architectural envelope from which the sounds emanate and then to the ambience or atmosphere of the altered environment created by the sounds-in-space. The rooms that host these performative interventions are no longer so many inert or neutral spaces but rather charged with a particular mood, one that shifts according to the sounds propelled through them and the participants who send and receive them. By foregrounding the nature of the interaction of sound, material envelope, and bodies, the building is revealed as not so much a stable architecture of powerful beams and vibrating girders but a mutable, undulating space in which sound waves, listeners and performers activate the architecture.

Let us remember how, in Young and Zazeela's *Dream House*, the listener is impelled, to walk around the room, sensing the unique contours of the tones as they condense and release in moments where sine waves are reinforced by their mates or clash with other discordant ones. This inquisitive probing of the space itself leads to a unique form of architecture in which the itinerant inhabitant remains always on-the-go. While the invisible form whose contours the listener may be tracing follows a path established by sound waves, the listener is not following the directional cues offered by the room's architecture. She is caught, temporarily, in another space, both situationally grounded and yet apart from the strictures of the immediate physical environment. She is thus implicated in the tense push-and-pull between the space and the sound inside.

In terms of Alvin Lucier's performance space *I am sitting in a room,* the listeners may not be activated agents, but the work does foreground the body of the performer, Lucier himself. Specifically, it is Lucier's lone voice that triggers the room, makes it come to life. Again, through auditory perception we come to know and understand architectural space. As such, Lucier displaces the optical experience of architecture that has dominated architectural theory and discourse by emphasizing other sensory forms of knowledge.[21]

Likewise, it is important to cite Lucier's ongoing fascination with the idea of the chamber. Over the course of his career, the composer came to view all manner of objects, from seashells to canyons, as resonant chambers, or as sound-making devices. In his words, "I thought of them as rooms within rooms which impinge their acoustic characteristics on each other."[22] Seen in this light, Lucier, as the performer of *I am sitting in a room* is himself one more chamber, one more room. The distinction is thus eroded between the body and the architectural envelope that surrounds it. The architecture of a room is not a determining force affecting the bodies inhabiting it but is activated by the resonant chambers of the bodies taking up residence inside it at a given moment. Pallasmaa's atmospheric architecture again unites us, as resonant chambers, with the rooms we inhabit. We are all, ourselves, rooms within rooms.

Finally, it is not quite enough to merely state that sound is a spatialized medium. Instead, we must investigate what architectural claims given sound art works make. What sort of architecture is made through the introduction of sound into the built environment? Many sound-objects do indeed condition the body, wielding a sort of authority to literally put us in our place. It is, therefore, worth mentioning that the immediacy of atmospheric architecture and its ability to tap into our emotions make it an ideal medium for both consumer persuasion and political manipulation.[23] However, we might also mine sound art for an alternate, sly, and cunning architecture—one that is slippery, amorphous, and ambient. As Pallasmaa has noted, atmospheric architecture, in its sensory imminence, is primarily experienced and felt rather than known intellectually. It is "perceived in a diffuse and peripheral manner," and invites haptic curiosity.[24] It is in that space—where sound, bodies, and matter come into contact and conflict—that the dynamics and frisson of habitation come so pointedly to the fore. Young's and Lucier's works may condense and concentrate sound, suffusing space with auditory objects, but as both subjects and sounding vessels ourselves we might navigate them with a newfound agency now that these conditioning and conditioned interiors are geared toward uses for which they were never intended. Sound affords the possibility of new programs for habitable space, but it is up to us—the new producers of space—to determine their ultimate fate.

Notes

1. Certainly, a central figure in establishing the connection between sound and site is Brandon LaBelle whose many texts on this intersection have been foundational. See especially his *Background Noise: Perspectives on Sound Art* (London and New York: Bloomsbury, 2006); *Site of Sound: Of Architecture and the Ear* (Los Angeles: Errant Bodies Press, 1999), edited with Steve Roden; and *Surface Tension: Problematics of Site* (Los Angeles: Errant Bodies Press, 2003), edited with Ken Ehrlich. More recently, LaBelle's work has addressed the issue of the "site of sound" in terms of the politics of public space in *Sonic Agency: Sound and Emergent Forms of Resistance* (London: Goldsmiths Press, 2018). The term "architectural complex" here is borrowed from Hal Foster's *The Art–Architecture Complex* (London: Verso, 2013).

2. See, for instance, Steven Connor: "Much of the work that is characteristic of sound art has either gone outside or has the capacity to bring the outside inside… Sound art comes not only through the wall but round the corner and through the floor. Perhaps the greatest allure of sound for artists… is that sound, like an odor or a giggle, escapes." In "Ears have Walls: On Hearing Art," *FO(A)RM*, no. 4 (2005): 48–57. Reprinted in *Sound,* ed. by Caleb Kelly (London and Cambridge, Mass.: Whitechapel Art Gallery and The MIT Press, 2011), 130.

3. This point is made most cogently by Dan Lander in his "Introduction" to *Sound by Artists,* ed. by Lander and Micah Lexier (Toronto: Art Metropole, 1990), 10–14. It also serves as a grounding principle in William Furlong's "Sound in Recent Art," in *Audio Arts: Discourse and Practice in Contemporary Art,* ed. by Furlong (London: Academy Editions, 1994), 128–30.

4. See Christoph Cox, "From Music to Sound: Being as Time in the Sonic Arts," in Kelly, ed. *Sound,* op. cit., 80–87. First published in German as "Von Musik zum Klang: Sein als Zeit in der Klangunst," in *Sonambiente Berlin: Klang Kunst/Sound Art,* ed. by Helga de la Morte-Haber, et al. (Heidelberg: Kehrer Verlag, 2006).

5. See Chapter 5, "Minimalist Treatments: La Monte Young and Robert Morris" in LaBelle's *Background Noise,* 68–75. For more on the impact of Young's music on the

perceiving body (and its departure from Cagean acoustics), see Brandon W. Joseph, "The Tower and the Line: Toward a Genealogy of Minimalism," in *Grey Room* no. 27 (2007): 58–81.

6.   Keith Potter, *Four Musical Minimalists,* (Cambridge, UK and New York: Cambridge University Press, 2000), 78. The quotation here is taken from unpublished notes in Young's archives.

7.   In addition to the LaBelle and Joseph texts already mentioned, it is important to cite Keith Potter's essential *Four Musical Minimalists,* 67–80.

8.   Joseph, "The Tower and the Line," 69.

9.   LaBelle, *Background Noise,* 73.

10.   On notions of agonism, see especially Chantal Mouffe, *Agonistics: Thinking the World Politically* (London: Verso, 2013).

11.   LaBelle, *Background Noise,* 74.

12.   Ibid.

13.   Gernot Böhme, "Urban Atmospheres: Charting New Directions for Architecture and Urban Planning," in *Architectural Atmospheres: On the Experience and Politics of Architecture,* ed. by Christian Borch (Basel: Birkhäuser, 2014), 43.

14.   Alvin Lucier, *I am sitting in a room.* Lovely Music, Ltd. CD 1013, 1990, Compact Disc.

15.   Alvin Lucier, "Careful listening is more important than making sounds happen: The propagation of sound in space," in *Reflections, Interviews, Scores, Writings* (Cologne: MusikTexte, 1995), 430.

16.   Lucier's pronounced stutter is the "irregularity" referred to in the recited text. Brandon LaBelle's reading of the work focuses intently on *I am sitting in a room* as a therapeutic effort to counteract the composer's disability. The work "allows an escape from such a body by stripping him of that nagging stutter and refashioning personality outside the identifying jag of his speech." See *Background Noise,* 132.

17.   Sylvia Lavin, *Kissing Architecture* (New York and Princeton, NJ: Princeton University Press, 2011).

18.   The literature on site-specificity is vast. Important texts include: Miwon Kwon, *One Place After Another: Site-Specific Art and Locational Identity* (Cambridge, Mass.: The MIT press, 2002); Nick Kaye, *Site-Specific Art: Performance, Place, and Documentation* (London: Routledge, 2000); Erika Suderberg, ed. *Space, Site, Intervention: Situating Installation Art* (Minneapolis: Univ. of Minnesota Press, 2000).

19.   Lucier points to this very disjunction when he states, "Conventional acoustic engineering practice has historically defied these phenomena [the unique sonic properties of individual sites] in an attempt to deliver the same product to everybody in the same space." See Lucier, op. cit.

20.   In referring to the *genius loci* of a given site or architectural object, I am referring to the phenomenological apprehension of space epitomized especially by Christian Norberg-Schulz in his *Genius Loci: Toward a Phenomenology of Architecture* (New York: Rizzoli 1980).

21.   Here, one should note the pioneering work of Juhani Pallasmaa, whose critical inter-
      vention into architectural discourse has prodded the field to consider other sensory
      means of understanding space. See especially his *The Eyes of the Skin: Architecture and the
      Senses* (Chichester, UK: John Wiley & Sons, Ltd., 2005).
22.   Lucier, op. cit.
23.   This point is made persuasively by Christian Borch in his essay "The Politics of Atmos-
      pheres: Architecture, Power, and the Senses," in *Architectural Atmospheres*, 60–89.
24.   Juhani Pallasmaa, "Space, Place, and Atmosphere: Peripheral Perception in Existential
      Experience," in *Architectural Atmospheres*, 19.

SECTION #02

Building Pitches

The Happiness of the World at its Birth: Acoustic Atmosphere in the 'General Effect' of Ledoux's Theater of Besançon

Paul Holmquist

In his initial proposal for the Theater of Besançon (1784), Ledoux wrote enigmatically that he knew what it would cost to "establish a new religion."[1] While fearing that the "progressive," more egalitarian social organization of the audience he envisioned would be resisted, if not rejected outright, by the citizens of the provincial garrison town in Franche-Comté, Ledoux was speaking directly to his larger sociopolitical ambition for the theater to become a new civic institution of moral transformation. Ledoux's commentators have generally interpreted this ambition in light of the ascendance of sight and vision in the theater reform movement of the latter half of the 18th Century, and particularly the visual and conceptual reciprocity between audience and performance that Ledoux enacted, in which spectators could see and recognize themselves as a newly reordered social body.[2] Yet theater reform sought to improve spectators' ability not only to see but also to hear the performance, and although Ledoux gave much attention to the acoustics of his theater and the spectators' aural experience, the particular role and significance of these aspects for his conception of the theater as a civic institution have not been considered. In this essay I examine Ledoux's acoustical innovations in the Theater of Besançon and their intended effect on the audience as presented in his treatise *L'architecture considérée sous le rapport de l'art, des moeurs et de la législation* (1804). Through a consideration of how Ledoux conceived of the audience's aural experience within the architecture of the hall in relation to his understanding of *caractère*, or architectural character, I outline how sound and acoustics were essential to Ledoux's social and moral ambition for the theater. I first discuss Ledoux's singular adoption of the semicircular form of ancient Greek and Roman theaters in the context of the French theater reform movement in the second half of the 18th Century. I argue that in taking the antique theater for a model, Ledoux tacitly followed Vitruvius to conceive of the theater as an acoustic instrument to amplify and clarify the voices of the actors, as well as the music of the orchestra. I show how Ledoux's acoustical innovations for the Theater of Besançon were intended to heighten the audience members' aural perception in order to harmonize them emotionally with the performance, and with each other. I then examine how, by virtue of its acoustics, Ledoux's theater partook of his expansive conception of architectural character as an affective, synesthetic atmosphere, capable of emotionally and morally attuning spectator-inhabitants in accord with nature. I show how Ledoux rhetorically invokes natural sounds and music to characterize the emotional, moral experience and effect of architectural character in key projects of his ideal city of Chaux presented in *L'architecture*, particularly the Oikema and Lavoir-et-Abreuvoir. I argue that Ledoux understood the architecture of the theater at Besançon to have a similar attuning effect by amplifying the emotional and moral power of the actors' voices and of the music, such that the spectators' experience of the architecture fused with that of the performance itself. I conclude by examining the role that Ledoux's acoustical innovations could be understood to have played in his conception of the theater as a morally transformative civic institution. I consider how the emotional attunement of spectators, brought about through their identification with the performance and with each other through their aural experience, could be understood to unify the audience through shared emotions. I argue finally that this emotional unity was essential to what Ledoux called the "general effect" of his theater, in which the spectators could recognize themselves within the auditorium as comprising a new, harmonious social body, potentially reconciled with nature, and manifesting an original, natural equality. By tracing the link between Ledoux's acoustical innovations, the 'musicality' of character and the shared emotional experience of spectators in the "general effect," I hope to show how sound and aural experience were as important as vision, if not more so, in his design for the Theater of Besançon and for his conception of the theater as a transformative civic institution.

Hearing Well

Ledoux's theater at Besançon was one of several new theaters built in France in the latter half of the 18th Century that were part of a reform movement in theater design to improve visual and acoustic conditions for both spectators and performers, while also mitigating the potential for audience unruliness and moral impropriety. This movement was increasingly concerned with the role of optics and acoustics in focusing audience attention on the performance, but also with retaining French theatergoing conventions and habits that considered the theater as a social space of public appearance.[3] Theaters in France had traditionally been located within existing spaces, such as indoor tennis courts or other large rectangular halls, in which the performance and audience often shared the same space, and wherein theatergoers were most interested in social display and performance centered around the king and court, rather than the dramatic performance. Audience members generally stood in an open area in front of the stage known as the *parterre*, while others viewed from private compartments encircling the hall, or even sat on the stage itself. Spectators openly moved about and socialized during the performance, freely interrupting it with their own exclamations or commentary, and often breaking out into arguments or even fights. The poor visual and aural conditions of theaters, in addition to the questionable morals and potential for social disorder associated with the theater in general, had long been sources of concern and calls for reform. As Louise Pelletier has written, the rise of a new, more "natural" and intimate form of theater in the *drame bourgeois* in the mid-18th century, and the increased attention—both visual and aural—to the performance that it demanded of the audience, gave impetus to the movement to reform theater design in the decades prior to the French Revolution.[4] In response, Ledoux and his contemporaries, such as Jacques-Germain Soufflot, Charles-Nicolas Cochin, Marie-Joseph Peyre, Charles de Wailly and Pierre Patte, drew upon increasingly scientific understandings of optics and acoustics to consider and debate the optimum shape, size and configuration of the auditorium and stage that would allow the audience to see and hear the performance more clearly. While their designs and proposals to replace the traditional rectangular theater sought to retain the distinct social dimension of the French theater experience, they had the effect of generally increasing the audience's primarily visual orientation to the performance.[5]

The ancient Greek and Roman theaters described by Vitruvius in *De architectura* were recognized as potential models for the redesign of French theaters, especially in their civic function and capacity to accommodate large audiences.[6] Andrea Palladio's Teatro Olimpico (1585) in Vicenza furthermore demonstrated how the Roman theater could be adapted to modern usages. Yet the problem remained of how best to adapt these antique models to the customs, conventions and practices particular to the French theater. The Theater of Besançon was the first to adopt the antique semicircular form in France (Figure 1). Ledoux succinctly expressed its advantages for accommodating the inherently social experience of French theatergoing: "One sees well from everywhere, and is well seen."[7] Yet Ledoux's near equal emphasis on "hearing well" from everywhere recalls the essentially acoustical nature of the antique theater according to Vitruvius.[8] While the semicircular configuration of Greek and Roman theaters evidently allowed the audience to see the performance clearly, Vitruvius describes the function of this geometry in terms of acoustics. He writes that the form of the theater conformed to the ascending circular movements of sound, which radiated outward from the stage like the rippling waves from a pebble dropped into

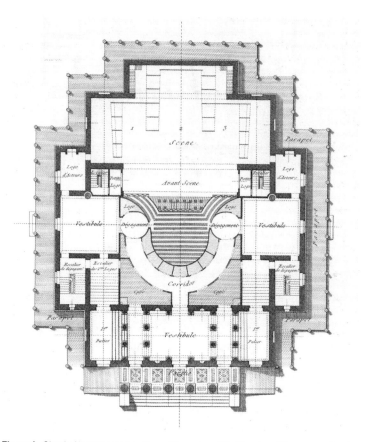

Figure 1: Claude-Nicolas Ledoux. Ground floor plan of the Theater of Besançon, showing rows of seating in place of the traditional *parterre* and the orchestra recess at the edge of the proscenium. From Claude-Nicolas Ledoux, *L'architecture considérée sous le rapport de l'art, des moeurs et de la législation,* Tome premier (Paris: Perronneau, 1804), pl. 114. Canadian Centre for Architecture.

still water.[9] The particular sound at issue was the actor's voice as a "flowing breath of air," and the acoustical objective was to preserve the distinctions of spoken words as they came into "contact" with the spectator and became perceptible to hearing.[10] The geometrical and proportional configuration of the theater was crucial for the clarity and reach of the voice, and thus for its reception and comprehension by the audience. Furthermore, as Vitruvius famously recounts, harmonically tuned *echea*, or sounding vessels, made of bronze or clay were to be distributed throughout the seating area in order to resonate in unison with the actor's voice.[11] For Vitruvius, acoustics was integrally associated with the theory of musical harmony, and the theater acted

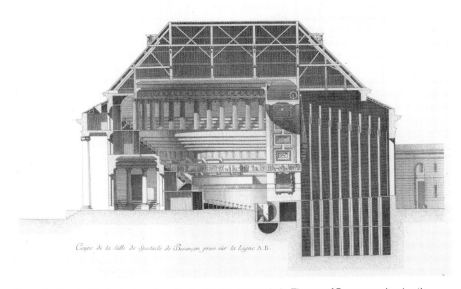

Coupe de la Salle de Spectacle de Besançon, prise sur la Ligne A.B.

Figure 2: Claude-Nicolas Ledoux. Longitudinal section through the Theater of Besançon, showing the orchestra recess in relation to the stage and auditorium. From Claude-Nicolas Ledoux, *L'architecture considérée sous le rapport de l'art, des moeurs et de la législation*, Tome premier (Paris: Perronneau, 1804), pl. 118. Canadian Centre for Architecture.

essentially as an acoustic instrument to strengthen, clarify and effectively harmonize the voice with natural order to intensify its emotional effect on the spectators, who listened and watched "spell-bound … their bodies motionless from enjoyment," with their "pores open."[12] While Ledoux explicitly asserts the primary role of vision in architectural and theatergoing experience in his famous engraving "Coup d'oeil du théâtre de Besançon," I argue that a complementary Vitruvian conception of the theater as an emotionally attuning, acoustic instrument emerges implicitly from his textual presentation of the Theater of Besançon in his treatise *L'architecture considérée sous le rapport de l'art, des moeurs et de la législation*.

Acoustical Attunement

In presenting his socially "progressive" design for the theater at Besançon in *L'architecture*, Ledoux invokes the authority of nature as the basis for his acoustical innovations and their significance for the audience's experience of sound, especially the natural voice as the carrier of human passion able to immediately impact the soul.[13] Throughout his exposition of the theater, Ledoux makes clear his intention to increase the audience's ability not only to see, but equally to hear, and to amplify the audibility, clarity and quality of the actors' voices and the music of the orchestra. He furthermore extols in effusive prose the sensuous, emotional beauty and power of the theater as a seductive, passionate, yet morally educative force for renewing a people's moral instincts by bringing them into accord with nature. Alongside natural geometry, Ledoux asserts the natural voice as one of the "first ideas" upon which to base the design of theaters and as a primary justification for adopting the form of the antique theater. Declaring that "all is circular in nature,"[14] he describes how a crowd gathers around a "charlatan" in the public square "in equal rays" in order that all may hear him equally well.[15] Like Vitruvius, Ledoux believed that a primary effect of the theater's semicircular geometry was to propagate and even harmonize the sound of voices emanating from the stage, whose "rays," like those of light, radiated outward in a spherical manner.[16] To this end Ledoux sought to remove any impediment to the natural geometric projection of the voice into the hall, as well as to clear the visual sightlines to the stage. For instance, he abolished the multiple levels of closed boxes found in traditional theaters, whose "angles" and "cheap" and tasteless ornamentation not only obstructed the spectators' view, but "confounded" the rays of sound and impeded the clarity, reach and emotional impact of the actors' natural voices.[17] In addition, Ledoux's filling in of the area traditionally reserved for the *parterre* with ascending rows of fixed seating had the effect of increasing general audibility and visibility within the hall, not least by relegating the potentially unruly spectators who would have otherwise stood in the *parterre* to seating at the back of the theater[18] (Figures 1, 2).

Yet the centrality of the voice to Ledoux's conception of the acoustical function and significance of the theater can be seen in his wholly original treatment of the orchestra. Declaring that "the orchestra, considered as an instrument identified with the voice, should not be visible,"[19] Ledoux relocated the musicians from their traditional place at the front of the hall, or even onstage, to a recess below the stage at the leading edge of the proscenium, out of view of the audience (Figure 2). While recessing the orchestra removed the visual distraction of the assembled musicians, Ledoux intended as well to prevent the discordant interference of the music with the voices of the actors. When the orchestra was in the hall itself, Ledoux writes, it produced a cacophony that obliterated actors' voices and violently assaulted the ears as the most "sensitive organs."[20] Placed below the stage, its action would be "subordinated to the organs [voices] that it will accompany."[21] Conceiving the orchestra recess as an instrument itself, he fashioned the space with a resonant underfloor void and a concave, fir-wood sounding volume at the back that would propagate the sound of the orchestra spherically into the hall[22] (Figure 3).

In radiating musical sound geometrically outward into the semicircular hall that was configured to receive it most clearly, the orchestra recess effectively extended its

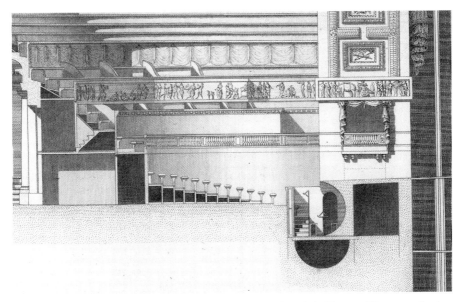

Figure 3: Claude-Nicolas Ledoux. Detail of longitudinal section through the Theater of Besançon, showing the orchestra recess and subfloor void. From Claude-Nicolas Ledoux, *L'architecture considérée sous le rapport de l'art, des moeurs et de la législation*, Tome premier (Paris: Perronneau, 1804), pl. 118. Canadian Centre for Architecture.

instrumental character and function to the architecture of the theater as a whole. In so doing, "obedient to the laws of harmony,"[23] it acted to harmonize the musicians' playing into proper symphony with the actors' and singers' voices, while ceding them their proper melodic priority. Considering this attuning function further in his text, Ledoux speculates that the orchestra recess, "treated in its entirety as an instrument," could be tuned to a pitch lower than that of a double bass.[24] He tacitly invokes Vitruvius in suggesting that it could furthermore be supplemented with *echea*, "vases of clay, bronze or brass, which forming among them a harmonic scale, would respond faithfully to the voices of the singers like so many artificial echoes."[25] While Ledoux does not specify the placement or arrangement of this "sonorous disposition," it would not be unreasonable to assume that these vessels might be distributed throughout the seating areas of the hall following antique precedents. Not only would these vessels, in principle, resonate in sympathy with the singers' voices, harmonizing and amplifying them as in Vitruvius's account, but their sounding would also resonate among the audience to obtain a similar attuning effect. Ledoux writes that "if the universal harmony of the world is composed principally of a certain proportion and certain relations of spherical and rectilinear actions, one must seek to imitate this proportion and its relations, as much as for the effects of light and of colors, as for those of sounds, in theaters."[26]

Returning to the sounding "vaults" of the orchestra recess, Ledoux describes the music of the orchestra itself as evoking the harmony of natural things and places in their multiplicity and variety, and thus heightening the emotional experience of the listening spectators:

> In these sonorous cavities the lion will add its voice to the concert of nature; its soft-ened heart will be forced to join the tribute of its roaring joy to sounds that restore the melodious harmony of compositions. The flute, in sighing, will awaken love; the breezes will encourage the whispering of leaves and the silvery frolic of streams; the oaks will sway their heads in rhythm, the thistle will soften, and the stinging nettle will become like velvet; all will yield to the dominating bow that conquers discord-ant elements; cymbals will lose their harshness, and the passions, now subjected to reason, will forgo their excesses to acquire the tone of a delicious sentiment.[27]

The spectators in turn are emotionally attuned by, and resonate in sympathy with, the musical harmony, as "joy spreads across faces, and bodies express the vibrations of the soul."[28] For Ledoux, the audience is thus brought to experience a reconcili-ation with the original harmony of primordial nature: "Such was the happiness of the world at its birth … Divine harmony! … [A]ll acknowledge your law, all comes to life by you, nature obeys your eternal command."[29] Like for Vitruvius, the theory of acoustics for Ledoux was essentially the theory of musical harmony, and of har-monization. Likewise, in extending the orchestra recess's attuning faculty to the hall as a whole, Ledoux's theater implicitly emulates the affective acoustical model of the antique theater as described by Vitruvius to intensify the emotional, even cathartic, power of the spectators' experience of the performance.

The Musicality of Character

In Ledoux's tacit conception of the theater as an attuning acoustic instrument, the spectators' experience of the performance and of the architecture itself would fuse into an ephemeral, synesthetic atmosphere belonging singularly to the event. Ordered within the hall according to the natural geometry of sound, the spectators would experience the potential harmonization of their passions with nature by virtue of the emotional power of the performance. Although vision would play an important role in this experience, the affective, attuning power of the performance would be carried by the sound of the actors' and singers' voices and the music of the orchestra, ampli-fied and harmonized by the architecture. Arising out of the combined effects of the

architecture within the spectators' perception, this atmosphere could be best understood as constituting the architectural character of the theater, according to Ledoux's
expansive notion of *caractère*.[30] In general, character for Ledoux can be understood as
the eloquent 'voice' of an *architecture parlante* that 'spoke' to the soul through sensuous images of perfected human passions, harmonized with nature. Character both
expressed "the image of feeling" of moral purpose and, as for Étienne-Louis Boullée,
was itself the effect felt by the inhabitant-spectator in the experience of the architecture.[31] Conveyed by the physiognomy of geometric forms and the colors and patterns
of light, shade and shadow, character not only encompassed a building's exterior and
interior qualities, but even those of its natural surroundings. Character was thus the
overall affective, attuning quality of complex architectural settings. While appearing
to be primarily visual in the plates of *L'architecture*, the character of Ledoux's architecture is depicted in the accompanying text as wholly synesthetic, including sounds and
scents, and evoking even qualities of touch and taste.

When describing his ideal projects in *L'architecture*, Ledoux often ascribes acoustic
and musical qualities to them to rhetorically express the emotional and moral attuning effects of architectural character, and to sensuously portray the experience of
harmony with nature, oneself and others that he envisioned it would provoke in spectator-inhabitants. In presenting the Oikema,[32] the brothel of his ideal city of Chaux,
for example, Ledoux evokes the passionate and even erotic quality of the natural
surroundings through the sounds of natural things, such as a "sweet" breeze "caress-
ing the atmosphere;" aromatic trees, herbs and flowers gently "breathing" their "per-
fumes," their foliage "rustling in whispers;" and the water of a stream "quivering"
within its banks, "sharpening the air," and then "bursting" in "echoes" of "delicious
sounds."[33] When he describes the interior of the brothel, however, he characterizes
the patron's moral dissonance through an eroticized inversion of nature's inherent
musicality, figured by the "languorous sounds of the harmonica [musical glasses],"
and an "instrument imitating the singing of Orpheus of the woods."[34] Likewise in
the allegorical description of his project for the Lavoir-et-Abreuvoir, or communal
laundry and watering pavilion, Ledoux draws upon musical analogies to recount a
veritable origin story of society born out of the state of nature, in which individual
voices remain harmonious with nature in becoming consonant with each other. He
describes the primeval world in atmospheric terms using aural musical metaphors to
express nature's original attuning beauty and harmony:

> Harmony holds all in perfect poise. Echoes respond from the bottom of valleys
> to the music of the air, and the zephyr, at the sound of its wings, unites all voices.
> Such were without doubt the first days of the world, in its infancy; all had been
> perfected by the author of nature; there were found all the benefits that the eyes of
> experience and of art could not yet foresee.[35]

Within this pristine setting, a solitary nymph discovers the company of others, and "excites her companions to gaiety," and to the spontaneous expression of their joyful desire to be together in singing and dancing.[36] Ledoux observes that "these fortunate children knew neither wrong nor injustice; reason [and] equity were the foundation of the laws that governed them."[37] Immersed within a proto-architectural atmosphere of nature's primeval beauty, embodying the concord of "all voices," the nymphs' nascent society emerges in accord with the natural order as their own voices remain consonant with it. The affective, attuning musicality of character appearing in both the Lavoir-et-Abreuvoir and the Oikema suggests how best to understand the role and significance of character in the Theater of Besançon, not only in emotional terms, but also in how it could potentially bear moral and even socio-political implications in light of Ledoux's ambition for the theater as a transformative civic institution.

The 'General Effect'

In summing up the advantages of his design for the Theater of Besançon in *L'architecture*, Ledoux advises the reader that "one should not lose sight of the fact that spectacles [dramatic performances], among the Ancients, were part of religion."[38] Although he was speaking more directly to the need for theaters to promote morality and preserve spectator decency, Ledoux was appealing as well to the comprehensive cultural and civic role of theater in antiquity, which he sought to recover in his theater. For Ledoux, this role consisted less in the moral effect of the performance than that of the theater itself, wherein the audience members, emotionally attuned and unified in shared feeling, could recognize themselves as a newly harmonized social body in what he called the "general effect" of his theater. As is well known, Ledoux's most controversial innovation at Besançon was his radical reorganization of the audience seating largely according to economic class, rather than social rank.[39] Whereas the arrangement of audiences conventionally reflected the traditional social hierarchy, centered on the king and court, Ledoux took it as a natural principle that "the strongest," or those who could pay the most, should be seated closest to the stage.[40] Following his description of a crowd forming "naturally" around the charlatan in the public square, with the strongest standing the closest, and the weakest, the farthest away, Ledoux arranged spectators generally by their ability to pay.[41] While the king remained, in principle, the symbolic center of the theater as a social space, Ledoux inset the royal boxes on either side of the stage within the depth of the monumental proscenium arch, thus removing them from direct view. The military command of Besançon was instead given priority of place in the center section of the first tier of boxes, flanked by members of the nobility and "notable citizens" of the wealthy bourgeoisie. The benches at the very front of the hall, in place of the traditional *parterre*, were reserved for distinguished visitors to be seated in full view. The middle-class bourgeoisie, workers and tradespeople were located progressively higher and farther back in the second and third tiers. Finally, those who could pay the least—the soldiers, lower-class townspeople, domestic workers and others who had typically stood in the *parterre*—were seated in the uppermost tier behind a monumental Doric colonnade. With all being, in principle, able "to see, and be well seen" within the hall, a new social body appeared in which the ascendant bourgeois and professional classes took their place on par with the nobility within a new economic order.

Furthermore, by reconfiguring the audience according to his view that economic "strength" was analogous to natural strength, Ledoux asserted a putatively natural basis for social distinction according to wealth. Yet in doing so, he also asserted an original, natural human equality underlying the meritocratic, socio-political order of the bourgeoisie over and against the social inequality of privilege in the ancien régime. Ledoux writes that, by virtue of the semicircular form of the hall,

> the moral system, united with political strength, will reestablish natural grada-tions. He who pays the most will be the closest; he who pays the least will be the farthest away; but all, in paying, will have acquired the right to be seated conveni-ently and safely; they will have acquired the right to see in an equal ray, and to be well seen.[42]

As seen in the Lavoir-et-Abreuvoir and other projects in *L'architecture*, the philosophi-cal principle of natural equality was the basis of social order for Ledoux, and thus of the unity of society and the social hierarchy, capable of reconciling its inherent differ-ences, whether inherited or acquired. By adapting the naturally egalitarian geometry of the antique theater and arranging the audience according to the "equal rays" by which all could "see and hear well," Ledoux enabled all "ranks and fortunes"[43] to equally take their proper place within the unified, hierarchical social space of the theater on the basis of an original, natural equality, in spite of actual social inequali-ties.[44] Ledoux describes the "general effect" as the visual presentation of the audience to itself as a unified whole, in which the new, egalitarian and economically based social hierarchy within the theater becomes manifest in a progressive array of splen-dor, with each rank assigned its place throughout the hall: "The finery of the first row is in gradual opposition to the last. What variety! What richness of tones! … [An incomparable] spectacle, arrayed with the most beautiful colors … [displaying] the magnificent unity of the assembly of people who applaud with enthusiasm the excel-lence of the first talents."[45] This "magnificent ensemble that seduces the spectator" is, for Ledoux, in perfect accord with nature.[46]

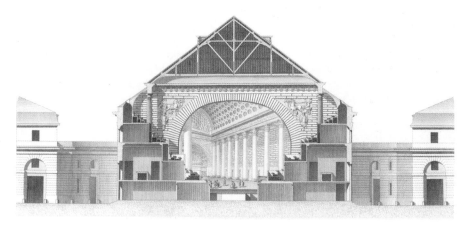

Figure 4: Claude-Nicolas Ledoux. Lateral section of the Theater of Besançon, showing the proscenium arch and orchestra recess below the stage. From Claude-Nicolas Ledoux, *L'architecture considérée sous le rapport de l'art, des moeurs et de la législation*, Tome premier (Paris: Perronneau, 1804), pl. 119. Canadian Centre for Architecture.

In describing the "general effect" from the point of view of the stage, Ledoux suggests that the radically "leveled," or egalitarian, social body of the audience comes to appear and be recognized in a theatrical self-presentation by virtue of the imaginative interplay enacted through the monumental proscenium arch between the auditorium and the stage (Figure 4). While Ledoux presents the "general effect" as a visual phenomenon, his conception of the theater as an attuning acoustic instrument suggests that the emotional effects of voice and music would play a primary, if not singular, role within it. If the architecture of the theater could be understood to encompass the experience of the performance, voice and music within its overall character as an attuning atmosphere, then the visual "general effect" of the assembled audience could be seen in turn as integral to this character-atmosphere. As an effect, it could furthermore be understood to belong first and foremost to the harmonization of the spectators in a shared emotional experience, as their souls vibrated together equally in sympathy with the voices of the actors and singers, and with the music of the orchestra. It would then be the harmonious unity of feeling born of this emotional attunement that would, properly speaking, manifest within the "magnificent" self-presentation of the audience, such that it could appear and be recognized. Through the attuning power of voice and music, amplified and clarified by architecture, individual voices could become consonant with each other in accord with nature, as in the Oikema and the Lavoir-et-Abreuvoir, and spectators could come to recognize themselves within a newly ordered, egalitarian social body, itself in harmony with nature. Aural experience can thus be seen to have played an essential role in Ledoux's ambition for the theater to become a civic institution for moral transformation. By virtue of its inherent moral and emotional affectivity, enacted through natural, circular geometry, in the theater "man rendered to his primitive state [found] again the equality that he should never have lost," and spectators recognized themselves as citizens within larger social and natural orders which transcended them.[47]

Recapitulation

Through the emotional power of the voice and music, amplified and clarified by the sonority of the architecture of the Theater of Besançon, Ledoux effectively sought to evoke the rebirth of society within the "divine harmony" of nature through aesthetic experience: "Such was the happiness of the world at its birth."[48] Ledoux's ambition for the theater as a morally transformative civic institution, if not a "new religion," appears finally to have been dependent on the capacity of audition to unite an audience in emotional sympathy and shared feeling, and of architecture to activate the acoustic and emotional oscillations between spectators and performance that would elicit the appearance and recognition of the audience as a social body reborn. As a built work situated in a specific place and time, the Theatre of Besançon appears ambiguously within Ledoux's presentation of the ideal city of Chaux in *L'architecture*, paradoxically highlighting the fact that no theater is included within the city's panoply of civic institutions. Yet by conceiving of the theater as an attuning acoustic instrument which acted affectively through character as "musical" atmosphere, Ledoux decidedly enfolded the Theater of Besançon within his larger institutional ambition for architecture as a form of legislation capable of "tying the seductive powers of art to the innate rights of man" and composing a "new social system."[49] In so doing, he asserted not only an affective moral and socio-political dimension of architecture, but also a renewed civic and institutional function for the theater in the ability to hear well.

Acknowledgments

I wish to acknowledge the School of Architecture at Louisiana State University for generously supporting the research for this essay and the opportunity to present it at the Society of Architectural Historians 72nd Annual International Conference in Providence, Rhode Island in April 2019.

Notes

1.   Claude-Nicolas Ledoux to Charles-André de La Coré, Intendant de Franche-Comté,
      August 24, 1775, in Michel Gallet, *Claude-Nicolas Ledoux: 1736–1806* (Paris: Picard,
      1980), 267.

2.   See especially Pannill Camp, *The First Frame: Theatre Space in Enlightenment France*, Kindle
      edition (Cambridge, UK: Cambridge University Press, 2018); Louise Pelletier, *Architec-
      ture in Words: Theatre, Language and the Sensuous Space of Architecture* (London: Routledge,
      2006); Daniel Rabreau, *Claude-Nicolas Ledoux (1736–1806): L'architecture et les fastes du
      temps* (Paris: Centre Ledoux; Bordeaux: W. Blake & Co., Art & Arts, 2000); Anthony
      Vidler, *Claude-Nicolas Ledoux: Architecture and Social Reform at the End of the Ancien Régime*
      (Cambridge, MA: MIT Press, 1990); Jacques Rittaud-Hutinet, *La vision d'un futur: Ledoux
      et ses théâtres* (Lyon: Presses Universitaires de Lyon, 1983); and Michel Gallet, op. cit.

3.   See especially Pelletier, *Architecture in Words*, 59–76; and Camp, *The First Frame*, Ch.1,
      passim.

4.   Pelletier, *Architecture in Words*, 77.

5.   Ibid., 77–103; Camp, *The First Frame*, 174–77.

6.   French translations of Marcus Vitruvius Pollio's *De architectura* likely known to Ledoux
      include *Architecture, ou Art de bien bastir*, trans. Jean Martin, Paris, 1547; and *Les dix
      livres d'architecture de Vitruve*, trans. Claude Perrault, Paris, 1673.

7.   Claude-Nicolas Ledoux, *L'architecture considérée sous le rapport de l'art, des moeurs et de
      la législation*, Tome premier (Paris: L'imprimerie de H.-L. Perronneau [chez l'auteur,
      rue Neuve d'Orleans], 1804), 232. All translations of Ledoux's text by author unless
      otherwise noted.

8.   Ledoux, *L'architecture*, 232.

9.   Marcus Vitruvius Pollio, *The Ten Books on Architecture*, trans. Morris Hickey Morgan
      (New York: Dover Publications, 1960), 139.

10.   Ibid., 138.

11.   Ibid., 143–45.

12.   Ibid., 137.

13.   This was particularly the view of Denis Diderot and other 18th-century philosophers
      and aestheticians. See especially Ellen R. Welch, "Diderot's Theatrical Acoustics,"
      Eighteenth-Century Studies 51, no. 4 (2018): 473–52.

14.   Ledoux, *L'architecture*, 223.

15.   Ibid.; Ledoux to La Coré, in Gallet, *Claude-Nicolas Ledoux*, 267.

16.   Ibid., 229.

17.   Ibid., 221.

18.   Here Ledoux followed the precedent of Marie-Joseph Peyre and Charles de Wailly in
      the Comédie-Française (1782) in Paris.

19.   Ibid., 229.

20.   Ibid., 220.

21.   Ibid., 230.

22.   Ibid., 229.

23.   Ibid., 230.

24.   Ibid., 229.

25.   Ibid.

26.   Ibid.

27.   Ibid., 230. Translation by author and Jacques Carré.

28.   Ibid.

29.   Ibid. Translation by author and Jacques Carré.

30.   For Ledoux, architectural character exceeded its conventional understanding in the 18th Century as the appropriate expression of the destination, purpose or intended use of a building. Rather than a property of the building itself, character for Ledoux arose in the emotional experience of places as a distinct feeling and existed, in effect, between the environment and sensing inhabitant. Similar to Étienne-Louis Boullée, character in the fullest sense for Ledoux was both expression and effect, and approached what has come to be understood in recent architectural discourse as atmosphere. I examine Ledoux's character theory more fully in *Educating the Desire for the City: Nature, Institution and Language in Claude-Nicolas Ledoux's Ideal City of Chaux*, PhD Diss., McGill University, 2015, Ch. 8.

31.   Ledoux, *L'architecture*, 17; Étienne-Louis Boullée, *Architecture: Essai sur l'art*, in Étienne-Louis Boullée and Jean-Marie Pérouse de Montclos, *Étienne-Louis Boullée: L'architecte visionnaire et néoclassique* (Paris: Herrmann, 1993), 180, 73.

32.   For a close reading of the moral dimension of the Oikema see Paul Holmquist, "More Powerful than Love: Imagination and Language in the Oikema of Claude-Nicolas Ledoux," *Chora 7: Intervals in the Philosophy of Architecture*, ed. Alberto Pérez-Gómez and Stephen Parcell, (Montreal and Kingston: McGill-Queen's University Press, 2016).

33.   Ledoux, *L'architecture*, 200.

34.   Ibid., 203.

35.   Ibid., 124. Translation by author and Jacques Carré.

36.   Ibid., 24.

37.   Ibid.

38.   Ibid., 232.

39.   See especially Rittaud-Hutinet, *La vision d'un futur*, 70–79; and Vidler, *Claude-Nicolas Ledoux*, 168–176.

40.   Vidler, *Claude-Nicolas Ledoux*, 168.

41.   Ledoux, *L'architecture*, 223.

42.   Ibid.

43.   Claude-Nicolas Ledoux, "Dernière réponse à M. Poyet," *Journal de Paris* 97 (7 April 1783): 403. Reprinted in Rittaud-Hutinet, *La vision d'un futur*, 150.

44.   Ledoux's apparent belief that wealth was analogous to natural strength, as well as his
       tacit invocation of the "natural law of the strongest" in economic terms for the sake
       of promoting social equality, will seem contradictory to many modern readers. Yet in
       the late 18th-century discourse on equality as a natural, social, and civil principle, the
       original, natural equality of individuals was not understood to be compromised by the
       inequalities of naturally given characteristics such as strength, health, talent and intel-
       lect. In principle, acquiring wealth and social position on the basis of one's own merit,
       rather than noble birth, validated the natural and just equality of persons as opposed to
       the unjust social inequality of inherited privilege. While Ledoux could not completely
       disregard traditional social rank in reorganizing the audience seating at Besançon,
       subsuming the "ranks and fortunes" within a common economic order effectively
       equalized them on a natural basis, despite their differences. For a concise summary of
       equality as an animating philosophical, social and political principle before and during
       the French Revolution see Mona Ozouf, "Equality," in *A Critical Dictionary of the French
       Revolution*, ed. François Furet and Mona Ozouf, trans. Arthur Goldhammer (Cam-
       bridge, MA: The Belknap Press of Harvard University Press, 1989), 669–83.
45.   Ibid., 233. Translation by author and Jacques Carré.
46.   Ibid.
47.   Ibid.; Pelletier, *Architecture in Words*, 88.
48.   Ledoux, *L'architecture*, 230.
49.   Claude-Nicolas Ledoux, *L'architecture considérée sous le rapport de l'art, des moeurs et de
       la législation: Prospectus* (Paris: C.- F. Patris, Imprimerie de l'Académie de Législation,
       1802), 24.

08.

Acoustics at 1:10: Miniaturizing Atmosphere

Carlotta Darò

Testing sound in acoustic models is a method that originates in the early history of architectural acoustics, at a time when the sound photography technique was practiced using two-dimensional models of concert halls. Despite the advent of digital modeling, the application of this empirical method for testing the acoustics of concert halls is nowadays more popular than ever, being employed for the extremely sophisticated acoustical properties of some of the most high-profile venues in the world.

Nowadays, physical acoustic models are three-dimensional, scale reproductions of the interiors of concert halls and auditoriums, capturing their material and decorative properties. These models have the capacity to create a sensorial environment to scale (normally at 1:10 or 1:20 scale) in order to provide an accurate prediction of a project's acoustic performance. Crucially, each acoustical parameter, such as the absorption coefficient of the materials and the frequencies of the sound, must be scaled down too. Furthermore, since the early beginnings of the science of acoustics, physicists have known that the composition of the air (i.e. temperature and humidity) changes the way acoustic waves travel, meaning that the composition of the atmosphere within these models also has to be modified to scale.

Compared to computer simulations, which allow the creation of mathematical models to reproduce the acoustic performance of architecture, the physical models method remains costly. Yet it not only offers a particularly effective tool for designers, it has also been proven highly effective as a promotional tool during the completion of high-profile building projects. This paper addresses both the historical genealogy behind acoustical models and today's practices based on a recent interview with Yasuhisa Toyota,[1] president of the firm Nagata Acoustics International and a leading figure in the field of acoustic modeling (Figure 1). Invented long before the digital turn, what is the current operative meaning of non-digital modeling?[2] How do the empirical roots of this practice interact vis-à-vis other methods? In what ways does the principle of scaled atmosphere constitute a fascinating experimental domain for architecture?

Figure 1: The first acoustic model used by Yasuhisa Toyota for the Suntory Hall project, Tokyo, 1986.
Nagata Acoustics. (Plate 3, p. 290)

Visualizing Sound

The prehistory of acoustic models goes back to the use of photography, applied to
acoustics since the early 20th Century in order to visually represent the experience
and movement of sound. As excellently argued by Sabine von Fisher, the photographic medium provided a sense of scientific objectivity (by fixing the actual movement of sound waves), combining it with a sensory visual impression used to discuss acoustical physics.[3] Examining the broad body of photographic research by the
Swiss acoustician Franz Max Osswald in the 1930s, von Fisher contends that despite
the ostensible (i.e. unproven) exactitude of Osswald's method, his interest in sound
photography instead demonstrates his obstinate belief in the necessity of involving
the human sensorium in the experience of modern science. Borrowing from previous acoustic experiments, the pioneer of architectural acoustics, Wallace Clement
Sabine, had briefly adopted the photographic technique, using it to illustrate a single
paper in 1913, only to rapidly abandon it again. Other acousticians continued to explore ways to visualize the behavior of sound waves in enclosed spaces, trying to progressively overcome the various limitations inherent in the method. In brief, so-called
schlieren photography (from the German *Schliere*—a stria, a streak) is a technique that
allows the movement of air around an electric spark to be captured by projecting
the inhomogeneous movement of smoke-filled air onto a photographic plate lit from
behind, while small sectional models of the hall are inserted into the photographic
apparatus. The most obvious initial impediment for this photographic technique was
the two-dimensional representation of space, which Sabine eventually overcame by
using longitudinal and cross-sections of the concert halls. In addition, the absence of
the temporal dimension in the pictures was also considered a constraint, which would

ultimately be addressed by practitioners such as the British scientists Alfred H. Davis and George W.C. Kaye, who in 1927 demonstrated cinematographic sequences of sound transmission. Finally, and perhaps most critically, the lack of atmosphere in the process of the abstract geometrization of the photographic models was another significant obstacle.

Other methods, explored during the late 1920s and 1930s—such as the ripple tank method (emitting light through a water tank), the light-beam method (2D) or the light-distribution method (3D)—changed the constitution of the atmospheric composition (air with water) or the vibrating source (sound with light) in order to visually simulate the behavior of sound in enclosed spaces.[4] Building on von Fischer's argument regarding the necessity of finding a visual translation of invisible acoustic phenomena, I would add the even more pressing need to find ways to visualize sound, dating from when acousticians first started collaborating with architects and furthermore sharing the same vocabulary through drawings. Even though Vitruvius in the 1st Century AD used the image of concentric waves created by a stone thrown in water to comprehend the movement of sound, and though the 17th-century Jesuit scholar Athanasius Kircher instead used straight lines to explain the effects of echoes in enclosed spaces, it was only during the modern period that acousticians tried to find precise and calculated graphic ways to predict the behavior of sound in architecture. In particular, the method established by the Frenchman Gustave Lyon—one of the first professional consultants in architectural acoustics, who worked directly with many renowned architects in the early 20th Century—led to a long list of collaborations that were almost exclusively achieved by tracing geometrical schemas onto architectural plans.[5] Having gathered empirical knowledge while making adjustments to the Salle de Trocadero in 1911, Lyon went on to define a geometrical formula that was able to establish potential echo points in a given drawn shape, which he then systematically applied in many different projects, until his death in 1936.

Nevertheless, it is also important to highlight how the different positions of the main protagonists of the field of acoustics in fact contributed to the establishment of various distinctive methods. For instance, Lyon's status as a professional private consultant, essentially as an entrepreneur, is obviously different from Osswald's, who was a lifelong researcher at the Swiss Federal Institute of Technology in Zurich, and also that of Sabine's, who even though he was involved in architectural consultancy remained a faculty member (and later dean) at Harvard University. The visual documents they produced therefore need to be contextualized in terms of their specific roles: Lyon's in finding concrete, rapid, and case-by-case solutions; Osswald's in searching for advanced ways of understanding sound within architecture and making it understandable to others; Sabine's in focusing instead on precise quantitative formulas to be universally applied in architecture. These different outcomes can be tied to differing specific functional aims, since in all their cases these forms of representation are selective and synthetic reductions of a real phenomenon, thus becoming what Bruno Latour calls "forms of mediation."[6]

Miniaturizing Atmosphere

Returning to the major shared limitation of these different methods, namely the lack of atmosphere within their scale replicas, or in some cases the presence of a medium which is different than that of the actual concert hall (water instead of air, light instead of sound), we can argue that the use of scale models marks a genuine turning point in terms of research. Despite still being projections of a thing to come, i.e. the architecture itself, these models are nonetheless conceived as replicas in terms of environmental perception, including the presence of the audience through the inclusion of sound-absorbing puppets on seats.[7] The actual instrument for measuring the acoustic outcome of the project is ultimately the genuine experience of reality. As a matter of fact, what is properly measured in scale models is not a seemingly objective visual drawing but the acoustic result, which is, however, most of the time recorded (i.e. still mediated) by microphones. In other words, scale models represent a fundamental switch from a quest for supposedly objective information to an assumed subjective judgment.

As Yasuhisa Toyota explains, physical scale models have the ability to reproduce the aleatory and still unpredictable results of acoustics, and as such have become particularly effective for today's highly sophisticated concert halls, which, paradoxically enough, can only be designed using digital tools. This hybrid combination of empirical and older testing techniques with advanced digital methods reflects an understanding of architecture as both a material experience and a virtual projection of data. Thanks to computer design, since the 1990s concert halls have been involved in an exponential race towards ever more articulated and expressive geometries that have ruptured the symmetry, regularity, and predictability of the traditions set by previous typologies, such as amphitheaters, Italian Renaissance theaters, shoebox- and vineyard-style halls, immersive spherical layouts, and so on. Despite the general confusion that subsumes most of the recent major projects within the blurry category of the vineyard style, renowned concert halls nowadays tend to have unique shapes and in the majority of cases a single embossed ornament that also functions as a detailed acoustic controller.[8] As Toyota expresses it, speaking about typology has hardly any relevance anymore because each auditorium is uniquely designed, and the only element in common with the first vineyard hall, Hans Scharoun's original Berlin Philharmonic, is the fact that the audience sits both in front of and behind the stage. This layout means that people can see each other and that communication, including its visual form, has actually become the primary requirement for concert halls. As the acoustic consultant Lothar Cremer commented when Scharoun first expressed his new idea of surrounding the stage with the audience: "Scharoun was giving less thought to the acoustic aspects of the hall than to the question of creating 'a new society.'"[9] The intention was for this new society to experience an environment that gave the impression of complete immersion, which as a correlate could only be tested by reproducing the material object together with its atmosphere on a reduced scale.

Indeed, designers no longer use such set typologies—e.g. vineyard *versus* shoebox— but instead make use of a variety of solutions taken case by case, and detail by detail, as part of an ongoing dialogue between architects and acousticians. Paradoxically, however, this is also the reason why scale modeling as a tool has seen a renewal today: as a complement, wherever possible, to digital modeling. The latter is applied from the commencement of the design-conception stage, when changes are often numerous and radical and where computer simulation can rapidly capture them. The former, on the contrary, is employed during the roughly completed phase of the work, when several empirical adjustments need to be made in the closest approximation possible to the real space. Scale models therefore intervene at the moment when the main shape is fixed and modifications can be made *in situ* without altering the overall form of the auditorium. Changing building parts or details into a 1:10 model has far less impact than the major work of amending a real ceiling, materials, or ornaments in the completed hall.

Setting a Method

Despite their recent emergence and proven value as complementary methods, physical acoustic models have a far longer pedigree than digital design and it is therefore worthwhile to trace their roots and history in order to understand their original role. In 1934 the German acoustician Friedrich Spändoch, who worked for the electrical engineering company Siemens & Halske, wrote the first report on a method of subjectively evaluating a room's acoustics by using three-dimensional models at a scale of 1:5.[10] To do so, he used a wax drum rotating at 60 revolutions per minute to record a sound signal, which was then played back at 300 revolutions per minute into the model. The result was then captured by reversing the process again, meaning the sound in the model was recorded at high speed and then played back at low speed.[11] While thoughts on the objectivity of acoustic science and its various methods were a bone of contention in the various debates during this period of modernism, Spändoch was perfectly aware that quantitative measures are only operative tests, completed by the best qualitative judgments of the capacity of human hearing: "Above all, this method should be suitable for testing the actual speech intelligibility and audibility of a projected room, which in the end is only decided by the ear, and to give an immediate impression of the acoustics to be expected at the different places before it is executed."[12] Scale models are in fact based on the principle of a scale reduction of all the physical elements, including the sound wavelengths. In later experiments, the surface materials would also be adapted to the correct absorption coefficient at the scaled frequencies, the physical size would be reduced to 1:10 and 1:20, and the air within the models would be adjusted by either adding nitrogen to saturate the air, thus reducing the level of oxygen (from about 20% to 3–5%), or by introducing very dry air (<3% relative humidity) so as to attenuate the way air filters high frequencies.[13] Manipulating the atmosphere in this context is also to be comprehended as a way to understand the invisible functioning of its related phenomena, such as acoustics. In this regard, this acoustic technique shares one of the founding themes of architecture, which is the "human desire to dwell inside a 'climate-controlled' environment."[14]

Photographic documents of the Berlin Philharmonic show a 1:9 model built to test the pioneering vineyard layout imagined by Hans Scharoun and acoustically adjusted by Professor Lothar Cremer, director of the Institute for Technical Acoustics at Berlin's Technical University, who collaborated on the project with the architect Werner Gabler, an acoustic specialist as well (Figure 2). Impressed by the powerful impact of the Berlin project, Jørn Utzon dismissed in turn an initial proposal by the engineer Vilhelm Lassen Jordan for a traditional shoebox layout and in 1962 turned to the newly formed consultancy Cremer and Gabler to seek advice on the Sydney Opera House. Jordan was a specialist in acoustic modeling in his own right, acknowledging the need to find numerical values beyond the reverberation-time criterion as correlated to subjective assessments.[15] Between 1957 and 1959 Jordan had already built a 1:10 model—30 feet (9 meters) wide and 12 feet (3.6 meters) high—to test a first rectangular layout for the Sydney major hall, using tape-recorded music speeded up in proportion to the scale of the model.[16] In fact, Cremer and Gabler pursued the same method as Jordan, but applied it to explore a "faceted" scheme, which was actually the very last design by Utzon for the major hall prior to his departure from the project.[17] The beginning of the typological complexification of concert halls—initiated by Scharoun's visionary Berlin vineyard design and advanced by Utzon's Sydney project to become the modern benchmark for concert hall design—likewise signals the point at which acoustic models came of age as effective working tools, constituting an advance that has been carried through to the digital-design turn. Acoustic models thus became highly valued investigation instruments even for architects.

Parallel to the process of reducing the physical properties of concert halls in models, the technique of acoustic modeling also progressed based on the evolution of the means for sound recording. One of the most widespread techniques is the use of dummy heads equipped with two symmetrical microphones, developed for the recording of binaural signals from the model. The binaural listening technique dates

Figure 2: Acoustic model (1:9 scale) of the Berliner Philharmonie by Hans Scharoun, 1963.
Photo: Archiv Akademie der Künste Berlin.

back to 1881 when the *théâtrophone*, a device allowing individuals to hear performances from the National Opera House in Paris in real time through paired microphones and headsets, was first revealed to the public during the International Exhibition of Electricity.[18] However, it was not until the 1930s that binaural recording was coupled with anthropomorphic simulations by using artificial heads and manikins, seemingly for research by Bell Laboratories into binaural hearing.[19] Binaural technologies improved during the 1960s and 1970s, firstly by perfecting the anatomic reproduction of the human ear, and secondly with the production of microphones small enough to insert precisely into the ears of the heads of the dummies. However, these studies focused primarily on other fields, ranging from military to industrial and communication applications, and it was only in the mid-1980s that hearing manikins were introduced for testing purely architectural acoustic outcomes. It was for the renovation of the Semper Opera House in Dresden that acoustician Walter Reichardt added miniature microphones in the ears of dummy heads in order to reproduce the binaural audience's hearing from a single seating point.[20] Thus, these kinds of manikins ended up having a double role: on the one hand they functioned as absorbent agents simulating the presence of real people, and on the other hand they acted as individual testing microphones. Once more, as Michael Barron emphasizes, "[these] tests can be either objective, i.e., delivering numerical values, or subjective, that is, where anechoic music is 'played' through the scale model and assessed subjectively."[21] Nowadays, acoustic modeling combines the physical replication of a real space with sound-capturing techniques at a minimum scale—a method that can numerically measure sound and also offer the experience of being in, as if in a real space, thus representing a groundbreaking moment not only for acoustics but also for architectural techniques of representation.

Tiny Acoustic Spectacles

Acoustic models are somewhat hybrid objects, situated between the architectural tradition of models that allow principles about the real building to be imparted by experimenting with a miniature version of it, and the scientific and technical tradition of models that are mainly used as investigative tools producing real information, or a measure, from their "autonomous" functioning. As Margaret Morrison and Mary S. Morgan argue, it is exactly this autonomous prerogative that enables scientific models to function at many levels, due to their being agents of mediation between the real world and its theoretical representation.[22] Technical models had already been developed during the 19th Century in order to test the mechanization and technical functioning of buildings.[23] These instruments generally reproduced specific aspects of modern networks within the construction—such as piping, lighting, sanitary appliances, etc.—without really showing the overall environmental outcome of a given building. In this regard, and as already mentioned, acoustic models are innovative tools since they combine a material representation of architecture with the reproduction of the functioning of at least one of its atmospheric aspects. Compared to other traditional models, in this particular case the concept of autonomy is pushed even further. In this regard, acoustic models are *objects* of presentation as opposed to forms of *representation* of a project. Many photographs of acoustic models underscore the way in which these 1:10 replicas are not simply entities that can be contemplated but can indeed be visited, can be experienced from inside. The relative bigness of these objects provides the possibility of becoming part of them, and hence they are actually interiorized models because the observer can enter them and perceive their atmospheric proprieties.

Physical acoustic models also have an undeniable "rhetorical" value and have been used in recent years as powerful objects of communication, beyond acoustics, for ambitious and heavily media-hyped (and also criticized) projects, such as the Paris (Jean Nouvel, 2015) and Hamburg (Herzog & de Meuron, 2016) Philharmonics (Figure 3). In the latter case, the model used by Nagata Acoustics International was later

Figure 3: Acoustic model (1:10 scale) of the Elbphilharmonie in Hamburg by Herzog & de Meuron, 2016. Nagata Acoustics. (Plate 4, p. 290)

put on prominent display in the precious cabinet of a pavilion, located in the public space of HafenCity, during the construction of the project itself. Tourists visiting the building site could entertainingly savor a rather physical representation of the actual project.[24] Even though it was never publicly displayed, in the project for the Paris Philharmonic, the model, which was stored in a prefabricated facility located in the construction site, apparently played an additional role in helping overcome some of the financial and political crises, between the project's authors and sponsors, caused by budget overruns.[25] The sensational aspect of the object contributed to raising a high level of expectation for the public venue, convincing the different actors, despite many difficulties, to pursue the project. This role of architectural models in general has already been discussed by scholars in terms of representation in 19th-century culture, emphasizing how as means of representation models are "not simply the projection of an idea, but they hold a particular reality of their own."[26] In this regard, models, and more specifically acoustic models, are analogous tools, since they share with the architecture-to-come their physical presence, along with a capacity to work on and stage the possible atmosphere, and a direct relationship to the public.[27] Compared to drawings, plans, sections and axonometries—which convey only very selective information about the building they represent—these special acoustic models offer experiences to live in, like "tiny acoustic spectacles."

In conclusion, if seeing has often been associated with an objective form of knowledge in science, as affirmed by Bruno Latour,[28] and scientific drawing is traditionally treated as a tool for transmitting that knowledge, as argued by Lorraine Daston and

Peter Galison,[29] then hearing commonly represents other ambiguous and physical values in scientific judgment that generally entail more subjective parameters. In this sense, Karin Bijsterveld and other scholars around her have studied a variety of historical instruments used in science, medicine, and engineering where sound was a complementary or a specific sensory modality for exploring and validating scientific knowledge.[30] She importantly distinguishes between three purposes of listening—monitory, diagnostic, and exploratory—which in turn correspond to three different acts, namely analytic, synthetic and interactive listening.[31] As far as acoustic models are concerned, seeing and hearing are tandem sensorial instruments for evaluating the outcome of an architectural project. However, if the visual allows informative material knowledge—testing and determining the shape, the size, and the interior ornamentation of a concert hall—an acoustic judgment is made by exploratory hearing, thus implying the experience of the physical immersion of the listener. This embodied interaction of the listener is based on the open assimilation of the subjective part of scientific analysis that is then seamlessly transferred to the architectural language of representation. Moreover, the perception of the model and its reduced atmosphere assists in a vital fusing of the visual and the auditory, constituting the ostensibly objective and subjective analytical methods for anticipating and testing a built project at reduced scale. While still being forms of mediation of real architecture, acoustic models attempt to bring the idea of the autonomous functioning of the object itself to a pinnacle by offering a more calibrated instrument for understanding the art of building, and thus architecture as an assemblage of both material forms and atmospheric effects.

Notes

1.   Author's interview with Yasuhisa Toyota, Tokyo, October 18, 2019. Nagata Acoustics International is a worldwide renowned firm, specialized in acoustical consultancy for concert halls and auditoriums. Starting with the design of the Suntory Hall in Tokyo (1986), Nagata Acoustics has been involved in some of the most prestigious projects of recent times, such as the Walt Disney Concert Hall in Los Angeles (2003) and the Elbphilharmonic in Hamburg (2017). I am deeply indebted to Mr. Toyota – President of the Nagata Acoustics International – for his time and generosity in enabling the discussion, and Marc Quiquerez – acoustic consultant at the same firm – for his insightful feedback on this paper. A first draft of this paper was presented at the CATDAWG group organized on the 5th of June 2020 by Jonathan Sterne and Burç Kostem, from Mc Gill University, gathering Sound Studies scholars from institutions all over the world. I am thankful for the inspiring discussion and creative ideas I shared with this widespread community.

2.   In this paper, I purposely use the term "non-digital" and "physical" modeling as op-
      posed to digital modeling to designate the fabrication of three-dimensional objects
      reproducing in scale an architectural project. As for the term analogous, which is com-
      monly used in opposition to digital, I rather refer to Jonathan Sterne's interpretation by
      arguing that physical acoustic models are analogous to the architecture itself, meaning
      that they share a physical relationship to the observer. See Jonathan Sterne, "Analog",
      in Benjamin Peters (ed.), *Digital Keywords, a Vocabulary of Information Society and Culture*
      (Princeton and Oxford: Princeton University Press), 31–44.

3.   Sabine von Fischer, "A Visual Imprint of Moving Air: Methods, Models, and Media in
      Architectural Sound Photography, ca. 1930," *Journal of the Society of Architectural Histori-
      ans* 76, no. 3 (September 2017): 326–48.

4.   See Jens Holger Rindel, "Modelling in Auditorium Acoustics—From Ripple Tank and
      Scale Models to Computer Simulations," keynote lecture, Forum Acusticum, Sevilla,
      September 16–20, 2002.

5.   Gustave Lyon was the author of the Salle Pleyel in Paris (this is the name of the concert
      hall designed by Lyon) (1927) and collaborated as acoustic consultant, among others,
      with Le Corbusier on two relevant projects: the League of Nations in Geneva (1927)
      and the Palace of the Soviets in Moscow (1932). See Carlotta Darò, "Lines for Listen-
      ing: On Gustave Lyon's Geometrical Approach to Acoustics," The journal of Architec-
      ture (special Issue), *Sound Modernities: Histories of Media and Modern Architecture*, ed. by
      Sabine Von Ficher and Olga Touloumi) 23, no.6 (2018): 881-902.

6.   Bruno Latour, "How to Be Iconophilic in Art, Science and Religion?" in Caroline
      A. Jones and Peter Galison (eds.), *Picturing Science, Producing Art* (London: Routledge,
      1998): 418–40.

7.   Research undertaken in 1968 demonstrated that the absorption power per person is
      not a standard coefficient, but that it varies according to different halls and conditions,
      and can be tested at scale. See Brian F. Day, "A Tenth-scale Model Audience," *Applied
      Acoustics* 1, no. 2 (April 1968): 121–35.

8.   See Kate Wagner, "How the Vineyard-Style Concert Hall Took Over the World (and
      Changed How We Hear Music)," *Metropolis*, May 28, 2019: https://www.metropolis-
      mag.com/architecture/concert-hall-acoustics-design/ (accessed March 13, 2020). On the
      digital mass-customization of architecture, see Mario Carpo, *The Second Digital Turn:
      Design Beyond Intelligence* (Cambridge: MIT Press, 2017).

9.   Cited in Rainer Esche, "Sounding Space," Berliner Philharmoniker official website:
      https://www.berliner-philharmoniker.de/en/philharmonie/acoustic/ (accessed March 17,
      2020).

10.   Friedrich Spandöck, "Akustische Modellversuche," *Annalen der Physik* 20, no. 4 (1934):
      345–60.

11.   See Rindel, "Modelling in Auditorium Acoustics" (see note 3).

12.   Spandöck, "Akustische Modellversuche" (see note 9), 351.

13.   As specified by Marc Quiquerez, due to the practical constraints and difficulties of hu-
       midity or oxygen control, nowadays many acousticians use a numerical compensation
       of air absorption on the measured signal (by calculating the air absorption according
       to temperature and humidity and applying the corresponding correction factors). See
       Alexander Burd, "Acoustic Modelling—Design Tool or Research Project?" in Robin
       MacKenzie (ed.), *Auditorium Acoustics: The Proceedings of an International Symposium on
       Architectural Acoustics* (London: Applied Science Publishers, 1975): 73–85.

14.   Yuriko Furuhata, "The Fog Medium: Visualizing and Engineering the Atmosphere" in
       Craig Buckley, Rüdiger Campe, and Francesco Casetti (eds.), *Screening Genealogies: From
       Optical Device to Environmental Medium* (Amsterdam: Amsterdam University Press, 2019),
       200.

15.   See Vilhelm Lassen Jordan, "Acoustical Criteria for Auditoriums and Their Relation
       to Model Techniques," *The Journal of the Acoustical Society of America* 47, no. 2 (1970):
       408–12.

16.   See Peter Murray, *The Saga of Sydney Opera House: The Dramatic Story of the Design and
       Construction of the Icon of Modern Australia* (London/New York: Spon Press, 2004), 16.

17.   In 1966 Utzon resigned from the project and architect Peter Hall was made appointed
       to complete the interior design of the opera house. Hall once again contracted Jordan's
       acoustic consultancy firm, who pursued the method of physical modeling at scale for
       the acoustical testing. See V. L. Jordan, "Acoustical Design Considerations of the Syd-
       ney Opera House," *Journal and Proceedings of The Royal Society of New South Wales* 106,
       pts. 1–2 (November 21, 1973), 33–53.

18.   See Melissa Van Drie, "Hearing through the *théâtrophone*: Sonically Constructed Spaces
       and Embodied Listening in Late Nineteenth-century French Theatre," *Sound Effects: An
       Interdisciplinary Journal of Sound and Sound Experience* 5, no. 1 (2015): 73–90.

19.   Stephan Paul, "Binaural Recording Technology: A Historical Review and Possible
       Future Developments," *Acta Acustica united with Acustica* 95 (2009): 767–88.

20.   Ibid. p. 780. See also, Lothar Cremer, "Reichardt, Walter 1903–1985," *The Journal of
       the Acoustical Society of America* 78, no. 5 (1985), 1915; and Michael Barron, *Auditorium
       Acoustics and Architectural Design* (London/New York: Spon Press, 2010 [1993]), 358.

21.   Michael Barron, "Developments in Concert Hall Acoustics in the 1960s: Theory and
       Practice," *Acoustics* 1, no. 3: special issue *Auditorium Acoustics* (2019): 538–48.

22.   Margaret Morrison and Mary S. Morgan, "Models as Mediating Instruments," in
       Mary S. Morgan and Margaret Morrison (eds.), *Models as Mediators: Perspectives on Natu-
       ral and Social Science* (Cambridge/New York/Melbourne: Cambridge University Press,
       1999), 10–37.

23.   For examples see the collections of technical models at the Science Museum in London
       or at the Musée des arts et métiers in Paris.

24.   It is worth noting that in order to be publicly displayed, the model itself was altered to
       become an essentially visual mean by providing more viewpoints and reducing the pos-

sibility of being inside the project, avoiding then to spoil the ultimately fragile object. No longer required as such in the public presentation, the slots cut for the microphones become peepholes, allowing a visual piercing of the envelop of the model. Author's exchange with Benjamin S. Koren, Paris, October 26, 2020. Koren is the founder and director of the society One to One, specialized in computer-aided design and digital manufacturing methods (and with offices in New York and Frankfurt), who helped fabricating the acoustic models for the Paris and Hamburg Philharmonics in collaboration with a German carpenter.

25.   See Claude Askolovitch, "Le chantier de la Philharmonie de Paris qui rend tous fous," *Vanity Fair*, January 14, 2015: https://www.vanityfair.fr/pouvoir/politique/articles/symphonie-inacheve-le-chantier-de-la-philharmonie-de-paris-qui-les-rend-tous-fous/14613 (accessed March 10, 2020).

26.   See Matthew J. Wells, "Relations and Reflections to the Eye and Understanding: Architectural Models and the Rebuilding of the Royal Exchange, 1839–44," *Architectural History* 60 (2017): 219–41.

27.   See note 3.

28.   Bruno Latour, "Visualisation and Cognition: Thinking with Eyes and Hands," *Knowledge and Society: Studies in the Sociology of Culture Past and Present* 6 (1986): 1–40.

29.   Lorraine Daston and Peter Galison, *Objectivity* (New York, NY: Zone Books, 2007).

30.   Karin Bijsterveld, *Sonic Skills: Listening for Knowledge in Science, Medicine and Engineering (1920s–Present)* (London: Palgrave Macmillan, 2019).

31.   Ibid., 18.

09.

The Electronic Campanile at Ronchamp

Joseph L. Clarke

Today, architectural pilgrims commonly experience the chapel of Notre Dame du Haut in Ronchamp, France in reverent silence, but when it was built and for years after, Le Corbusier was striving to realize an electronic sound installation adjacent to the building. The drawings he submitted to his Dominican clients in November 1950—and many of the Ronchamp drawings and models his studio produced through the project's five-year gestation—show a large metal grid, his version of a campanile or bell tower, next to the north portal (Figures 1–2). At set times of day, loudspeakers mounted on this structure would make the atmosphere resound with unsettling noises.

To create the auditory program, he sought to enlist Edgard Varèse, the radical Franco-American composer who preferred the term "organized sound" over "music" to describe his work. In a 1954 letter, Le Corbusier proposed that Varèse might use traditional Christian music as an *objet trouvé*, splicing it together with jarring new sounds:

> I am sending you three photos. You will see, for your reference, a campanile, consisting of a metal frame to hold the platforms that will be used to support sound machines intended to realize a new kind of broadcast [*émission*] (electronic). [...] Musical elements will be recorded on a wire or ribbon one after another, as at a disco. The director of the broadcast will cut together fragments of this ribbon music. In the present case, I can readily imagine that at key moments, magnificent liturgical music of the past might be directly framed by a background of modern music, by interventions which are violent, impersonal, etc.[1]

Given that Notre Dame du Haut is one of the most written-about buildings of the 20th Century, it is astonishing that the—ultimately unbuilt—installation has received scant attention, especially since Le Corbusier's own statements about the project are replete with mentions of sound. The chapel's "acoustic architecture [...] will make

Figure 1: Le Corbusier, Chapel of Notre-Dame-du-Haut, Ronchamp. Plaster model from 1950. Photo: Lucien Hervé. Fondation Le Corbusier / SODRAC.

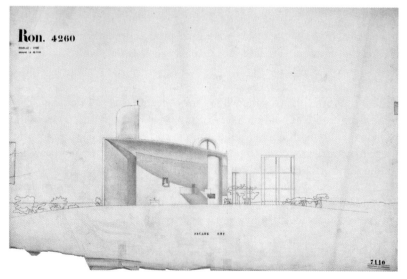

Figure 2: Le Corbusier, Chapel of Notre-Dame-du-Haut, Ronchamp. Elevation from November 1950. Fondation Le Corbusier / SODRAC.

it 'sing' among the Vosges mountains," he told an interviewer in 1953.[2] Later he wrote that the building manifested "an acoustic component in the domain of form."[3] Scholars have generally interpreted his assertions of this kind as esoteric metaphors unrelated to the project's actual auditory environment. Architectural history's reliance on visual media has meant that until recently, sound was often considered only in abstract terms, or—in the case of Ronchamp—as an arcane analogy. Discussions of experimental music and sound technology in Le Corbusier scholarship have tended to focus on his design of the Philips Pavilion for the 1958 World Expo and the audio-visual *Poème électronique* it housed, but, as argued here, the architect first conceived key elements of the Philips project earlier, for Ronchamp. Le Corbusier had, in fact, been keenly interested in the power of sound throughout his career. The son of a piano teacher, he counted music critic William Ritter among his earliest mentors.[4] The architect's brother Albert, a composer, was a close confidant throughout his life.

This essay begins by considering the evolving relationships of sound, place, faith, and electronic media in Le Corbusier's artistic consciousness. It then examines his shifting ideas for the Ronchamp campanile in the context of the Catholic Church's internal debates over liturgical music and bell-ringing. Because no music was ever created for the installation, it is impossible to know exactly how it would have sounded, but Le Corbusier's auditory intentions can be at least partially evoked based on his drawings, published texts, and private correspondence pertaining to Ronchamp, along with his more general remarks about music and electroacoustic media. The essay concludes by arguing that the overall project for chapel and campanile would have staged a dialectic between a sense of consonance with the landscape that Le Corbusier identified with geometric acoustics and the experiences of dislocation he associated with electronic media.

"The Melody of the Soul Joined with the Rhythm of the Machine"

In early 1950, Le Corbusier was approached by Lucien Ledeur, secretary of the Diocese of Besançon's Sacred Art Committee, to design a hillside chapel dedicated to the Virgin Mary. Ledeur was affiliated with the journal *L'art sacré*, whose editor, the friar Marie-Alain Couturier, championed modern art in the Catholic Church. Supported by Couturier, Ledeur sought Le Corbusier's assistance in reimagining the practice of pilgrimage through a chapel that would draw a new wave of seekers. He was unconcerned that the architect was a self-described agnostic raised in Protestant Switzerland.[5]

While Le Corbusier did not feel any particular allegiance towards the Catholic Church, he was by no means hostile to religion in general. Like many in the European avant-garde, he was fascinated by occult philosophy. His architectural practice was characterized by fervent pursuit of an ideal of reason and geometric order that

Tim Benton describes as a sublimated religious belief, and that Le Corbusier himself associated especially with music.[6] "I declare: 'I like Bach, Beethoven, Mozart, Satie, Debussy, Stravinsky,'" the architect wrote. "Architecture and music are instinctive manifestations of human dignity. Through them, mankind affirms 'I exist, I am a mathematician, a geometer, and I am religious. That means that I believe in some gigantic ideal that dominates me and that I can achieve.'"[7] He was certain that his distinctive belief system shared common roots with modern Christianity, and when he later invited Varèse to collaborate on the Ronchamp project, he identified himself cryptically as "a veritable Christian, but a Christian from 5,000 years before Jesus Christ."[8]

If this fascination with religion made Le Corbusier receptive to Ledeur's overtures, what finally convinced him to accept the chapel commission was the aura of the site, just outside the town of Ronchamp, on a hillside near the Vosges mountains said to be the location of a pagan temple and an early Christian sanctuary. Sound may well have played a role in his attraction. The echoic properties of mountainous areas and the human tendency to ascribe supernatural significance to such places and their acoustics have been noted since antiquity.[9] At any rate, from the outset of the project, Le Corbusier thought about how the sound of liturgy would activate the Ronchamp landscape. Recognizing that audibility would be a crucial concern at outdoor Masses attended by tens of thousands of worshipers (Figure 3), he sketched a pulpit and a "sound deflector" (*abat-son*).[10] Over the next few months he conceived the freestanding campanile, whose perpendicular relationship to the chapel entrance suggests that it might also have served as an entry baldachin for processions.

At first, he intended for this structure to house the chapel's existing bells. Since the Middle Ages, the bells of French cathedrals, abbeys, and parish churches had been rung to call villagers to prayer and to warn of impending crisis, forming what Alain Corbin calls a "web of sound" across the countryside.[11] Peals radiating out from villages set a rhythm for labor and communal life. The fact that one could not avoid being immersed in their auditory summons made them a powerful means to "sacralize space and time."[12] Corbin emphasizes how even in the ostensibly secular 19th Century, bell-ringing was a widespread yet contested practice, which proved instrumental in France's development into a modern nation. Bells shared certain characteristics with minarets—structures that had made a strong impression on Le Corbusier during his 1911 journey through the Ottoman Empire: "Flanking the sanctuary [of a mosque], there must be minarets so tall as to carry afar the shrill voices of the *muezzins* chanting and calling the devoted to prayer at hours regulated by the sun," he recorded in his diary. "Impressive notes filter down from above."[13] He marveled at how the call to prayer pervaded the surrounding environment and gathered a community of listeners, bringing order and structure to the day, and thus seemed to parallel architecture's vocation to organize space.

Figure 3: Pilgrimage Mass at Ronchamp, October 1962, postcard. Public domain.

His experience of the traditional sounds of religious worship was not the only influence on his campanile idea. After all, he had also witnessed how these devotional sounds had been substantially drowned out, during the years of his own childhood and adolescence, by a crescendo of industry. In 1933, a French magazine identified as "the most striking characteristic of our modern world" the "noises of motors, auto horns, the jerky crackling of drilling machines demolishing the roadways, the beep-beeps of traffic horns, the whistles of policemen, [and] the rumbling of the autobus […] making houses tremble from the basement to the attic."[14] Urban cacophony was further intensified by the rise of public address loudspeaker systems, which proliferated after World War I.

Le Corbusier was intoxicated by these new sounds. He found them a fitting sonic accompaniment for the new monuments of the industrial metropolis, which he conceived as modern answers to religious edifices. In his travelogue of his 1935 lecture tour of the United States, significantly titled *When the Cathedrals Were White*, his fascination with American-style skyscrapers and new urban sounds is palpable. Jazz seemed to him to capture the energy of American technological innovation. He expressed his enthusiasm in racial language: "Negro music has touched America because it is the melody of the soul joined with the rhythm of the machine. […] The music of an era of construction: innovating. It floods the body and heart; it floods the USA and it floods the world. Hence, everything in our auditory habits changes. […] The radio broadcasts the Negro spirit into the home."[15] These remarks, like his account of the Islamic call to prayer, show how Le Corbusier was particularly captivated by the "exotic" sounds he associated with nonwhite people. He thought he heard, in jazz, an atavistic *élan* that he conceived as a dialectical counterpart to the calculating rationality of modern engineering.[16] He also framed the success of jazz as a function of its technical mediation. Issuing from radios and loudspeakers, it seemed to pervade society as a new soundtrack for everyday life.

Liturgy Electrified

It is easy to understand how, upon receiving the Ronchamp commission, Le Corbusier could conceive that a modern electroacoustic equivalent to church bells might evoke a fusion of primal vitality and technological modernity similar to his impressions of jazz. He was also well aware that, since the turn of the century, the Catholic Church had been vexed by internal debates over liturgical music. There was widespread discontent with sacred music composed in grand, operatic styles, and in 1903, Pope Pius X had directed Catholics instead to pursue sacred music exemplifying holiness, beauty, and universality. "These qualities are found most perfectly in Gregorian chant," the Pope declared, warning against secular-sounding music "reminiscent of theatrical pieces."[17]

To some Catholics, this turn away from 19th-century styles seemed to present an opening for modernism. Marie-Alain Couturier's *Art sacré* movement developed out of the *Ateliers d'art sacré*, a workshop established in 1919 by Maurice Denis and Georges Desvallières for the renewal of Catholic painting and crafts. Couturier and his associates commissioned leading modern artists—regardless of their personal faith—to create religious works. Their advocacy reached a high point in 1951 with the consecration of the Chapel of the Rosary in Vence, France, for which Henri Matisse designed interior furnishings, stained-glass windows, and vestments. While Couturier was concerned primarily with visual art, he advocated for modernist music as well, in particular the work of the radical Catholic composer Olivier Messiaen.[18]

While Le Corbusier's idea for sound at Ronchamp was shaped by all of these contextual influences, he does not appear to have given much thought to a specific sonic program for the campanile until late in the design process, and even then his accounts were inconsistent. His decision to pursue Varèse rather than Messiaen or another Catholic composer was probably motivated by the favorable impression he had received in 1947 when he heard one of Varèse's works in progress.[19] It was likely the composer's monumental *Déserts*, which, in its final form, alternates between orchestral segments and a track recorded on tape. In the instrumental sections of *Déserts*, meditative, otherworldly passages alternate with rhythmic onslaughts that evoke the commotion of heavy industry. The tape music develops these associations further.

"I went to various factories in search of certain sounds I needed for *Déserts* and re-corded them," Varèse explained. "These noises were the raw material out of which, after being processed by electronic means, the interpolations of organized sound were composed."[20] This procedure, involving artistic appropriation of the sounds of the modern world, may have reminded Le Corbusier of the formal references to indus-trial structures such as grain silos in his own buildings.

Le Corbusier's letter to Varèse in January 1954, quoted at the beginning of this chapter—in which the architect proposed a collage of ancient church music and the "violent, impersonal" sounds of electrified modernity—recalled the juxtaposition of two kinds of sound in *Déserts*. While this idea seems to have been consistent with *Art sacré*'s goal of embracing modern culture, its further development was cut short as Pope Pius XII, who was generally suspicious of cultural modernism, turned decisively against Couturier's Dominicans. In February 1954, Couturier was suspended from publishing and other ecclesiastical activities. He died soon thereafter.[21] At this point, construction on the chapel had already begun, but the campanile seemed out of the question. As hostile as Pius XII's Vatican was to experimentation in the visual arts, it was even more emphatic on the subject of music. In 1955, the Pope issued new instructions singling out church music for special regulation and stipulating that new sound technologies could never be used liturgically:

> The use of "automatic" instruments and machines such as the automatic organ, phonograph, the radio, dictaphone, or tape recorder, and other similar devices, are absolutely forbidden in liturgical functions, or pious exercises, whether inside or outside the church. [...] It is strictly forbidden to use in place of bells any ma-chine or instrument for the mechanical or automatic imitation or amplification of the sound of bells.[22]

These emphatic prohibitions explain why the campanile was not built in 1955. Yet in a sign of Le Corbusier's determination, he almost immediately conceived that a similar audiovisual program might first be realized in a secular project. When execu-tives of the Philips corporation invited Le Corbusier in early 1956 to design their corporate presence at Expo 58, they claimed to have observed, at Notre Dame du Haut, "elements also potentially applicable to our pavilion."[23] They specifically cited photographs of the chapel's interior, but may also have been aware of Le Corbusi-er's published comments about the electronic campanile. After all, since the 1920s, Philips had been one of the largest producers of audio equipment, and its engineers were at the forefront of research on electronic sound.[24]

Once again, Le Corbusier approached Varèse, and this time his entreaties were successful. As the music for the pavilion's *Poème électronique*, the composer created a multichannel electronic composition consisting of sampled mechanical noises, synthesized tones, and various percussive sounds. The work also contains repeated references to Christian worship: It begins with the deep, resonant sound of church bells, a motif that recurs several times during the eight-minute work. Toward the end, fragments of choral music and a pipe organ are heard alongside explosions and a jet engine.[25] In many respects, then, Varèse's *Poème électronique* music corresponds to Le Corbusier's earlier idea for Ronchamp of "magnificent liturgical music of the past" interspersed with modern sounds.

Still, there is evidence that even at this point, Le Corbusier thought of the pavilion project as a test bed for the architectural integration of electronic sound he remained determined to realize at Ronchamp. Catholic reformers had not stopped advocating for cultural modernity. Their hopes were buoyed after the election in 1958 of Pope John XXIII, a reformer who quickly began preparations to convene the Second Vatican Council. Le Corbusier, meanwhile, continued to speak out for the construction of the campanile. In 1959 he told an interviewer:

> They will be able to make incredible music, an unbelievable sound when they have twelve thousand people outside, with amplifiers. I said to the priest, "You should get rid of the kind of music played by an old maid on an old harmonium— that's out of tune—and instead have music composed for the church, something new, not sad music, a loud noise, an unholy din."[26]

This statement is Le Corbusier's most direct suggestion that his sound system might be used during services to replace other forms of liturgical music. Likewise, in a letter to his brother Albert in 1960, he described an electronic system that "could be heard indoors or outdoor" and might serve as "a kind of Matins."[27] By contrast, in a 1961 book on the chapel, he suggested that the installation would function separately from the Mass, perhaps with no human agent at all: "Music should come forth (even if nobody were there to hear it), automatic music emanating from the chapel at regular times, and addressing the occasional unknown listener, inside and out."[28] The following year, he told Albert that he and the chaplain, René Bolle-Reddat, had discussed the campanile over lunch. Le Corbusier described how brief "*coups de musique*" would issue forth every day at set times and "spread through the atmosphere."[29] Still nothing happened. Finally, the year before he died, the architect wrote to Bolle-Reddat with a last appeal:

> Our imperative duty is to make for Ronchamp a voice—not of a more or less worthy artist, but a voice without limits, coming from faraway centuries and arriving today in modern times. A selection will be made, with a direct connection to the loudspeaker. The hill of Ronchamp will thus speak properly at one o'clock in the morning, at noon, and at eventide. In this way we will follow tradition, and Ronchamp will be open and not closed to music.[30]

In these various descriptions of the campanile, what comes through most of all is the tenacity of Le Corbusier's campaign. All architects have occasional design notions that never make it off the drawing board—proposals they sketch and later think better of—but the sound installation does not belong in this category. The architect's persistence over fifteen years demonstrates that he considered it essential to his idea for Ronchamp. It was never built; instead, a diminutive structure designed by Jean Prouvé to hold three bells was eventually placed inconspicuously on the chapel's little-trafficked west side.[31]

If the electronic installation had been realized, it would have represented Le Corbusier's most important contribution to an emerging area of artistic experimentation with sound that defied the conventions of Western musical performance. In 1952, John Cage's *4'33"* had brought new attention to the space of the concert hall and the tiny ambient sounds that filled its putative silence. Three years later, Karlheinz Stockhausen composed his *Gesang der Jünglinge* for voice and electronic sound, to be played on four loudspeakers spread around a performance hall. When the term "sound art" was finally coined around 1980, such works—along with the *Poème électronique*—were recognized as important forerunners. It is not hard to imagine that Ronchamp would have had a similar stature. The considerable discrepancies between Le Corbusier's accounts of the campanile make it impossible to say with precision exactly *how* it would have been used liturgically and how its sound would have altered vistors' experience of the Haute-Saône landscape. What all his descriptions share, though, is an insistence that it should draw on the Church's musical traditions while expressing an experience of modernity that was both exuberant and disconcerting. Moreover, he clearly conceived the installation as integral to both the chapel's liturgical function and its relationship to the site.

Call and Response

There is no question that Le Corbusier conceptualized the chapel's complex relation with the landscape in quasi-acoustic terms. He referred in his design to the formal motif of curved sound reflectors, and in his writings about Ronchamp to the rhetoric of sound propagation. His initial plan sketch of the chapel resembled a horn with a flared opening (Figure 4).[32] This figure survives in the inflection of the south and east walls, concave to the exterior. While their contours have often been ascribed to free-form sculptural intuition, Robin Evans points out that their double curvature could only be realized through precise calculation. He discerns in these walls the figure of parabolic acoustic listening dishes.[33] The geometry at Ronchamp is actually more complex than this: the south wall is defined in plan as a concave profile comprising straight and curved segments, and in the vertical dimension, it twists from an oblique

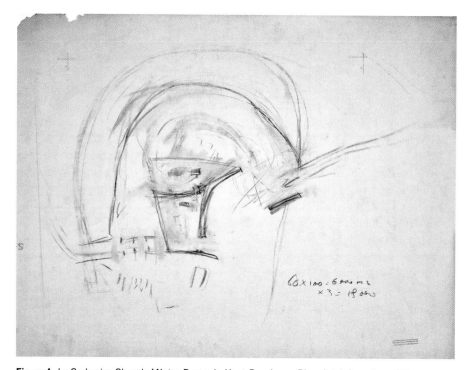

Figure 4: Le Corbusier, Chapel of Notre-Dame-du-Haut, Ronchamp. Plan sketch from June 1950.
Fondation Le Corbusier / SODRAC.

slant at the door to plumb vertical at the southeast corner.[34] Still, there is an unmistakable resemblance to the acoustic reflecting surfaces Le Corbusier had designed for earlier projects, such as his unbuilt Palace of the Soviets auditorium (Figure 5). Moreover, Christopher Pearson has noted many instances when the architect used sonic language to argue that significant features of a building should be located at particular "mathematical points" in space.[35] In this spirit, Le Corbusier's *Oeuvre complète* entry for the Ronchamp chapel declares, "One begins with the acoustic of the landscape."[36] One of his other publications describes the project as a "speech addressed to the place," and includes a photograph of the horizon with a line from Catholic poet Paul Claudel: "Grasp this word in the ear of your soul."[37]

If one disregards the electronic sound system, such locutions come across as pure esotericism. Pearson, for example, argues that the chapel was fundamentally based on a "paradigm of metaphorical acoustics," intended to suggest an aesthetic fit between built form and landscape.[38] A perennial theme in the architectural reception of Ronchamp has been the "sculptural" character of the building, often ascribed to an ethos

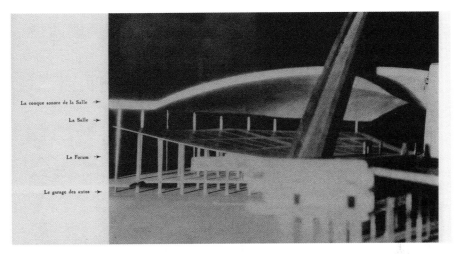

Figure 5: Le Corbusier, Palace of the Soviets project, 1931. Model of auditorium published in *L'architecture vivante*, 1932, showing "sound shell" (*conque sonore*). Public domain.

of rootedness in place and a regressive sensibility.[39] Christian Norberg-Schulz went so far as to praise Ronchamp as "the great turning point" in a reaction against the International Style and toward a renewed appreciation for *genius loci*.[40] The idea of a mystical, notionally acoustic connection between chapel and landscape meshes with the premise that there is something vaguely "phenomenological" about the chapel, at odds with a visually-oriented modernist way of thinking and associated instead with an elemental intuition of the spirit of place.

When the acoustic rhetoric is considered alongside the campanile proposal, however, a different reading of the project emerges. The appearance of the campanile itself conspicuously avoids any notionally "acoustic" form. It is a generic grid, whose extreme anonymity seems to express the way a loudspeaker's propagation of sound was independent of geometry. The side-by-side placement of chapel and campanile can thus be read as a poetic encounter between multiple ways of experiencing and conceiving the propagation of sound: the older technology of architectural reflectors and the newer one of electroacoustics. It is as though the formally vacant campanile would project music out to the surrounding hills and the chapel building would listen for the answering report, registering it in its three-dimensional form and thereby affirming its awareness of its own position in space, like an animal checking its bearings by echolocation. In the process, the music would defamiliarize the surrounding topography through the introduction of startling and disturbing noises. The acoustic fable Le Corbusier created for Ronchamp suggests the project was simultaneously at home in its hillside setting and also deeply foreign.

To determine "the meaning" of Ronchamp is, no doubt, an impossible enterprise. Moreover, given the absence of a fully worked-out sonic program for the campanile, it is hard to go beyond informed speculation about how it would have transformed the experience of the chapel. Notwithstanding this limitation, the project as a whole reads as an exploration of communication—and hence of communion—at a time when new technology seemed to threaten traditional ideas of place, the sacred, and the sacrality of place. It suggests an expanded conception of architecture's scope, in which the task of the designer could include the development of a soundtrack for the building and its environs. The consternation this idea prompted among some church leaders is a testament to the difficulty of achieving in the modern world the organic integration of architecture, sound, and ritual Le Corbusier had observed at the mosques of Istanbul many decades earlier. He had enough self-awareness about the unattainability of such integration, at least, to thematize this problem in the deliberate disjunction between the project's two different acoustic modes. Although the "voice without limits" was never realized, the silence of Ronchamp speaks volumes.

Notes

1.   Le Corbusier to Edgard Varèse, January 21, 1954. Fondation Le Corbusier G2-16.
2.   "Corbusier Designs a Hilltop Chapel Shaped Like a Fiddle," *Architectural Forum* 99 (July 1953): 35.
3.   Le Corbusier, *Oeuvre complète*, ed. Willy Boesiger, vol. 5 (Zurich: Les Éditions d'Architecture, 1970), 72.
4.   Peter Bienz, *Le Corbusier und die Musik* (Wiesbaden: Vieweg, 1999), 38–45.
5.   André Wogenscky, *Le Corbusier's Hands*, trans. Martina Millà Bernad (Cambridge: MIT Press, 2006), 18–19.
6.   Tim Benton, "The Sacred and the Search for Myths," in *Le Corbusier Architect of the Century* (London: Arts Council of Great Britain, 1987), 238–45. Also see Jan Birksted, *Le Corbusier and the Occult* (Cambridge: MIT Press, 2009).
7.   Le Corbusier, *Precisions on the Present State of Architecture and City Planning* (1930; Cambridge: MIT Press, 1991), 11.
8.   Le Corbusier to Varèse, January 21, 1954.
9.   Lucretius, *On the Nature of Things*, trans. Martin Ferguson Smith (Indianapolis: Hackett Puublishing, 2001), 116.
10.   Le Corbusier, sketch of Ronchamp chapel, May 20, 1950, reproduced in *Le Corbusier Sketchbooks, Volume 2: 1950–1954* (New York: Architectural History Foundation, 1981), no. 274.
11.   Alain Corbin, *Village Bells: Sound and Meaning in the 19th-Century French Countryside*, trans. Martin Thom (New York: Columbia University Press, 1998), 7.

12.   Ibid., 3.

13.   Le Corbusier, *Journey to the East*, ed. and trans. Ivan Žaknić with John Gery and Nicole Pertuiset (Cambridge: MIT Press, 2007), 104.

14.   "Le bruit," *Guérir: Revue mensuelle de vulgarisation médicale et scientifique*, May 1933, no. 9, trans. in Rebecca P. Scales, *Radio and the Politics of Sound in Interwar France, 1921–1939* (Cambridge: Cambridge University Press, 2016), 4.

15.   Le Corbusier, *When the Cathedrals Were White*, trans. Francis E. Hyslop (1937; New York: McGraw-Hill, 1947), 158–60.

16.   See Mardges Bacon, *Le Corbusier in America: Travels in the Land of the Timid* (Cambridge: MIT Press, 2001), 221–6; Adrienne Brown, *The Black Skyscraper: Architecture and the Perception of Race* (Baltimore: Johns Hopkins University Press, 2017), 170–4.

17.   Pius X, *Tra le sollecitudini, motu proprio*, November 22, 1903, translated in Robert F. Hayburn, *Papal Legislation on Sacred Music: 95 AD to 1977 AD* (Collegeville, MN: Liturgical Press, 1979), 224–5.

18.   Olivier Messiaen, "Autor d'une oeuvre d'orgue," *L'art sacré* 5, no. 40 (April 1939): 123. Translated in Stephen Broad, "Messiaen and *Art Sacré*," in *Messiaen Perspectives 1: Sources and Influences*, ed. Christopher Dingle and Robert Fallon (Burlington, VT: Ashgate, 2013), 273.

19.   Le Corbusier to his mother, May 6, 1947, in Le Corbusier, *Correspondance*, vol. 3: *Lettres à la famille, 1947–1965* (Paris: Fondation Le Corbusier, 2016), 34.

20.   Edgard Varèse quoted in Wilfrid Mellers, *Music in a New Found Land: Themes and Developments in the History of American Music* (London: Barrie and Rockliff, 1964), 165–6.

21.   Richard Stockton Dunlap, "Reassessing Ronchamp: The Historical Context, Architectural Discourse and Design Development of Le Corbusier's Chapel Notre Dame-du-Haut," Ph.D. thesis, London School of Economic and Political Science, 2014, 22–32.

22.   Pius XII, *Musicae sacrae disciplina*, encyclical, December 25, 1955, translated in Hayburn, *Papal Legislation on Sacred Music*, 348–9. Congregation of Sacred Rites, *De musica sacra et sacra liturgia*, instruction issued September 3, 1958, translated in Hayburn, *Papal Legislation on Sacred Music*, 370–2.

23.   Louis Kalff to R. d'Aboville, January 9, 1956. Getty Research Institute, 870438-2.

24.   See Kees Tazelaar, *On the Threshold of Beauty: Philips and the Origins of Electronic Music in the Netherlands, 1925–1965* (Rotterdam: V2_Publishing, 2013).

25.   Jan de Heer and Kees Tazelaar, *From Harmony to Chaos: Le Corbusier, Varèse, Xenakis, and Le poème électronique* (Amsterdam: Uitgeverij Duizend & Een/1001 Publishers, 2017), 165–79.

26.   1959 interview with Le Corbusier quoted in John Peter, *The Oral History of Modern Architecture* (New York: Harry N. Abrams, 1994), 146.

27.   Le Corbusier to Albert Jeanneret, September 21, 1960, in Le Corbusier, *Correspondance*, vol. 3, 574.

28.   Le Corbusier, *Le Livre de Ronchamp*, ed. Jean Petit (Paris: Cahiers Forces Vives/Editec, 1961), 18.

29.   Le Corbusier to Albert Jeanneret, February 19, 1962. Le Corbusier, *Correspondance*, vol. 3, 686.

30.   Le Corbusier to René Bolle-Reddat, June 19, 1964, quoted in Le Corbusier, *Textes et dessins pour Ronchamp*, ed. Jean Petit (Paris: Editions Forces-Vives, 1965), n.p.

31.   Danièle Pauly, *Le Corbusier: The Chapel at Ronchamp*, trans. Sarah Parsons (Basel: Birkhäuser, 2008), 60–3.

32.   Le Corbusier, *Livre*, 17.

33.   Robin Evans, *The Projective Cast: Architecture and Its Three Geometries* (Cambridge: MIT Press, 1995), 307.

34.   Le Corbusier, *Livre*, 119.

35.   Christopher Pearson, "Le Corbusier and the Acoustical Trope: An Investigation of Its Origins," *Journal of the Society of Architectural Historians* 56, no. 2 (June 1997): 168–83.

36.   Le Corbusier, *Oeuvre complète*, 72.

37.   Le Corbusier, *Livre*, 18.

38.   Pearson, "Acoustical Trope," 180.

39.   James Stirling, "Ronchamp: Le Corbusier's Chapel and the Crisis of Rationalism," *The Architectural Review*, March 1956, reprinted in James Stirling, *Writings on Architecture*, ed. Robert Maxwell (Milan: Skira, 1998), 40–9. Nikolaus Pevsner, *An Outline of European Architecture*, 6th ed. (Harmondsworth, UK: Penguin, 1960), 698–99.

40.   Christian Norberg-Schulz, *Genius Loci: Towards a Phenomenology of Architecture* (New York: Rizzoli, 1980), 196–7.

10.

Chromesthesia and the Multiverse of Listening in Music and Architecture: Luigi Nono in Collaboration with Renzo Piano

Federica Goffi

Post-war avant-garde composer Luigi Nono (1924–1990) collaborated with architect Renzo Piano and philosopher Massimo Cacciari to create what became Nono's last composition: *Prometheus: Tragedy of Listening* (1981–1985).[1] This chapter addresses Piano's and Nono's early multisensory sketches, drawings, and scores, analyzing questions of spatiality concerning the unique character of the "mobility of sound,"[2] as articulated through Nono's musical experimentation. As will be demonstrated, the awareness of the aural qualities of architecture is apparent in Piano's sketches for the *Ark,* the musical vessel that he designed for *Prometheus'* original performance. Nono strived to design music not just for but *with* the architectural space of the performance, which is like an instrument in and of itself. Furthermore, it will be evidenced how "participatory creative imagination" was essential to reading and interpreting texts, musical scores, and architectural drawings in the endeavor to realize the spatialized condition of mobile sound as synesthetic apperception.[3]

Mobile sound in Nono's work was both a philosophical and compositional element of unconstrained experimentation. In his own words: "mobile sound […] is not tied statically to a given intonation imposed according to scales chosen to the exclusion of others: thoughts, systems, and mindsets that excluded or denied other thoughts, other systems, and other mindsets."[4] Live performers would be able to listen to themselves and quite literally "compose on themselves,"[5] responding to their own voices, which they could hear amplified by loudspeakers and affected by the space itself participating in the creation of the piece in real time as a unique event linked to a place. Nono did not aim at creating a "unified whole," but rather a "diversified mul-tiplicity," attained through real-time responses of performers listening to one another, to live electronics, to the space, and to everything around them.[6]

Nono and Piano's visualizations of sound through musical scores and architec-tural sketches of the performance space in plans and sections were based on sensory associations of one sense modality with another through the use of colored notations: allowing for chromesthesia—a silent "color hearing" through "sound seeing."[7] With this approach, scores and sketches do not represent a static reality but rather an-ticipate time and sound, however ephemerally. Moreover, as allographic arts, music and architecture are developed through an interposed representational medium that Nono and Piano used to invite participation between interdisciplinary collaborators.[8]

In *Prometheus,* the aural event is inseparable from *the-space-where-and-the-time-when* it was performed. Together, the deconsecrated space of the 1595 San Lorenzo Church in Venice—where the first performance took place (on September 25, 1984)—Piano's *Ark*—a temporary and adaptable "wooden musical instrument" installed within the Church—and the musical composition created the appropriate setting for a spatial-ized condition of listening. The event went beyond an acoustic experience to achieve the aural immersion of the participants in the socio-cultural and political conditions that defined the world at that time.[9] Nono's work and collaborations affirm the im-portance of listening not just to space, collaborators, and their craft, but also to socio-political events. He intended to realize a condition of active participation between the audience and the creators, for which spatialized sound and embodied experi-ence were essential. The spatialization of mobile sound was achieved by conceiving the piece *with* the space in mind, carefully choreographing the placements of sound sources, such as loudspeakers and performers.

On December 6, 1983, while preparing for *Prometheus,* Nono wrote: "No opera/ no director/ no set designer/ no traditional characters/ but/ dramaturgy-tragedy with mobile sounds that/ read discover/ empty/ fill up space."[10] His avant-garde approach to composition questioned established ways of composing music. Nono asserted his philosophies through negative statements to break with tradition, setting the trajecto-ry of the work as an experimental and collaborative search for the unknown, stretch-ing the ear into that which is not yet encoded through critical listening.

The Venetian lagoon soundscape of industrial production that awakened his so-cio-political consciousness is reflected in his work. His attention to the working condi-tion of industrial workers was translated earlier on in *The Lighted Factory* (1964), into which he incorporated recordings of piercing sounds of metalworking. He dedicated the piece to the workers of Italsider, a steel factory in Cornigliano, Genoa. The piece, sponsored by Italian national television (RAI), was censored as anti-government propaganda and not broadcast nationwide. Only later, Nono was able to perform it at the Theater La Fenice, during the XXXII Venice Biennale of Contemporary Music.

Figure 1: Italian composer Luigi Nono in his house. Zattere, Venice, 1988 (ALN FE500R0034).
© Marcello Mencarini/Rosebud2.

Undoubtedly, Nono's works disrupted what was commonly understood as a bourgeois medium. His intent was arguably to bring different worlds into close proximity with each other, enhancing the capacity for listening to social inequities.

In Nono's work, the ability to listen to spaces reflects the greater ability to participate in humanity's strife for social justice, emblematically represented in his last work by the figure of Prometheus. Under this premise, listening to music cannot be reduced to esthetic experience; instead, it is part of the ethical engagement with societal struggles.[11]

Nono's Listening and Chromesthetic Spatial Scores

Nono's criticism of the ocular-centric experience that still dominated the stage of sound performances in the post-War avant-garde period, and which goes back to Renaissance theatre, informs the spatialized condition of mobile sound in *Prometheus'* "acoustic multiverse."[12] This concept was part of an agenda developed with Cacciari, author of the *libretto,* "to break with schematism, with formulas, with mannerism, with givens, and the taken for granted."[13] In 1988, photographer Marcello Mencarini captured a serendipitous portrait of Nono, offering an implicit critique of the one-eyed perspectival constructions of traditional European opera (Figure 1),[14] where the stage was designed for a privileged point of view evidencing a stratification of the social structure.[15] Mobile sound—a key tenet in Nono's work—cannot be captured with the eyes.[16] I speculate that Nono covers his left eye with a music sheet to reference the mobility of a sound that is heard but cannot be seen. The composer intended to break the fixity of stage and audience relations in traditional Western theatres based on the dominance of vision, to turn it into what the human condition of listening affords when sounds originating from a plurality of sources reflect in multidirectional ways: far/near, above/below, spatialized through interaction. Every listener is at the center of a unique experience, where space is architectural, musical, and social all at the same time.[17] The mythological condition of Prometheus evoked by Nono, which defines the utopic plane of the work, is not a form of abstraction from reality but rather a call for the awakening of human consciousness.

As sound director Alvise Vidolin explained, mobile sound lives in real space and is inseparable from it. Each performance needs tuning into the acoustic of its space. However, mobile sound exceeds its kinetic qualities and depends on the interpreters' creative use of the voice, instruments, breathing techniques, live electronics, and the capacity to listen to one another. Space is recognized as an active element that participates in the play of sound—a "creative component" contributing to define "a spatial listening with no beginning and no direction."[18]

In another photo by Mencarini, Nono sits next to a print by Andreas Cellarius, titled *Atlas Coelestis. Harmonia Macrocosmica* (1660).[19] An interest in the infinite newness of the micro-universe of sound complements his interests in Giordano Bruno's infinity of possible worlds based on the Copernican worldview.[20] Nono's compositional technique of "cosmically scattered fragments of sonic material" does not 'create music.'[21] Rather, it allows him to participate in what could be called the phonosphere—a world of sound, synesthetic aurality, and socio-political conditions. The Venetian composer intervenes in a phenomenon for which he is present and to which an attentive listener could attune their ears. The multidirectional sounds in the lagoon reveal a multiverse characteristic of the polycentrism of Venice's soundscape, which influences his conception of the "acoustic multiverse" permeating *Prometheus*. In Nono's words:

> Venice is a complex system that affords precisely that pluridimensional listening [...] the sounds of the bells are diffused in various directions: some combine, are conveyed by the water, transmitted along the canals [...], others vanish almost completely, others connect to other signals from the lagoon and the city itself. Venice is an acoustic multiverse, the opposite of that hegemonic system of transmitting and listening to sound that we have been used to for centuries.[22]

In 1988, Nono described Venice's "sound fields" as infinitely magical, especially when the sound of the bells marks the location of distant islands on foggy days.[23] Venice was the acoustic multiverse in which he operated. Sounds reaching from different directions are the signs of life, inviting work, and participation. Nono's spatio-temporal concepts were defined two decades earlier. In a letter to dramaturge Giuliano Scabia, with whom he was collaborating on *The Lighted Factory,* he wrote: "The relationship between phonemes or sounds is created each time, not in linear temporal succession but continuously, polivalently, and in all directions; there is no single center, but a multiplicity of centers chasing, determining, inventing one another."[24] Venice's aural condition, which Nono experienced in day-to-day life, allows immersion in a sound field where "multidirectional listening" is possible.[25] The concept of time was not the linear progression that manifested orderly notational sequences; rather, it was characterized by the permeability of sounds originating from various directions in a multitemporal condition. The choir, live instruments, and live electronics merged in a "ritual labyrinth" of sound paths.[26]

Throughout his career, Nono intended to create a politically engaged "new musical theater" that partakes of history.[27] His compositions bear the mark of cultural activism that saw him involved in denouncing historical events: the persecution of the Jewish people (*Remember What They Did to You in Auschwitz,* 1966); the post-war socio-economic class struggles; the factory workers' condition in a capitalist society (*Illuminated Factory,* 1964).[28] Nono believed that it was necessary to "learn to live with the plurality of times and spaces, with multiplicities and with differences,"[29] to be immersed in what Cacciari called the "tragedy of listening,"[30] towards engaged participation of the listeners, partaking in the struggles on the world's stage. In spaces for listening, ideas are shared, debated, taken apart, or augmented. Listening invites the creation of empathic connections.

While earlier works directed attention to specific historical events and situations of societal oppression and inequalities, *Prometheus* transfers human suffering and struggle in the dimension of the myth. Symbolically, the second performance of *Prometheus* took place in a disused space at the Ansaldo Factory (1985) rather than in a bourgeois performance venue. In 1983, citing Eschilo's *Prometheus,* Nono wrote that "even when they saw, they could not see, and even when they heard, they could not hear."[31] In this "new musical theater," sound sources are interspersed in the space through a spatialization of sound inspired by historical images of St. Lorenzo showing two choirs at higher levels, opposite each other, the so-called *"cori battenti"* (counterpoint choir). Nono implements the *"percorsi rotti"* (broken paths), inspired by the 1500's *"cori spezzati"* (divided choirs) used in polyphonic music at St. Mark's Basilica, Venice, creating a dynamic relationship between choirs at different heights in counterposed locations, thus engaging the upper vaults.[32]

Nono studied the spatialization of mobile sounds for *Prometheus* by making plan and section sketches (Figure 2). Mobile sounds envelop participants from different directions. The historic church is a 'found instrument' with given aural qualities. Nono, who had been attentive to the history of the relationship between spaces and music, engaged the cultural history of the sound qualities of the deconsecrated church, which became a freed instrument reinvented in the present context: "Now I feel as if my

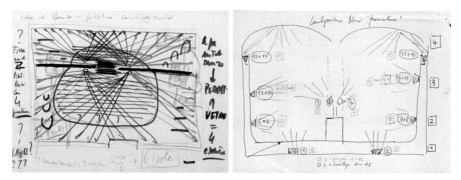

Figure 2: Luigi Nono, *Prometheus. Tragedy of Listening* (1984), Church of San Lorenzo, Venice. Left: Plan studies of multidirectional light paths. 51.38.02_02 ALN, Archivio Luigi Nono, Venezia © Courtesy Eredi Luigi Nono. Right: Sketch of the vertical section of the church by Nono, showing the position of the loudspeakers. 51.36.01_018_r ALN, Archivio Luigi Nono, Venezia © Courtesy Eredi Luigi Nono. (Plate 5 and 6, p. 291-292)

head *were* San Lorenzo. […] I feel that I occupy it and try to be fully occupied by the space."[33] Nono's spatializations through 'sound-sketches,'[34] and Piano's drawings for the *Ark,* came to life, in the Church of St. Lorenzo, as a reconceived vessel for sound.

Piano designed the *Ark* to stand freely within the interior space of the church. This was an acoustic choice, since the gap between the *Ark* and the interior church walls defined a double volume for sound reflections; it became possible to hear two spaces: one internal (the wooden *Ark*) and the other external (the walled stone church), creating a sense of sounds originating from afar. The *Ark* was composed of three levels of footbridges that allowed live sound and live electronics to be played at different levels in the space, implementing the "broken paths" and taking advantage of the spatializing effects of double choirs.[35] Loudspeakers were placed beneath the deck, which stood three meters off the ground. Each audience member was at the center of an unrepeatable aural experience where sound reflected from the ceiling to the floor, and from below upwards—the space participated in the music, and the music was composed for the space.

The search for multidirectional listening was present in Nono's early works. Nono's friend, Carlo Scarpa (1906–1978), understood this well, and when he traveled to Japan in 1956, he sent him a postcard showing a kabuki theater with a footbridge (*hanamichi*), which allowed performers to move from the stage to the stalls all on one level,[36] offering the opportunity for sound to come from different directions. This configuration echoes the use of footbridges on multiple levels in the *Ark,* allowing performers to move from one location to another surrounding the audience, in contrast with Western theaters where audience and performers remain separate, and sound sources are located exclusively on stage. Architect Shunji Ishida, who worked on the *Ark* project with Piano and Nono, was aware of this kind of performance space in Japan.

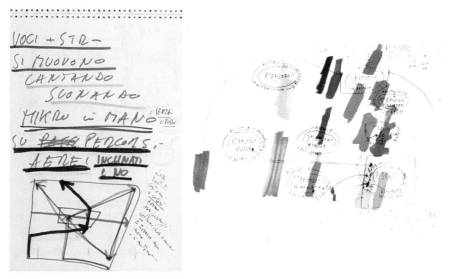

Figure 3: Luigi Nono. *Prometheus*. Left: Preparatory sketch showing the sound paths. 51.35.01_08 ALN, Archivio Luigi Nono, Venezia © Courtesy Eredi Luigi Nono. Right: Sketch showing *Prometheus'* five islands and associated colors. 51.38.02_15v ALN, Archivio Luigi Nono, Venezia © Courtesy Eredi Luigi Nono. (Plate 7 and 8, p. 293-294)

Nono's preparatory sketch shows that the loudspeakers were meant to engage the ceiling (Figure 2, right), the walls, and the church floor, allowing multidirectional sounds to permeate each other in an omnidirectional way, achieving the mobility of sound around the centralized audience.[37] Nono writes that "Prometheus is all in the air."[38] In one of his plan sketches, where he also indicates the possibility of using colored laser lights designed by Emilio Vedova, which were not ultimately realized, he noted that Piano suggested placing the audience at the center of the space (Figure 2, left). Sound is not seen but rather felt, generating a memorable experience by enveloping listeners. Air is the medium of sound, but it is also associated with the church's high ceiling. The warning sounds of the "tragedy of listening" were to originate and be amplified by a series of loudspeakers that engaged the vaulted ceiling, reflecting sound downwards.[39] The sonorous church accomplishes more than the reverberation of sound—it is a shared listening space.

Regarding Nono's compositional method, Marinella Ramazzotti explained how discovery implied moving beyond the sketching stage or annotating drawings and scores to spatialize a temporal phenomenon. Different colors were used to visualize sound paths. Chromatic sound scales on the same sheet are seen concurrently yet remain distinguishable in the eye of the composer (Figure 3).[40] The composer's extensive production of sketches, especially with *Prometheus,* allows us to argue that the chromesthetic notations reveal that the visual phenomenon may also be an auditory one, in which one could "listen to sketches" with the eyes.

Hearing through sketching is a form of "silent listening," a "colored hearing," or chromesthesia.[41] In a notebook for *Prometheus,* Nono marks down his notational use of colors to express the "broken paths" of sound relative to the five islands, or episodes, into which the work is divided (Figure 3, left).[42] Fabrizio Gay observed that Nono noted down the Pantone® color numbers, codifying, for example, the use of the color red for *Prometheus* (Figure 3, right).[43] Nono's sketches do not just make sound visible; they facilitate the concurrent perception of sound events, allowing the composer to hear their synchronous co-presence (Figures 2, 3). Furthermore, synesthetic percepts are vividly remembered, and synesthetes use their synesthesia as a mnemonic aid.[44]

However, the realization of the performance was not a matter of an accurate translation of visual representation into auditory phenomena. Musicologist Alessandro Mastropietro explained the "infinite possibilities" in Nono's work as a free logic of combinatory elements essential to the permanently open state of the work, active listening, and the mobility of sound.[45] Converting the work into a live event is about liberating possibilities "under authorial instruction."[46] Nono's scores breathe, coming to life when interpreters perform the score by inhaling or exhaling air to bring voices and sounds to life. According to the composer, even the stones of the Renaissance church and so too Piano's wooden musical instrument are sources of "infinite breaths."[47]

Renzo Piano's *Ark*: Sensorial and Geometric Architecture Drawings

When it comes to the relation between sound and architecture, a gap is yet to be bridged between acoustic and "aural design," dealing not just with the measurability of sound but also its immeasurable synesthetic qualities based on cultural associations.[48] Architectural theorist Marco Frascari (1945–2013) argued that architects do not merely design 'space' with attention to primary measurable qualities of Cartesian geometry (i.e., solidity, figure, motion/rest, number), but rather design 'air,' including considerations on secondary qualities, like non-measurable experience through multisensory perception (i.e., color, smell, taste, touch, hearing).[49] This design approach, which includes the experience of physical embodiment in space, reflects different tactics towards the production of meaning in architecture: a synesthetic one in the case of air and a visual one in the case of space. Frascari also argued that architectural representation never achieved a stable graphic codification due to the synesthetic design process.[50]

In *The Soundscape of Modernity*, a book on acoustic issues that notably also affected Italian architecture, Emily Thompson discussed the "silencing of architecture" during the modern period as a normative design objective. She explained that sound was perceived as a negative element, and the so-called "non-reverberant criterion" took hold in the design of schools, offices, and hospitals. Since the early 1900s, sound became an engineering problem to be solved by controlling materials, geometry, and dimensions.[51] Notably for Piano, however, sound was not understood as such, but rather as an aural element to work with in the design of performance spaces.

The *Ark* has been described as an "attempt to work on the synchronism between space and music."[52] While architectural representation relies on agreed conventions, the color choices to represent volumetric expansions and sound reverberations in Piano's drawings are subjective but not arbitrary. Moreover, the reading of such notations invites interpretation, making visible invisible aural qualities through sensorial notations.

Making sound visible in drawings is not about a rendering technique. The representation of sound in architecture and music has a history. In the 17th Century, Athanasius Kircher (1602–1680) used straight dashed lines rather than continuous lines in *Phonurgia Nova* (1673) to demonstrate geometric reflections of sound.[53] Nono used red dashed lines in one of his sketches for *Prometheus* to show the sound paths (Figure 2, right), while blue circular segments define enveloping sound waves, referencing the invisibility of sound, emphasizing a notational process through which an aural phenomenon is translated into a two-dimensional visual representation.

The score is critical in "sensing time,"[54] operating a silent listening. However, seeing the music is different from hearing the music. In musical notation, sign and signifier belong to different sense modalities—vision and hearing, respectively. Line weighted orthographic plans and sections offer the opportunity to sense the sequencing of spaces and events synchronically, opening the gaze to the temporal aspect. Horizontal and vertical sections reveal the thickness of time, defining what I like to call 'chronosections'—drawings that allow us to be here and there, in the before and after, at the same time.

Piano's sketches for the *Ark* represent sound sources with concentric arcs of an increasing radius (Figure 3, right). The graphical notation is based on a visual analogy of water ripples, which has been used to understand sound propagation since antiquity.[55]

The theories of specialization of the visual brain by British neuroscientist Semir Zeki suggest that in the absence of color and relying on black and white graphics, the brain specializes in reading geometric outlines.[56] The *Ark*'s design drawings rely on a translation of synesthetic representation in the mono-color blueprint graphic to the exclusion of multi-color effects; therefore, the final design drawings do not communicate explicitly the sought-after sensorial stimulation, tuning to a "specialized reading" of the visual brain in an appreciation of geometric form. *Prometheus'* musical scores translate Nono's sketches in the graphic of black and white notes on a score, keying into reading the temporality of sound.

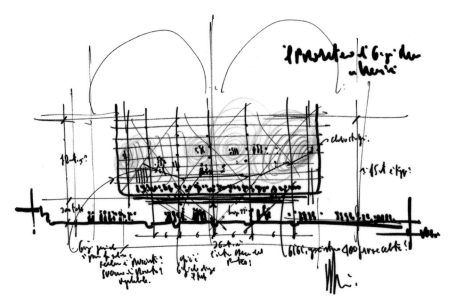

Figure 4: Preparatory sketch for the *Ark* by Renzo Piano (1984). © Courtesy of Fondazione Renzo Piano. (Plate 9, p. 295)

In a sectional sketch for the *Ark*, titled "Il Prometeo di Gigi" (*Gigi's Prometheus*), Piano uses a black marker to expediently draw the vaults with airy lines while marking the floor of the church and the *Ark* with heavier line weights (Figure 4). An intermediate line weight is used to draw the body of the *Ark*. The performers are in the stalls, and the music is played. Concentric sound marks visualize the multiplication of sound sources. Red circular segments suggest the presence of sharp sounds projected into the church's space, while orange marks project softer enveloping sounds. Sensorial drawings, such as this, emerged in the early stages of design, while geometric drawings were used in later design developments.

The *Ark* is a musical instrument rather than a stage. Its design enhances the capacity to listen: the color of the wood structure provides warmth to the space, coloring the music; mobile concave plywood panels diffuse sound; footbridges allow musicians to change position during the performance; the gap between the *Ark* and the church creates a double volume; the laminated timber structure functions as a scaffolding for the positioning of loudspeakers all around and at different heights. The metal stairs used to reach the footbridges are curved, like concentric sound waves, as if bent by sound, visibly anticipating the presence of music. The design enables a multisensory integration of the participants through cross-modal associations in the mediated experiencing of aural atmospheres.

Piano's drawings include geometric information while describing the pervading tone of place through synesthetic representation, adding to the technical aspects of geometrical acoustics and rewiring architecture's sensorium through layered representation. Looking at the *Ark*'s plan and section drawings, it is possible to distinguish two representational modes. On the one hand, there are "proprioception drawings," which focus on quantifiable information and define geometrical outlines and relative positions of spaces in relation to one another. On the other hand, while inclusive of this information, synesthetic drawings are not reduced to proportional or measured outlines and broaden their scope to account for a mediated sensorial experience, relying on cross-modal associations through two or more senses, analogically relaying synesthetic experiences.

Conclusions

In Nono's work, the gap between score and music is a listening space open to performers' interpretation, not unlike the translational gap between drawing and building.[57] While sketches and drawings release immediate sensory content in drawn music and architecture, they also relay a delayed sensory content: the performance or the executed architecture.[58]

Nono made use of synesthetic representation to visualize sounds in musical scores. As Roberto Favaro argued, spatio-temporal compositions made him a composer but also a "musician-architect."[59] Arguably, Piano's representational approach demonstrates the architect's role as 'aural composer' engaged with sound in and by architectural space.

Analogous to a musical score, architectural drawing is a notational system that makes time visible. The value of architectural representation as a notational system is well beyond visual duplication. Architectural representation is pre-eminently a representation of a process, demonstrating the on-site performance of construction assembly. To draw architecture based on one of the senses denies our synesthetic experiences and overlooks the sensory qualities of place. Even though nowadays design drawings often represent buildings in a state of completion, the architect, like a composer, can visualize the sequence of events on a construction site, imparting meaning through each drawing act, rather than show the 'blind' external appearance of a finished building.

Through the representation of time in architectural drawings, Piano's sketches construct pensiveness through making. Orthographic drawings offer an opportunity to sense time through the synchronic representation of spatial sequences and cross-modal associations. Such drawings make aural qualities visible through appropriate graphic notations. While, as Emmons stated, synesthesia has been codified to a degree in drawings,[60] it is vital to cultivate memorable representations evoking the synesthetic qualities of ambiance.

Frascari believed that "the future of construction drawings is to become emotion raising drawings."[61] Piano's drawings for the *Ark* allow one to ponder the possibility of tuning architecture for the human sensorium. While *Prometheus* continues to be performed and travels from place to place to this day, the *Ark* is stored in a warehouse in Milan, which reduces its potential as mobile architecture. Nevertheless, it still travels in our imagination of the first and second *Prometheus* through photographs and drawings, which are part of what is left behind when the music pauses, and we begin to listen in the silence to musical scores and architectural drawings.

Acknowledgments

The author acknowledges Architect Shunji Ishida (Renzo Piano Building Workshop), Curators Nicoletta Durante and Chiara Bennati (Renzo Piano Foundation), Nuria Schoenberg Nono and Valentina Burini (Fondazione Luigi Nono), Sound Director Alvise Vidolin and journalist Mario Gamba for support with the research. I thank photographer Marcello Mencarini for sharing memories of his encounter with Nono in 1988.

Notes

1.   Friedmann Sallis, "Luigi Nono (1924–1990)," in *Music of the Twentieth-century Avant-garde: A Biocritical Sourcebook,* edited by Larry Sitsky (Westport, CT: Greenwood Publishing Group, 2002), 329–331.

2.   Alvise Vidolin, "Il suono mobile in Prometeo. Tragedia dell'ascolto," https://www.youtube.com/watch?v=7vf1SPtugqY, accessed on May 8 2020.

3.   Luigi Nono, "Toward Prometeo: Journal Fragments," in *Nostalgia for the Future. Luigi Nono's Selected Writings and Interviews,* edited by Angela Ida De Benedictis and Veniero Rizzardi (Oakland, CA: University of California Press, 2018), 245. Nono collaborated with music director Claudio Abbado (1933–2014), sound director Alvise Vidolin, director of sound electronics Hans Peter Haller (1929–2006), painter Emilio Vedova (1919–2006). Peter Buchanan, *Renzo Piano Building Workshop: Complete Works,* Volume One (London: Phaidon Press, 1993), 87. Massimo Cacciari, ed., *Verso Prometeo* (Milan: Ricordi, 1984).

4.   Nono, "Toward Prometeo: Journal Fragments," 237, 239.

5.   Ibid., 241.

6. Carola Nielinger-Vakil, *Luigi Nono: A Composer in Context* (Cambridge, UK: Cambridge University Press, 2015), 211.

7. See Simon Shaw-Miller, *Eye hEar. The Visual in Music* (Farnham, UK: Ashgate, 2013), 11–12.

8. Nelson Goodman, *Languages of Art: An Approach to a Theory of Symbols* (Indianapolis and Cambridge: Hackett Publishing Company, 1976), 115, 118.

9. De Benedictis and Rizzardi, *Nostalgia for the Future*, 246.

10. Stefano Cecchetto and Giorgio Mastinu, eds. *Nono Vedova, Diario di Bordo, da" Intolleranza '60" a "Prometeo"* (Torino: Umberto Allemandi & C. 2005), 102.

11. Gianvincenzo Cresta, *L'Ascolto del Pensiero. Scritti su Luigi Nono* (Milano: Ruggienti, 2002), 7. Jonathan Impett, "The Tragedy of Listening. Nono, Cacciari, Critical Thought and Compositional Practice," *Radical Philosophy* 125 (May/June 2004), 31.

12. Enzo Restagno, ed., *Nono* (Torino: EDT, 1987), 262.

13. Impett, "The Tragedy of Listening," 32. Angela Ida De Benedictis and Veniero Rizzardi, eds., *Luigi Nono. Scritti e Colloqui* (Lucca: Casa Ricordi, 2001, II), 262.

14. Photographs taken during Mario Gamba's interview, *Non Sono un Maestro Ma* (De Benedictis and Rizzardi, *Luigi Nono,* II, 467–70).

15. De Benedictis and Rizzardi, *Nostalgia for the Future,* 197, 214–217.

16. Marinella Ramazzotti, *Luigi Nono* (Palermo: L'EPOS, 2007), 38–41.

17. Vidolin, "Il suono mobile in Prometeo. Tragedia dell'ascolto."

18. De Benedictis and Rizzardi, *Nostalgia for the Future,* 237–41, 243–4.

19. See https://rosebud2.it/search?q=luigi+nono+mencarini, accessed July 5, 2020.

20. Sthephen Davismoon, "Many possibilities…," *Contemporary Music Review* 18, no. 2 (1999), 3–9.

21. Nicolaus Huber, "Nuclei and Dispersal in Luigi Nono's 'A Carlo Scarpa Architetto, ai Suoi Infiniti Possibili per Orchestra a Microintervalli'," *Contemporary Music Review* 18 (1999), 19–36.

22. Jonathan Impett, *Routledge Handbook to Luigi Nono and Musical Thought* (Oxon and New York: Routledge, 2019), 407.

23. See *Archipiel Luigi Nono,* a film directed by Olivier Mille (1988).

24. Translation by author, from a letter of Nono to Scabia, March 11, 1964. See, Incontri. Il Diario Italiano per la Musica di Luigi Nono, Giuliano Scabia, 2008 (documentary, P31 ALN).

25. Restagno, *Nono,* 262.

26. In a preparatory sketchbooks for *Prometheus,* Nono writes about the "ritual labyrinth" as a series of "broken paths" between five islands (ALN 51.38.02/11). Impett, "The Tragedy of Listening," 31.

27. De Benedictis and Rizzardi, *Luigi Nono,* I, 118–131. Impett, "The Tragedy of Listening," 31.

28. Ramazzotti, *Luigi Nono,* 15–66.

29.   Jürg Stenzl, "Note Introduttive all'Incisione," *Prometeo, Tragedia dell'Ascolto,* (Cologne: EMI and Ricordi, 1995), 49–50.

30.   Nono, "Toward Prometeo: Journal Fragments," in De Benedictis and Rizzardi, *Nostalgia for the Future,* 245.

31.   De Benedictis and Rizzardi, *Luigi Nono,* I, 373.

32.   Roberto Favaro, *Spazio Sonoro. Musica e Architetttura tra Analogie, Riflessi, Complicità,* (Venezia: Marsilio, 2010), 208. Cacciari, Verso Prometeo, 24. Nielinger-Vakil, *Luigi Nono: A Composer in Context*, 192.

33.   Impett, *Routledge Handbook,* 407.

34.   I introduce the locution of 'sound-sketches' to refer to how sounds play in and through sketches through chromesthesia.

35.   Laura Moretti, "Architectural Spaces for Music: Jacopo Sansovino and Adrian Willaert at St Mark's," *Early Music History* 23 (2004): 156–7.

36.   Federica Goffi-Hamilton, "Carlo Scarpa and the Eternal Canvas of Silence," *ARQ* 10, no. 3–4 (December 2006): 292.

37.   See 51.38.02_02 ALN.

38.   Preparatory sketch by Nono (51.35.01_06v. © ALN).

39.   Federica Goffi, "Under-standing Counter Ceilings: The Multiverse of Gazing and Listening in the Ambiances of Carlo Scarpa and Luigi Nono," in *Ceilings and Dreams. The Architecture of Levity,* edited by Paul Emmons, Federica Goffi, and Jodi La Coe (New York: Routledge, 2019), 128–140.

40.   Nono, Das Atmende Klarsein, in De Benedictis and Rizzardi, *Luigi Nono,* I, 487.

41.   Shaw-Miller, *Eye hEar,* 50.

42.   Nielinger-Vakil, *Luigi Nono,* 193.

43.   Fabrizio Gay, "Partite e Partiture tra Luca Pacioli e Luigi Nono," in *Le Vie dei Mercanti da Luca Pacioli all'Ecogeometria del Territorio,* edited by Carmine Gambardella e Sabina Martusciello (Napoli: Edizioni Scientifiche Italiane, 2003), 447–9. See also 51.38.02_15r, ALN.

44.   Richard Cytowic, *Synesthesia, A Union of the Senses* (New York: Springer-Verlag, 1989), 65.

45.   Alessandro Mastropietro, "Luigi Nono: L'Ultimo Decennio 1979–1990. Lo Stato della Ricerca. Le Ultime Opere con Strumenti Elettronici," (Rome: La Sapienza, 1994), V.

46.   Elaine Scarry, *Dreaming by the Book* (New York: Farrar, Strauss and Giroux, 1999), 6.

47.   De Benedictis and Rizzardi, *Nostalgia for the Future*, 246.

48.   Barry Blesser and Linda-Ruth Salter. *Spaces Speak. Are you Listening? Experiencing Aural Architecture* (Cambridge, MA: MIT press, 2007).

49.   Marco Frascari, Lecture, "On Air," (Nottingham, UK, June 19, 2006).

50.   Marco Frascari, *Eleven Exercises in the Art of Architectural Drawing. Slow Food for the Architect's Imagination* (London and New York: Routledge, 2011), 143–5.

51.   Emily Thompson, *The Soundscape of Modernity. Architectural Acoustics and the Culture of Listening in America, 1900–1933* (Cambridge, MA: MIT Press, 2002), 3, 169–228.

52.   Renzo Piano, *Architecture and Music* (Milano: Edizioni Lybra Immagine, 2002), 11.

53.   Athanasius Kircher, *Phonurgia Nova. Sive Conjugium Mechanico-physicum Artis & Naturae Paranympha Phonosophia Concinnatu* (Rome: Hyacinthus Libellus, 1673), 94, 101, 149.

54.   Mamiya Michio, "Sensing time," *Contemporary Music Review* 1, no. 2 (1987): 45–52.

55.   Vitruvius, *The Ten Books on Architecture*, translated by Morris Hicky Morgan (New York: Dover Publications, 1960), V, 3–8.

56.   Semir Zeki, *Inner Vision. An Explanation of Art and the Brain,* (Oxford: Oxford University Press, 1999).

57.   Robin Evans, *Translations from Drawing to Building and other Essays* (London: Janet Evans and Architectural Association, 1997).

58.   Scarry, *Dreaming by the Book*, 6.

59.   Favaro, *Spazio Sonoro,* 192.

60.   Paul Emmons, *Drawing Imagining Building. Embodiment in Architectural Design Practices* (London and New York: Routledge, 2019), 141–2.

61.   From Marco Frasari's notes for the book "Eleven Exercises. Digital Notebook Livescribe 26: 11, 30 October, 2009, Architectural Archives of the University of Pennsylvania.

11.

Tools of Immersion: Drawing the Acoustic Atmosphere of the Philips Pavilion

Elisavet Kiourtsoglou

"I will not make a facade for Philips, but an electronic poem. Everything will happen inside: sound, light, color, rhythm. Perhaps, a scaffolding will be the pavilion's only exterior aspect,"[1] Le Corbusier provocatively stated for one of the most eccentric buildings of the 20th Century: The Philips Pavilion for the 1958 World's Fair in Brussels. Le Corbusier's long-lasting obsession with creating a total work of art, a kind of *Gesamtkunstwerk*, lined up perfectly with the initial idea of the firm's board: The Pavilion would be the place for a large-scale demonstration—not an exposition—of professional sound and light equipment by Philips Eindhoven, featuring a projection of still images accompanied by music and a shower of color-changing lights inside the entire building. Le Corbusier's original ideas for the design of temporary exhibition spaces—an example of which was his *Pavillion des Temps Modernes* in 1937—were quickly abandoned. His first drawings for the Philips Pavilion, a scaffolding rising up from a plan which resembled literally a "stomach," were transformed by Iannis Xenakis into a non-orthogonal space, made entirely of ruled surfaces (hyperbolic paraboloids). As Xenakis himself explained later, these surfaces were also chosen for their acoustic qualities. They did not generate multiple reverberations as the parallel surfaces of an orthogonal space would do, and they did not accumulate reverberation as the angles of a triangular space (in its trihedrons) would do.[2]

During the World's Fair, approximately two million visitors entered this peculiar space, to experience the automated running of the audio-visual spectacle of *Le Poème Electronique*. This consisted of a video, made by Le Corbusier with the assistance of Philippo Agostini, and an eight-minute musical piece accompanying the video, composed by Edgard Varèse. Xenakis, besides the design of the Pavilion, was also assigned the two-minute musical composition *Interlude Sonore*, an introduction to *Le Poème Electronique*. Visitors were meant to be immersed in an *avant la lettre* multime-

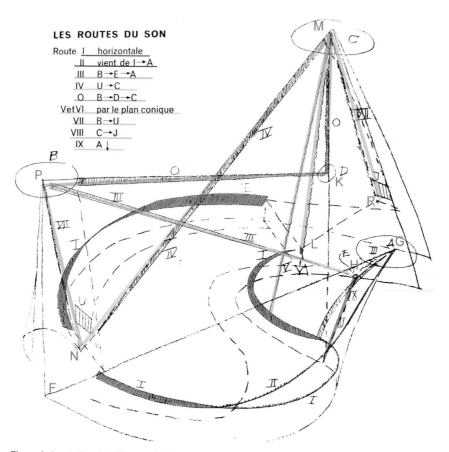

Figure 1: Iannis Xenakis, "Routes de Son" ("Sound Roads") showing the placement of the loudspeakers across the main lines of the Philips Pavilion's geometry used for the music spatialization, as shown in Petit Jean (ed), *Le Poème Electronique-Le Corbusier* (Paris: Les editions de Minuit, 1958). © Archives Famille Xenakis. Colors and letters added by the author. Red letters coincide with the projections of generatives lines on the sketch of the first page of Xenakis' *Partition de Stereophonie*. (Plate 10, p. 296)

dia art installation heavily based on the technological advancements of the firm, a pioneer in electronic equipment for both recording and broadcasting sound.[3] The modern soundscape the audience perceived was produced by a sound that was not only uniformly clear, loud, controlled and non-reverberant, but was also constantly emerging from multiple directions as it run through 350 loudspeakers installed along specially designed "sound roads" inside the Pavilion[4] (Figure 1). The musical performance of both *Poème Electronique* and *Interlude Sonore*, based on special sound effects and stereophonic technology, created a whole-body experience. The audience was meant to experience a series of embodied sensations, like loss of orientation, a sense of immobility or an urge to make sudden movements, a feeling of expansiveness or tightness. In other words, the composers were asked to create with sound a bodily felt space.[5]

Le Corbusier, Varèse and Xenakis used multiple types of "time-based" scores to study in advance what kind of acoustic and visual stimuli the visitors would perceive. While the history of the Philips Pavilion has been extensively discussed,[6] less attention has been paid to how the staging of its atmospheres was envisioned. An exception to this noted lack of bibliography are Le Corbusier's "minutage" tables, showing second-by-second written descriptions of the still images and color projections, which have received a detailed analysis.[7] Regarding the music, the main focus has been the collection and analysis of the sound material of *Poème Electronique*,[8] and the reconstruction of the spatialization for *Interlude Sonore* from a technological point of view.[9]

Both Varèse and Xenakis, beyond their fascination with the available stereophonic technology, cared for the sound experience of the audience. As media theorist Gascia Ouzounian argues, technological devices—especially tape recorders, automatization systems and loudspeakers that considered musical time in terms of the tape's length—transferred "culturally significant properties of visual space onto the acoustic imagination."[10] Using these devices, avant-garde composers were initiated into a world of lines, masses and surfaces that could represent parameters of sound (either electroacoustic or instrumental) such as rhythm, dynamics, volume and direction. These composers wished to create with their music an "acoustic space," that is a mental space where sound is perceived as moving or is placed inside a non-inert three-dimensional space (having reverberation, multiple focal points, etc.). Time-based graphics were compositional tools that allowed them to represent this "acoustic space." Indeed, Xenakis studied the spatialization of *Interlude Sonore* in a three-page geometrical graphic score (called *Partition de Stéreophonie*), while Varèse used free-hand sketches to work out the spatial dimensions of *Le Poème Electronique*.[11]

How did the representation of "acoustic space," through these graphic scores, help these two composers foresee the atmosphere that would be perceived by the public? Are free-hand drawings and sketches representing sound able to communicate felt experiences and bodily sensations and, if so, what is the difference with a geometrical notation of music? In a broader sense, what is the relation between electroacoustic music representation and its production?

Firstly, I argue that Xenakis, by introducing into his geometrical notation *Partition de Stéreophonie* a Euclidean "acoustic space" built up by points and lines, integrated into his composition the possible physical experiences of the audience. By doing so, he wanted to preview the way the *Interlude Sonore* could establish the atmosphere for the people entering the pavilion, by what Bohme described as a process "affecting the mind, manipulating the moods, and evoking emotions."[12] It produced and empowered a certain acoustic atmosphere, which progressively calmed the roar of the audience's agitation as they entered the pavilion and stimulated their senses. Secondly, I argue that this kind of geometrical notation used by Xenakis is not a prior stage but an integral part of the production of electroacoustic music, literally a tool of immersion, because it works with three-dimensional space. Staging an immersive sound atmosphere requires finding ways to represent space in musical notation.

In the following paragraphs, I will initially discuss Philips' artistic intentions, analyzing the technical text *Les effets sonores*, written by William Tak, Philips' acoustic engineer. Then I will move on to Varèse and Xenakis' graphic notations. I will focus on the three pages of Xenakis' *Partition de Stéreophonie* and I will compare them to Varèse's preparatory compositional sketches for the *Le Poème Electronique*. My aim here is to underline that immersion is a strategy followed by both composers, as part of a general trend of atonal music at the beginning of 20th Century, supported by the technical achievements of the music industry. More specifically, I will show that Xenakis' strategy of immersion is to predict an acoustic atmosphere by representing the mental "acoustic space" in his score, by using the three-dimensional, Euclidean elements (lines, points). Throughout this chapter, the term 'spatialization' of electroacoustic music refers to composers' techniques or the devices used by the producers to introduce movement into the perception of music. The term 'production' of electroacoustic music here is taken in its common definition, that is, the process by which music is created and manipulated, so it can be distributed and affect the public.

Philips and *Les effets sonores*

Philips' intentions regarding the new venue's acoustic character were clear: the sound effects and the automatization of the performance were presented by the engineers W. Tak and J. de Bruins respectively in the 1958 special edition of the *Philips Technical Review*.[13] The brief text by Tak on *Les Effets Sonores [Sound Effects]* deserves attention, because it puts forward the perception of acoustic atmospheres as a key intention for the whole project:

> In acoustics, we have already known for a long time now *the various effects that influence the perception of sounds*. Among these phenomena, the most well-known are reverberation and echoes. They provide us, disregarding visual perception, with *an impression*—acknowledged by experience—*of the atmosphere*. Reverberation and echoes can be created not only in a natural way but also artificially. That allows us to differentiate notably the acoustic impression that the audience acquires by the atmosphere from the visual impression. This contradiction of impressions could

give to the audience the impression of experiencing something unexpected. *The possibility of provoking, through electroacoustics, such emotions* will possibly become for the music a precious acquisition.

Equally remarkable effects are obtained by means of stereophony: a sound could be perceived from one direction where no sound source is found and purely electric manipulations *allow the impression to be created that a sound source is moving,* whereas in reality everything remains immobile. These effects came to our mind, when at the end of 1956, we were discussing with Le Corbusier the acoustic part of his "Poème Electronique". We could give to the audience *the illusion that varied acoustic sources move around them,* rise and fall again, meet and separate once again, while the interior in which all this takes place would be sometimes "dry", sometimes endowed with the [acoustical] dimensions of a cathedral.[14]

Creating illusion, as a possible audience *sensation*, was part of the original intention of Philips. *Emotions,* such as surprise, astonishment or even confusion, could be provoked by a constantly moving sound and multiple artificial echoes. Familiar soundscapes, such as the non-reverberant "dry" acoustic environment of a recording studio or the multi-echoing cathedral, were also mentioned as references of atmospheres to be achieved by Philips and the composers, inside a space where natural echoing had been neutralized by plastering the walls with asbestos.

In February of 1957, Tak also wrote a test scenario to illustrate vividly the technical possibilities the company offered: "rumble sounds from underground […] sounds move up the wall […] a melody with additional reverberation […] the reverberated sound decays rather quickly and disappears towards the horizon […] the echo crossfades into a zooming sound […] a sound that moves along the walls horizontally."[15] At that time, the Philips engineers believed technology could affect the audience's sensations in the same way. Today, according to Ouzounian, we are more inclined to suggest that sound, space and sensation occur in the intersection of the body, its gender and culture, and the mental "acoustic space" produced by appropriate sound technology.[16] Sound effects do not affect all people in the same way.

However, at that point, Varèse and Xenakis were invited to imagine the way the audience as a whole would be immersed in such acoustic impressions. According to musicologist Makis Solomos, sonic immersion—the possibility of being completely involved and submerged in a specific sound atmosphere—was one of the features that raised sound to a central compositional element of 20th-century music. Immersion, along with full exploration of timbre, broader use of noise and new methods forms of spatialization and listening, were compositional strategies that transformed the avant-garde, and progressively the popular, musical scene. Many of these composers (both instrumental and electroacoustic) hitherto focused on immersion, on the "internal life" of sound, by progressively abandoning sound as an inert point (notes related or not to a tonal system), and opened up to spatial definitions of it: sound has dimensions like *thickness* and can drive us into an *abyss* or *wrap* us *up*.[17]

Both Varèse and Xenakis, prompted by the Philips technology, focused on the spatial dimensions of music. Yet their preparatory graphic scores show different approaches. More precisely, thirteen sketches, traced by the Italian musicologist Leo Izzo and found in the archives of Paul Sacher Stiftung, reveal successive "sound images" drawn by Varèse during the composition of *Poème Electronique*.[18] The variety and the heterogeneity of notation in these sketches is astonishing: multicolored collage plans, textual notes of evocative-symbolic nature, diagrams on squared paper, parts of a traditional musical staff, rhythm patterns, instructions on tone or frequency progression. Different types of notation correspond to different types of sound material, according to Izzo: electronic glissandi, for example, were represented by curved lines that look like a section of the pavilion's hyperbolic paraboloids. In another sketch, a red curve stands for the envelope of dynamics (how sound's intensity changes over time). The whole sequence of the thirteen sketches offers a structural segmentation of Varèse's piece and takes the role of "a technical score," helping the composer to cope with technical problems since he lacked previous experience in electroacoustic composition. In these thirteen sketches it is the gradual progression over time of parameters such as dynamics, volume and pitch that are studied, as in a "classical" music score. Varèse represented *spatially on paper* the evolution of various "sound objects" to be recorded and mixed together, or elements that generated "sound masses."[19] The graphic alternation of these characteristics of sound evokes various effects that could have been perceived by the audience, but mostly helps Varèse to oversee the progression of his work. Yet the overall acoustic atmosphere cannot easily be imagined while reading these sketches, as we lack information related to the Pavilion as a space. How and where sound would be heard (the spatialization of sound) was not discussed by the engineers until the final staging of the entire spectacle.[20]

Xenakis and the *Interlude Sonore*

On the other hand, Xenakis' familiarity with electronic technology, along with his training as an engineer, allowed him to work early on with spatialization of sound as immersion strategy. The *Interlude Sonore* was meant to be broadcast while the public was entering and exiting the pavilion and to introduce Varèse's *Poème Electronique*. Xenakis composed "clouds of punctual sounds varying in intensity and density as well as [moving] inside the pavilion's space."[21] Assisted by Pierre Arnaud, he almost set fire to the DMS studio in Paris, in order to record ten "clouds of sound" produced by charcoal burning.[22] Moreover, he made a graphic score to be sent along with the three tapes, showing the spatialization of the music: the way sound would be distributed among the 350 loudspeakers. Considered lost for a long time, this graphic score, eventually found in the Xenakis family's archives, provides precious insights into the acoustic atmospheres inside the Pavilion. While nowadays we know that the spatialization as imagined by Xenakis was not technically feasible, it is still worth studying.

The *Partition de Stéréophonie* of *Interlude Sonore*

The *Partition de Stéréophonie* [Stereophony Score], dated April 1958, consists of three A3 sheets. The total duration of the piece is 1'52" and Xenakis proposes three independent channels (I, II, III) to be played on an appropriate magnetophonon in order to distribute sound into the loudspeakers placed in the pavilion. On the first page (Figure 2), Xenakis drew a plan of the Pavilion where he projects the generative lines of the hyperbolic paraboloids.[23] These same geometric lines are called "routes de sons" [sound roads], labeled FG, GK, etc., and used as "acoustic lines" to build the "acoustic space" of his piece, that is, its spatialization. Next to this plan, in a two-axis system, the abscissa stands for time (in seconds) and the ordinate for the sound's speed, as the slopes give the distance traveled per second. What Xenakis shows is not the exact distance between two points of the pavilion, but the direction of sound movement (from group A to group B of the loudspeakers or along the "sound roads") and whether the vector of sound speed is constant or variable (in magnitude or direction).

Deciphering this score provides us with two distinct, though complementary, types of observations. We can make quantitative and qualitative comments on the movement of sound according to the geometric variations of lines, and we can also indirectly infer the intended acoustic atmosphere caused by these sound movements.

The first page shows the spatialization of the sound during the first 30 seconds (-30" to 0"):[24] Tracks (I) and (II) are silent, while track (III) is broadcast simultaneously by all of the pavilion's speakers, which means whatever is heard will be perceived as motionless, while also surrounding the public. This first page also provides the one and only indication of the sound's volume. Xenakis calls for a maximum volume of all three tracks of his music as soon as Varèse's *Poème Electronique* stops. As Tazelaar suggests, that is logical, even if it seems excessive, since Varèse's music is so much more complex and violent compared to Xenakis' homogeneous and mild music.[25] The *Interlude Sonore* had to be played more loudly in order to make a statement next to Varèse's composition.

During these first 30 seconds, sound coming from all the corners and surfaces of the pavilion, along the horizontal belt and up to the vertical sound routes, wraps up the audience. While the listeners are kept in the dark (the visual projection of *Poème Electronique* starts as soon as Xenakis' music stops), new spatial boundaries are created by the sound. Because of the granular nature of sound (sound masses of charcoal

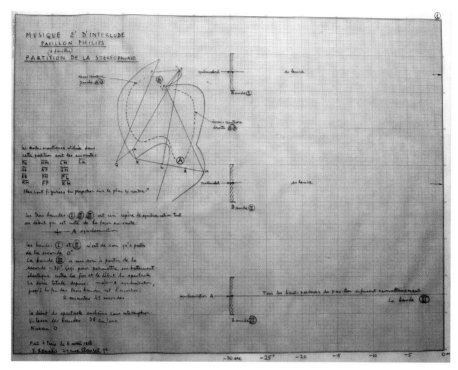

Figure 2: Iannis Xenakis, *Partition de Stéreophonie*, Stereophony Score, page 1, 1958. © Archives Famille Xenakis.

burning), a three-dimensional "acoustic space" redoubles point by point the existing physical space of the pavilion, which is no longer visually perceivable. The audience probably feels a boundary around them that keeps them fixed in their place. This seems like a perfect way to introduce an atmosphere of stillness, which gradually takes away the initial excitement of the audience when entering the space.

On the second page of the score (Figure 3), sound starts to move. During the next 30 seconds (0" to 30"), tracks (I) and (II) "are identical and are diffused synchronically," according to Xenakis' text, in opposite directions: Track (I) moves from A to B along the periphery of the pavilion at constant but not identical speeds, while track (II) takes the inverse path, moving from B to A , at the exact same time. Track (III) continues to be played simultaneously by all the loudspeakers of the pavilion. The audience is still inside the previous acoustic atmosphere: sounds of the same nature as before (charcoal burning) hit their ears from multiple directions, while gradually the audience feels more and more "tightened up" as sound moves back and forth around the pavilion's belt.

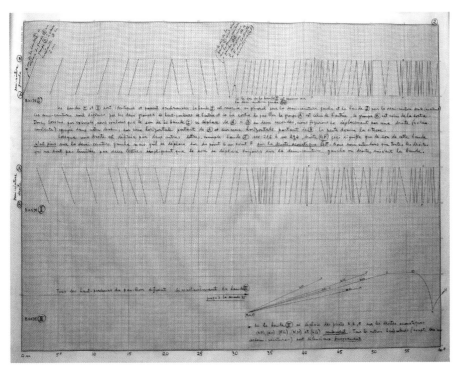

Figure 3: Iannis Xenakis, *Partition de Stéréophonie*, Stereophony Score , page 2, 1958. © Archives Famille Xenakis.

During the next 30 seconds (30" to 60") changes of constant speeds are more and more frequent in tracks (I) and (II), accelerating up to 200 meters per second. These same tracks (I) and (II) stop moving exclusively around the pavilion's belt and occasionally follow certain acoustic lines (GF), (PL), (PH). During the same time period, track (III) also accelerates, though at lower speeds, starting from the ground and moving along the "sound roads" (NP), (KM), (FG), (NM) and (KG). These abrupt sounds are labeled "thunderbolt" by Xenakis in one of his sketchbooks.[26] All these acoustic lines are produced by loudspeakers placed along some of the generative lines of the hyperbolic paraboloids of the pavilion. A complementary three-dimensional sketch (Figure 1) also made by Xenakis shows these same "sound roads" (although using different letters), helping us imagine these movements. Sound climbs towards the upper part of the pavilion, following the ascending "sound roads" (NP), (KM), (FG), (NM) and (KG), and ending up in the peaks, a kind of funnel, made by the intersections of two hyperbolic paraboloids. As the speeds of the sound accelerate, it eventually becomes impossible for the audience to register precisely the source and

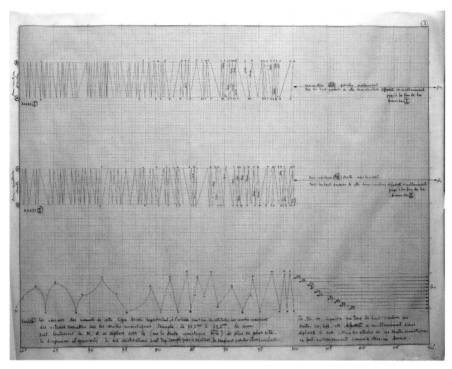

Figure 4: Iannis Xenakis, *Partition de Stéréophonie*, Stereophony Score, page 3, 1958. © Archives Famille Xenakis.

the direction of the sound around the pavilion's belt. A kind of surrounding sound cloud emerges, probably creating the impression of a "ring" forming around the audience's hips, a ring that confines them. Yet the audience is also surprised by "thunderbolts of sounds" (very fast passages of 2 seconds each) climbing up the acoustic lines. Having felt "tightened up" until now, this shift to linear ascending movements again changes the focus of the audience's attention: looking up, into the darkness, they grasp through their ears for the first time the inclined edges of the pavilion that they have only seen from the exterior.

As we now turn to the last page (Figure 4) of the spatialization score (60" to 100"), the composition reaches its climax. The sound cloud of the very fast sound movements is still here. Tracks (I) and (II) go around the half-belts AB and BA in opposite directions, changing speed constantly. The sound of the same tracks also climbs up to certain acoustic lines more and more often, but it stops abruptly at 100". Track (III) uses the remaining vertical sound routes, moving at variable speeds (creating the appearance of curves between certain points in space (K, G, R, etc.). Xenakis mentions that the abscissa of this broken line of track (III), formed by curves and lines, represents the altitudes of the pavilion's space, on a scale of 1cm = 4m. This way, we are able to grasp how fast sound accelerates, as it climbs towards the highest points in the three-dimensional space of the Pavilion. The intention is to still have the audience surrounded by an accelerating sound cloud, but now as the sound goes up and down along acoustic lines more and more frequently, it might feel like the violent "drops" of a sound storm that come from constantly higher points in space, faster and faster.

After this "sound storm" (from 100" up until the end of the piece), a homogeneous and quiet atmosphere gradually settles in. Track (I) is broadcast simultaneously by all the speakers of the left half-belt, while the speakers of the right half-belt play track (II). The spinning sound cloud is replaced by individual, directional sounds that arise from the periphery and point at the audience, who might still feel dizzy from the previous cataclysm, in the center of the pavilion. This shift might help people to calm down. At the same time, track (III) is broadcast gradually on certain "sound roads," using all their loudspeakers. Here, sound is stationary, coming from the inclined edges of the pavilion. It stops completely at 120". On the other hand, tracks (I) and (II), transmitted by the loudspeakers in the pavilion's belt, continue for a few seconds, giving the impression that the sound progressively "touches down" on the pavilion's floor. The audience is immersed in a new, stable soundscape, generated by various immobile sources around and along the pavilion's edges. This might give the impression of a familiar three-dimensional space. Acoustic space no longer reserves any surprises for them, an ideal way to conclude this prelude. The audience is now in the mood to be immersed in Varèse's and Le Corbusier's spectacle, which starts right away.

Conclusions: A Body inside the Drawn Acoustic Atmosphere

At the first post-war World's Fair at 1958, Philips wanted to make a statement about the new perceptions modern people could have, thanks to the new technologies. Moreover, the pavilion's space, due to its geometrical qualities, offered a unique acoustic environment. The hyperbolic paraboloids, generated by the simultaneous translocation of straight lines into two axes, keep reverberation low in comparison to orthogonal and spherical spaces. Meanwhile, the pavilion's constantly variable geometry helped to influence the perception of sound, as the 350 loudspeakers placed on the curves broadcast sound from and in multiple directions.

Xenakis and Varèse, adhering to Philips' intentions, worked to create a unique immersive experience for the audience inside the pavilion. In order to prepare this experience, Varèse created a graphical representation of the evolution of sound masses, rhythm patterns, intensity, and pitch throughout the eight-minute piece. On the other hand, Xenakis put the emphasis on drawing "the acoustic space" built up by the moving sound, to invoke immersion, since the early phase of composition. He channeled the audience's excitement when entering the pavilion's space and gradually staged a certain acoustic atmosphere that implied bodily stillness and concentration. His spatialization score, as analyzed in this chapter, represents sound movements along the circular belt and the generative lines of the Pavilion's hyperbolic paraboloids—in other words, inside the Euclidean space of the Philips Pavilion. In a way, these two composers worked with different strategies of immersion. On the one hand, Varèse worked on new kinds of sounds by representing on paper the evolution of sound parameters (pitch, volume, duration). In fact, Varèse made free-hand drawings of the spatial evolution of the sound parameters using a conception of space that is already present on a musical staff. In this kind of notation, we use spatial metaphors (up, down, converging) to represent the perception of sound: a high-pitched sound is placed *higher* on the staff than a low-pitched sound, while two *converging* lines represent a crescendo/decrescendo. On the other hand, Xenakis introduced the geometrical representation of the movements of sound and focused on where sound would be heard: points and lines in his musical notation built literally an "acoustic space," the mental perception of how the pavilion's space could be felt in the body when *Interlude Sonore* would be heard. It is possible to detect atmosphere in musical notation when actually three-dimensional, Euclidean space is represented. Xenakis tried to theorize this shift.

In a text published that same period he argued that whatever is valid for the Euclidean space could be transposed into an "acoustic space" with the use of the electroacoustic chain (the tape, the tape-recorder and the loudspeakers).[27] Euclidean space consists of points, while lines and surfaces could be generated inductively by applying the fundamental principles. Euclidean space could be also introduced as an abstract vector space. Given that a loudspeaker could be considered as a point, the sound broadcast by at least two sound points (loudspeakers) could form a straight "acoustic line," the multiplication, translocation and rotation of which could generate "acoustic surfaces." Of course, sound itself cannot be put down in paper; it is sound speed that has been represented as a vector inside the "acoustic space" in the three pages of the *Partition de Stereophonie* of the *Interlude Sonore*.

Yet, in Euclidean geometry, the position and magnitude of one vector is grasped relative to another vector or compared to the origin. The relativity of the vector's definition reflects the relativity of the "acoustic space" itself: the latter is a mental space that does not exist independently of the listener's position in space. A listener who felt more motivated to move as sound was moving from one loudspeaker to another would have hardly perceived the same audible impression as someone who stayed immobile. The listeners' reactions were of course also influenced by their different emotions at the given moment or their ways of interacting with space based on their cultural background, race or gender. In a way, to proceed with algebra of vectorial "acoustic space," Xenakis had to take into consideration the position and direction of another vector, i.e. the human body, inside the Pavilion's space. This is how geometrical notation helped him predict atmospheres of closeness or distance, dizziness, momentary loss of orientation, tightness or expansiveness: the vector of sound speed is manipulated as a body in a three-dimensional space, introducing the Pavilion's space into the composition phase and its notation. As Nicholas Cook argued, musical notation should not be considered dissociated from performance or interpretation, while production choices, especially in electroacoustic music, are in fact manners of interpretation and performance.[28] In this chapter, I have tried to show that by using geometrical notation, the composition, production and performance of music could be merged. For Xenakis, the geometrical representation of sound becomes a tool for immersion that builds up and foresees specific acoustic atmospheres.

Acknowledgments

This article is part of my postdoctoral research which is co-financed by Greece and the European Union (European Social Fund-ESF) through the Operational Program "Human Resources Development, Education and Lifelong Learning" in the context of the project "Reinforcement of Postdoctoral Researchers – 2nd Cycle" (MIS-5033021), implemented by the State Scholarships Foundation (IKY).

Operational Programme
Human Resources Development,
Education and Lifelong Learning

Co-financed by Greece and the European Union

Ευρωπαϊκή Ένωση
European Social Fund

Notes

1. Le Corbusier, as quoted in Jean Petit, *Le Poème Electronique,* (Paris: Editions Vives, 1958), 23.
2. Iannis Xenakis, "Le Pavillon Philips à l'aube d'une architecture," *Musique, Architecture,* (Tournai: Casterman, 1971), 123–142.
3. The Philips Research Laboratories in the Netherlands, established in 1914, advance important technological innovations. Roelof Vermeulen, who was in charged, was granted a patent for a loudspeaker in 1928. See more Kees Tazelaar, *On the Threshold of Beauty. Philips and the Origins of Electronic Music in the Netherlands, 1925–1965,* (Rotterdam: V2_Publications, 2013), 17–37.

4.   As historian Emily Thomson has shown, technologies of acoustic control, at the
     beginning of the 20th Century in America, initiated new standards for reverberation
     in concert halls which progressively transformed how modern sound should be heard:
     "[It] should be uniformly clear and direct, controlled and non-reverberant." Emily
     Thomspon, *The Soundscape of Modernity. Architectural Acoustics and the Culture of Listening
     in America, 1900–193,* (Cambridge: The MIT Press, 2004), 321.

5.   German philosopher Gernot Böhme introduces the concept of atmosphere as a bod-
     ily felt space. See Gernot Böhme, *Atmospheric Architectures: The Aesthetics of Felt Spaces*
     (Bloomsbury Publishing Plc, 2017).

6.   Marc Treib, *The Philips Pavilion. Space Calculated in Time* (Princeton New Jersey:
     Princeton University Press, 1996); Tazelaar, *On the Threshold of Beauty*; Peter Wever,
     Inside Le Corbusier's Philips Pavilion. A multimedia Space at the 1958 Brussels World's Fair,
     (Rotterdam: nai010 Publishers, 2015); Carlotta Darò, *Les Murs du Son* (Paris: Editions
     B2, 2015); Sven Sterken, "Immersive Strategies in Iannis Xenakis' Polytopes," *Immersed.
     Sound and Architecture, OASE*, 78, (2009), 116–120, Joseph Clarke, "Iannis Xenakis and
     the Philips Pavilion", *The Journal of Architecture*; 17, no. 2, (2012): 213–229.

7.   Jean de Heer & Kees Tazelaar, *From Harmony to Haos. Le Corbusier, Varèse, Xenakis and Le
     Poème Electronique* (Amsterdam: Duizend en Een Uitgeverij, 2017).

8.   For the virtual reconstruction of both sound and image spectacle of *Le Poème Electron-
     ique* see Vincenzo Lombardo, Andrea Valle, John Fitch, Kees Tazelaar, Stefan Weinzi-
     erl, and Wojciech Borczyk, "A Virtual-Reality Reconstruction of Poème Electronique
     Based on Philological Research," *Computer Music Journal*, 33, no. 2, (2009): 24–47.

9.   For the spatialization of Xenakis *Interlude Sonore* see Heer & Tazelaar, *From Harmony to
     Haos,* 179–185; Valle, A. & Tazelaar, K. & Lombardo, Vincenzo, "In a concrete space.
     Reconstructing the spatialization of Iannis Xenakis' Concret PH on a multichannel
     setup," *Proceedings of the 7th Sound and Music Computing Conference,* SMC 2010.

10. Gascia Ouzounian, "Visualizing Acoustic Space," *Circuit: musiques contemporaines*, 17,
     no. 3, (2007) : 45–56.

11. Comments on Varèse's preparational sketches on Meyer Felix, Zimmerann Heidy (ed),
     Edgard Varèse, composer, sound sculptor, visionary (Bâle : The Boydell Press ; Paul Sacher
     Stiftung, 2006).

12. Böhme, *Atmospheric Architectures,* 28.

13. This was a monthly publication of the Research Laboratories of N.V Philips Gloe-
     ilampenfabrieken, first released in 1938.

14. William Tak, "Les effets Sonores," *La Revue Technique Philips*, n°2/3, (1958): 47. Origi-
     nal text in French, translated and undersigned by the author.

15. Tazelaar, *On the threshold of Beauty,* 120–126.

16. Cf. Gascia Ouzounian, "Embodied sound: Aural architectures and the body," *Contem-
     porary Music Review*, 25, no. 1–2, (2006): 69–79.

17.   Makis Solomos, *De la musique au son. L'emergence du don dans la musique des XXe-XXie siècles* (Presses Universitaires de Rennes, 2013), 235–278.

18.   Leo Izzo, "La Genesi compositiva del "Poème Electronique" di Edgard Varèse," *Il Saggiatore musicale*, 22, no. 1 (2015): 61–96.

19.   A "sound mass" results from various compositional techniques in which, texture, timbre, and dynamics are primary shapers of gesture and impact instead of individual pitches, blairing in this way, the limits between sound and noise.

20.   It was by splitting the final composition in three individual channels, that allowed both Varèse and Philips engineers to create "three sound images" coming from different directions; the choice of points in the composition to be spatialized was indicated separately in another tape. Cf Tazelaar, *On the threshold...* ,147–152.

21.   Letter of Xenakis to Kalff, 02/12/57, Fondation Le Corbusier.

22.   Xenakis has recorded again this masterpiece of electroacoustic music in 1962 in GRM laboratories as *Concret PH*, named it after the Hyperbolic Paraboloids of the Pavilion. Cf Tazelaar, *On the threshold of Beauty*, 153; Delalande Francois, *"Il faut être constamment un immigré", Entretiens avec Xenakis*, (Paris, Buchet/Chastel-INA, 1997), 36.

23.   The Hyperbolic Paraboloids is a doubly ruled surface produced by the simultaneously rotation of a two families of straight lines. A hyperbolic paraboloid can also be defined as the union of the lines joining two points moving at constant speed on two non coplanar lines. This non coplanar lines are its generative lines.

24.   The timing on the spatialization score contains also negative numbering.

25.   Tazelaar, *From Harmony to Chaos*,181.

26.   In a sketch found in his notebooks, Xenakis describes the various acoustic routes as: "thunderbolt of sounds = straight lines at once". Archives Famille Xenakis, Carnet N°20, p. 20.

27.   Xenakis describe his theory about acoustic space in his article Iannis Xenakis, "Notes sur un 'Geste électronique'," *in* Jean Petit (éd.), *Le poème électronique Le Corbusier*, (Paris: Éditions de Minuit, 1958), 226–231.

28.   Nicholas Cook, *Beyond the Score: Music as Performance*, (Oxford, New York, Oxford University Press, 2013), especially chapter 11 & 12.

SECTION #03

———————————

City Tunes

The Instrumentarium of Kircher: Premises of a Universal Phonurgy

Cécile Regnault

The Imaginary of a City-Instrument

Whether natural or built, rural or urban, outdoor spaces sound. Like concert halls, public spaces have acoustics, which can be compared to the sounding boards of musical instruments. Used to discuss urban ambiances, seminal ideas of a "city-instrument"[1] or *urban instrumentarium*[2] date back to times when acoustics, which was not yet a science, already fueled the sounding imagination of scholars. The hypothesis of instrumentation supported here argues that the sounds of our environments cannot be studied outside the architectural and symbolic contexts that shape their expression, and hence their understanding. Indeed, the etymology of the word *akustike*, which means "to hear," reminds us that acoustics is a science that deals not only with properties of production and dissemination of the physical phenomenon but also with those relating to its reception, requiring systematic questioning of the conditions of perception. Therefore, we can argue that the complexity of acoustic knowledge was nurtured throughout the centuries by an auditory imagination that influenced our perception and its space-sensitive impact. Based on these hypotheses, this article explores the extraordinary freedom of the sound inventions proposed by the German Jesuit monk Athanasius Kircher (1602–1680), author of the first acoustics treatise in the West, *Phonurgia Nova* (1673),[3] which was published in the second half of the 17th Century, a turning point for the advent of modern science.

By proposing a new phonurgy, this illustrated *in folio*[4] book reveals the design of a sounding city, through a series of perfectly situated acoustic experiments, for example the engraving presenting the phenomenon of natural echoes based on a site's topography, or that of artificial echoes triggered by configurations built based on precise dimensions and distances[5] (Figure 1).

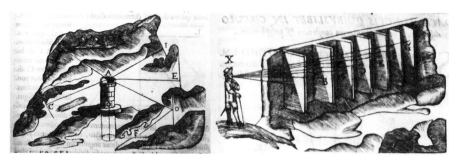

Figure 1: Natural echo – Wall of echo, Kircher, 1673, p. 41 & 47.

One could presume that the "phonurgic" postulate was a prelude to a certain aesthetic of acoustics, which is nowadays supplemented by two closely related concepts, the theory of ambiances and the aesthetics of atmospheres. The theory of ambiances, which is based on a phenomenological approach, was initiated fifty years ago in France by the Cresson team, founded by the philosopher Jean-François Augoyard.[6] According to him, sound ambiance is a phenomenon located at the crossroads of three polarities: the physical frame that shapes the acoustics of the space, the sound practices that interact with that frame, and the feelings elicited by that meeting.[7] In a recent paper retracing the ambivalence of the concept, the sociologist Jean-Paul Thibaud[8] showed that the theory of ambiances was enhanced by the aesthetics of atmospheres, a more pragmatic approach, whose main initiator, Gernot Böhme, managed to launch an inspiring international school of thought for many architects.[9] Regardless of the contexts in which atmospheres are deployed—natural milieus or artificial environments, public spaces or private spaces, theatrical scenographies or museum facilities—these contexts, according to Böhme, generate spatial qualities that offer living beings the immersive feeling that they belong and exist.[10]

To support the affiliation between the 17th-century treatise and the two 20th-century theories, I will first reaffirm the unprecedented character of Kircher's book regarding the advent of a new science: acoustics. I will briefly recall the impact of the historical context at the end of the Renaissance on the polymath's prolific work, and I will then explain how his metaphysics was the initiator of what we nowadays call pragmatics of sound ambiances, meaning an approach that is based primarily on active hearing of space through concrete sound experimentations. Throughout the article, I will be guided by the graphic expression of the treatise's engravings, which solidify my hypothesis of the "city-instrument."

An Unprecedented and Pioneering Acoustic Science: Phonurgy

Considered in his lifetime the "Phoenix of Scholars,"[11] Kircher was curious about everything. He wrote an impressive number of wonderfully illustrated books on a wide array of fields: astronomy, optics, geology, music, magnetism, hieroglyphs, alchemy, the Kabbalah and acoustics. Rather than the accuracy of the explanations of physical phenomena—his commenters indeed point out that he was not up to date with the contemporary scientific advances—it is the sum and diversity of knowledge which makes these writings a precursor to multidisciplinarity. The historical interest of this first treatise of acoustics does not lie in the accuracy of the scientific demonstrations, but rather in the invention of instruments or sounding machines that suggest an experimental spirit based on praxis rather than on a logical-deductive approach.[12]

Therefore, it is not by chance that the late publication of *Phonurgia* within the scholar's body of work gives a prime position to iconography. Written in scientific Latin,[13] the *in folio* provides suggestive drawings of a rare graphic quality.[14] Following an innovative practice at the time, the drawings were directly incorporated into the body of the text. More than mere illustrations, these architectural representations are precise enough in their geometry to show the acoustic impact of the "sound devices" on the overall perception of a territory. For example, the map of acoustic lines (Figure 2) shows the length of the acoustic distances between different horns and a network of villages several kilometers apart. Simple lines trace the directions of the sound waves.

Therefore, after the publication of *Musurgia Universalis*[15] in 1650—which is considered a textbook largely full of mathematical models applied to music[16]—we can affirm that the late publication of *Phonurgia Nova* (1673) complements the musical theories of the time by extending them to the outside sound world. The transition from music to phonurgy is doubly original. On the one hand, the treatise was based on a wide spectrum of applications, encompassing every notable auditory phenomenon, without making distinctions between natural sounds, voices or music. It thus prefigures the theories of Concrete Music (*Musique Concrète*). According to Jean-François Augoyard, "phonurgy is the sound universe. It is the world re-thought, built from the sounds. It is not a simple metaphor."[17] Linking his argument to the pioneering results in sound ethology, the philosopher tries to define the sound ambiance of a place, insisting on a necessary detachment that can free one from the categories and value-based judgments attached to the different types of sound sources. On the other hand, sounds act jointly on the real construction of the environment, the representations of sound space and the symbolism of places, as shown in the map of sound territories (Figure 2). This reasoning offers the first argument for my hypothesis of the city-instrument: the atmospheric space[18] of the engravings is suggestive of its acoustic performance, foreshadowing in a way the schematic elements of a contemporary theory of atmosphere.

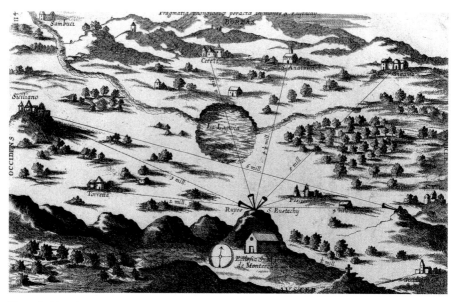

Figure 2: Map of acoustic lines between "talking horns", Kircher, 1673, p. 141.

At the Limits of the Analogy between Optics and Acoustics

Studying Kircher's engravings means looking for the unity of scientific fields, in this case the analogy between optics and acoustics. It is worth recalling that in the 17th Century, acoustics was not yet an established and independent science, but it could be defined as an applied one, in which empirical knowledge on the propagation of sound was used not only to explain musical harmony, but mainly to build instruments. This period also signals a break in the understanding of vision: the physiological parameters attributed to the eye are abandoned in favor of understanding how light works. The *camera obscura* became the absolute model for the eye. Taking for granted that sounds "mimic" light, Kircher applied the laws of optics[19] to acoustics by using the analogy of how beams of light are reflected off surfaces. He borrowed the principles of the Snell-Descartes law, which describes the behavior of light at the meeting point of two milieus, and applied it to sound beams. This transfer from the laws of optics to acoustics, still used nowadays in simplified models of so-called "geometric" acoustics, is valid in certain conditions.[20] While geometric acoustics is good at explaining the behavior and reflection of sound waves when they come into contact with surfaces, the arrows symbolizing how the sound propagates inside the acoustic horns can be

Figure 3: Up left: Incorrect diagram of sound propagation in the horns, Kircher, 1673, p. 67. Visionary drawings of megaphones, Kircher, 1673, p. 133.

wrong in terms of their details but not in terms of the general principle of a horn on the scale of the landscape (Figure 3).

Kircher was convinced that the voice was conducted better through curved horns than through straight ones. The graphic aesthetic of his cross-sectional drawings nonetheless did not account for the phenomenon of vibrations. In the absence of a theory on vibrating objects[21] (which emerged only at the end of the 17th Century),[22] Kircher's explanations of physical phenomena are thus not always scientifically valid and are mainly conveyed by simplistic images accompanied by a text that is more descriptive than demonstrative.

Metaphysics Grounded in Myths: Metaphysics of the Living

As we have already mentioned, the treatise appeared at a turning point when acoustic science was emerging. Between empiricism and wave theory, the field of acoustics grew out of the observation of natural phenomena, such as the echo (Figure 1) and the symbolic image an echo conveys. Kircher developed in particular esoteric theories (imaginary mechanics) of the echo effect, which he tried to explain by using inaccurate distance ratios. It is mainly due to the verbal and written dissemination of Ovid's myth of the nymph Echo that the phenomenon became common knowledge. As the acoustician Pierre Liénard explains, myths broadened the history of acoustics, leading to scientific experiments and finally to the fundamental discovery of the phenomenon of vibrations.[23]

In its conception of the living and its sensorial manifestation, Kircher's treatise outlines this metaphysical connection. This kind of thinking brings him close to theoreticians who belong to an aesthetics of perception. Unlike his "modern" contemporaries (Mersenne, Newton, Galileo), who contributed to an understanding of acoustics as a rational science, Kircher initiated in *Phonurgia Nova* a conception of the field as being tied to the world of the living. In that world, the sounds from nature (wind, echo, water, etc.) are part of a cultural vision of the sonic universe in which humans walk alongside the divine. The drawing on the treatise's frontispiece, with its angels blowing air, is an explicit introduction to the scholar's religious cosmogony, which recalls Aristotle or Genesis.[24] If Kircher's work did not align with scientific progress, it is because it was celebrating the wonders of creation, the results of a "natural magic"[25] stemming from universal magnetism. Moreover, Kircher's fascination with the East, emphasized in remarkable drawings of Chinese gardens, is not unconnected to his sensitivity to sounds and lights, or to his interest in water machines or Aeolian harps. In a drawing representing such a harp, Kircher suggests that the force of the wind will be able to vibrate a set of strings at the heart of the device (Figure 4).

By providing this biographic background, too often ignored, my intention is to demonstrate that Kircher's acoustic curiosities have been infused with metaphysics, a fact that opens up the possibility of studying his work in relation to the contemporary aesthetics of atmospheres.

Atmospheric Halo of the Engravings: Communicating Acoustics

Acoustics is one of the sciences that has left the fewest traces. Sound is stealthy, elusive. It disappears as soon as we stop producing it, and the reverberation of a room lasts only a few seconds. Above all, sound is also difficult to represent. According to Godwin,[26] *Phonurgia Nova* demonstrates a graphic inventiveness that is very close to

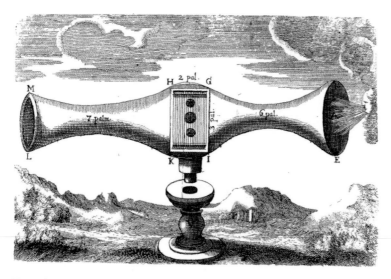

Figure 4: Aeolian harp, Kircher, 1673, p. 144.

the scientific thought of the Renaissance period, which was not yet detached from an artistic and naturalistic vision of the cosmos. In line with Leonardo da Vinci's drawings, where art meets calculation, Kircher's treatise demonstrates that imagination can be as determinative as logical deductions are for humans. His refined perspectives convey the presence of weather phenomena, the change of scales of instruments, and are distinctive of a "technological and anthropological symbolism."[27] The high quality of the drawings and their technique, close to *sfumato*,[28] communicate an atmosphere in which the cosmos and divine presence are connected. The drawings represent true artistic pieces with a strong symbolic value: to convey an auditory world while representing nature as precisely as possible. For example, in the engraving of an Aeolian harp (Figure 4), Kircher proposes an "acoustic curiosity" that uses wind power to highlight the rustling sounds of the natural environment. Its scale and its position within the landscape express the unrealistic character of this curiosity. Trévoux's dictionary (1771) offers three words to define a curiosity: *curiosus, cupidus, studiosus* – attention, desire, and passion for knowledge. Even in its late period, the Renaissance represents the golden age of curiosities. Indeed, many pages of Kircher's treatise present acoustic curiosities in scenes in which angels fly and the divine power blows through the windmills, as proclaimed in the frontispiece. Such an approach underpins the thesis of the imaginary power of legends told through these images: they thus work to represent the sensory world in which such auditory experiences and acoustic performances could be opportunities to make scientific progress.

Figure 5: Talking Statues, Kircher, 1673, p. 162.

In the engraving called "Talking Statues" (Figure 5), the precision of the architectural drawing does not prevent the imagination from considering the humans'
position in the world, as they listen to their environment. The outdoor space of the
square, as well as the interior space of the building, are represented as resonant bodies
inhabited by the human voices that pass through them. In the same image, Kircher
captures shifts of scales and meanings: the buildings include original devices built
into their walls (talking statues, auditory canals) that are similar to ancient horns and
trumpets. The classical modes of architectural representation (perspectives, axonom-
etry, sections), which describe precisely the geometry and nature of the materials, also
demonstrate innovative sound practices. They suggest vocal exchanges between the
inside and the outside, recalling the communicative power of such devices. Therefore,
the different elements present in this engraving are part of the definition of what we
nowadays call sound ambiance:[29] the physical framework of architecture, sound practices and the feelings conjured by the scene.

This image bolsters my second hypothesis by considering empiricism as a source
of innovative experiments to study sound in architecture. Architects are interested in
these acoustic curiosities because they connect to the construction of machines, in
which experience denounces the artificial separations between the subject and the

architectural object in line with the contemporary theories of atmosphere[30] or ambi-ance.[31] Kircher's thinking belongs to a time when there was no dichotomy between art and science, when music and acoustics were one. Artistic creations and scientific demonstrations lived side by side within modes of experience in which not the object but hearing is conjured, meaning the relationship between the "hearing subject" and the "sounding object." In this model, sound does not exist independently from the space that makes it ring or the listeners. Sound and sounding space blend together. Hearing predominates.

Furthermore, sound phenomena are considered within the totality of their spatial context of propagation and reception: wind, echoes against the walls or propagation inside pipes. Contextualized sound phenomena deal with both the aesthetics of com-position and a form of pragmatism, in which sensory experiences and the observation of phenomena guide their interpretations. At no point does Kircher's thought try to objectify sound or turn it into an "object," since it is close to an existential concep-tion of technical objects, as also defended by the philosopher Bruno Latour.[32] The "Talking Statues" (Figure 5) are like auditory windows on the environmental sounds. The "Aeolian Harps" (Figure 4) are the signals of weather events perceived by all of the senses. In these examples, empirical experiences lead to the invention of a novel form of music instrument making and a way of considering anew the permeability of architectural envelopes, in which classic windows appear to have the capacity of genuine hearing.

From Curiosity to Acoustic Utopia: Images Witnessing the Sounding City

Lastly, I would like to emphasize the formal aspect of the urban *instrumentarium* de-scribed by Kircher. *Phonurgia Nova* is the culmination of a lengthy work on musical lutherie.[33] Kircher changed scales and transferred, even without accuracy, the acous-tic principles of musical instruments to the built space: he imagined acoustic pipes and horns at the scale of architecture, city and landscape that were conceived ho-mothetically and accompanied by geometric diagrams. Moreover, he made sure that this system was reversible. Was he the first to invert the function of horns, trumpets and other wind instruments, emphasizing not the emission of sound but the recep-tion of sound by the ear? Before instrument-making, seashells and animal horns were undoubtedly the first objects used by humans to enhance their hearing. In Antiquity, sailors and fishermen in the Mediterranean used whelk shells as horns. While his-torians do not mention the importance precedence of such inventions, in medicine, the physician Renner[34] considers Kircher to be a pioneer in the description of ear trumpets. Inspired mainly by wind instruments, Kircher "reversed" their function.

It is hard to tell if Kircher had the opportunity to really test out these curiosities. He might have simply been inspired by sound devices that he had seen or heard in gardens during his travels. The visionary drawing of megaphones (Figure 4) depicts the delicate passage from acoustic science to the concept of sound culture. Kircher used his purely geometric demonstrations of the propagation of sound inside the horns to convert them to a megaphone's dimensions, ten times larger. Re-drawn on the scale of a large open site, these instruments, "catapulted" into the landscape, suggest the desire to overcome the natural powers of the ear in order to allow it communicate easily over a distance, like the hearing devices developed by military staff in the 20th Century during the two World Wars, in order to hear from afar and send signals between camps. These large acoustic horns demonstrate the broadening of knowledge from musical lutherie to the emergence of a soundscape culture. On the architectural scale, Kircher used pipes or giant acoustic horns to reveal the sound porosity of walls, between the building and the city, as well as between the city and its underground levels.[35] While such representations must be considered cautiously, they demonstrate how instrumental lutherie can resonate with urban morphology. As such, there is an instrumentation taking place in the proper sense of the word, between the sound effects of the drawn instruments and the built space of the city. For example, in another engraving, the shape of a new instrument imagined by Kircher refers to the profile of church bells, which can be considered the oldest instruments of our cities.

Whether we study Kircher's cross-section of the bowels of the earth, the ear trumpets in a building, or the megaphone drawings, all these images indicate a sensitive imagination that does not distinguish the utopic from genuine acoustic inventions. Among technical utopias, Kircher's *instrumentarium* is unique, particularly because of the diversity of acoustic scales involved. From the musical instrument to the landscape, via architecture, Kircher aimed to represent nature with as much accuracy as possible, like a miniature world where sounds have their place.

Conclusions

Very often reproduced but rarely situated in their metaphysical context, the *Phonurgia Nova* engravings have been cited for their extraordinary evocative power. Presented to contemporary eyes, they become visionary objects of the history of science, images that serve as witnesses in the history of acoustics while resonating strongly in our ears, which are overwhelmed by our noisy environments that never seem to quiet down. Beyond the fact that these acoustic curiosities expressed a creative vision of acoustics as a science, they remain, four centuries later, fertile imaginary resources for the architects and sound designers of our time. The reason is that these acoustic curiosities explicitly draw our attention to the importance of listening to space and qualifying the sound exchanges between indoor and outdoor environments. The other prominent element of the treatise is the crossing of different scales, varying from body-sized "sounding objects" to sound sculptures integrated into the landscape and architecture, by way of spatial devices incorporated into buildings. The convergence of environmental, architectural and acoustic data represents an alternative approach to the contemporary design of the city suggesting a synthesis of sound arts that requires collaboration between musicians, designers, acousticians, landscapers and architects. Indeed, to conceive the atmosphere of a place, the manufacture of sound space naturally requires the project management teams as well as the design teams to transcend scales. Finally, beyond Kircher's ability to combine the scales of sound, the universal phonurgical thought of this great scientist of the end of the Renaissance testifies to a tension between science and philosophy, between empirical analysis and myth, between sound as an object and listening, as something that was lost in the normative practices of the academia during the European Enlightenment. As a consequence, Kircher's treatise invites us to imagine and animate the necessary interrelation between different professions, useful in the invention of sound atmospheres.

Notes

1.   Cécile Regnault, "Les représentations visuelles des phenomènes sonores. Applications à l'urbanisme", PhD thesis, (Université de Nantes, 2001).

2.   Jean-François Augoyard, "Un instrumentarium urbain," in *Urbanités Sonores*, ed. Michel Grosjean and Isaac Joseph (Paris, 1989), 14. https://hal.archives-ouvertes.fr/hal-02104257 accessed march 6, 2022.

3.   Athanasius Kircher, *Phonurgia Nova* (Kempten: R. Dreher, 1673).

4.   In the 17th Century, *in-folio* were usually very big – 10 kilograms per book – reference books and were close to our modern A3 format.

5.   Measurements that will prove to be wrong.

6.   Jean-François Augoyard, "Éléments pour une théorie des ambiances architecturales et urbaines", in *Les Cahiers de la Recherche Architecturale*, 3, no. 42-43 (1998): 7–23.

7.   Jean-François Augoyard, "L'environnement sensible et les ambiances architecturales", in *L'espace géographique* 24, no. 4 (1995): 310.

8.   Jean-Paul Thibaud, "Petite archéologie de la notion d'ambiance", in *Communications: Les Bruits de la Ville,* 90 (2012): 155–174.

9.   Peter Zumthor and Philippe Rahm, two contemporary architects and defenders of the concept of atmosphere.

10. Gernot Böhme, "Atmosphere as a Fundamental Concept of a New Aesthetics", in *Thesis Eleven*, 36 (1993): 113.

11. Sylvain Matton, *Kircher Athanasius – (1602–1680), Encyclopædia Universalis*.

12. For example, the second edition of his treatise on light re-use principles of the magic lantern. The adjective "magic" corresponds to Kircher's metaphysics, depicting the spiritual and evil dimension of science.

13. In the Germanic part of Europe, where Roman law was in effect until the end of the Empire, Latin remained for a long time the language of important scientific publications in order to be disseminated across Europe.

14. The precision of the line is possible with the technique of copper engraving.

15. *Musurgia Universalis* (1650) is by far one of the most comprehensive syntheses of musical knowledge at the time.

16. As part of scientific knowledge on music, we can mention the theory of vibrating strings, known by the Chinese, or the struck plates already observed in ancient civilizations.

17. Jean-François, Augoyard, "Expérimenter et analyser un parcours de phénomènes sonores," in *Hors les murs*, no. 8 (janvier 2013): 5. https://www.artcena.fr/sites/default/files/medias/etu.aut-50.pdf accessed march 6, 2002.

18. Including both people, built spaces and nature, according to Böhme, "Atmosphere as a Fundamental Concept of a New Aesthetics", 114.

19. In *Ars magna lucis et umbrae* (1646), the summation of proto-scientific and artistic theories from the observation of light and colors (*chromocritica*), Kircher developed the evil (*magia*) part of geometry and optics that were practiced according to empirical processes from the 16th Century in Italy (Matton, *Encyclopedia Universalis*).

20. The geometric method remains valid, provided that the wavelength does not exceed the dimensions of the obstacle.

21. This theory consists in no longer modelling sound as a simple beam but as a variation in air pressure from an issuing body.

22. Theory published by Huygens in 1690.

23. Pierre Liénard, *Petite histoire de l'acoustique. Bruits, sons et musique* (Paris: Lavoisier, 2001).

24. Jocelyn Godwin, *Théâtre du monde* (Paris: Actes sud, 2009).

25. Ibid.

26. Jocelyn Godwin, *Athanasius Kircher: Un Homme de la Renaissance à la Quête du Savoir Perdu* (Paris : Homes and Hudson, 1980).

27. Ibid.

28. The word originates from "*fumare*" in Italian, which means "misty." It is a painting technique conceived by Leonardo da Vinci. It represents the effect obtained by superimposing several delicate layers of paint, which give the outlines of a subject an evanescent aspect.

29. Brice Begout, *Le Concept d'Ambiance* (Paris: Seuil, 2020).

30. "We are not sure whether we should attribute them to the objects or environments from which they proceed or to the subjects who experience them." Böhme, "Atmosphere as a Fundamental Concept of a New Aesthetics", 114.

31. Augoyard, "L'environnement sensible et les ambiances architecturales," in *L'Espace Géographique* 4 (1995): 302–317.

32. Latour. *Enquêtes sur les Modes d'Existence: Une Anthropologie des Modernes.* (Paris: La Découverte, 2012).

33. *Musurgia Universalis* (1650) is by far one of the most comprehensive syntheses of musical knowledge at the time.

34. C. Renner. "Sur l'histoire des cornets acoustique," in *Annales françaises d'Oto-rhino-laryngologie et de Pathologie Cervico-faciale*, 129, no. 1 (2012): 75–81.

35. Kircher's intuitions were applied for the first time in the 18th Century with the sound tubes of military buildings used to communicate from one blockhouse to another, as well as with the phonic pipes set up on ships. The sound tubes used in castles and large houses, described in the monk Dom Gauthey's memoirs, could reach dozens of meters to carry orders to the domestic servants. Initiated by physicians, the construction of sound horns and tubes appears to be later than the 18th Century. It stopped in the second half of the 20th Century with the closure, in London in 1962, of FC Rein & Son, the most emblematic manufacture of sound horns (cf. Renner, ibid.).

13.

Dissolving in the Air: *Mrs. Dalloway's* Sonorous Modern London

Angeliki Sioli

London as Protagonist

Virginia Woolf's iconic modernist novel *Mrs. Dalloway*, published in 1925, is often summarized as a day in the life of the homonym protagonist in post-World War I London. Approaching the book with an architectural and urban interest in mind, one quickly realizes that the city is actually more of a protagonist than Mrs. Dalloway, or any of the narrative's other figures. Through the characters' various activities, urban walks, preoccupations, memories, thoughts or dreams, London emerges with a sticking clarity and precision. Professor of English Carl Ray Woodring actually argues that Woolf's characters exist in two worlds: the subjective world she creates for them (and out of them), and the physical world that she holds too much in awe to alter for a merely fictional pattern.[1] Indeed the city of London is portrayed without fictional elaborations, vibrant and palpable during a June day in 1924. Richard Hughes, a British novelist who wrote one of the first critical reviews on the novel, supported that Woolf made readers, for the first time, experience the city of London as a crystal, rather than a fog.[2]

The city is moreover depicted not as a neutral background setting but as an active interlocutor. Susan Squier highlights that the European metropolis appears through the novel with its fascinating capacity to influence the characters' thoughts and guide their actions.[3] The characters are defined by the streets they pass through. Elements of the urban atmospheres affect their decisions. And although critical interest in Woolf's London has turned to questions of space, mobility of characters and narrators across the city, as Tamar Katz explains, scholarly interest on these walks often omits the study of extant urban atmospheres and the effects they have on the protagonists' walking through them.[4] In agreement with Katz, I wish to add, that even less emphasis has been placed on the role of sound in the creation of these urban atmospheres, and how these acoustic phenomena impact the protagonists.

Sound plays an important role in the creation of ephemeral, momentary, brief—and thus difficult to study—urban atmospheres throughout the novel. Margaret Church argues that Woolf introduces short-lived elements such as "moments of explosion, of *ricorso*; (...) the boom of sound, the striking of Big Ben," in an attempt to "make something permanent of the moment, to arrest the mysterious and continual flux seen in the ambience of the great city."[5] The novel is actually exemplary in recording ordinary, random, fleeting and thus usually unnoticed everyday sounds of London: the roaring of the traffic, the tinkling and darting of the motorcars, the bell of the ambulance, the chimes of the city clocks, the beating and stirring of galloping ponies, the tapping of cricket bats, or even the silence, the hum on entering Saint James Park. It is in this layered polyphony—consonant with the urban qualities, sociopolitical life and cultural aspects of London—that, in the very opening pages of the narrative, Mrs. Dalloway immerses herself:

> in the swing, tramp, and trudge; in the bellow and the uproar, the carriages, motor cars, omnibuses, vans, sandwich men shuffling and swinging; brass bands; barrel organs; in the triumph and the jingle and the strange high singing of some aeroplane overhead was what she loved; life; London; this moment of June.[6]

Acoustic Atmospheres of London

Amidst this vibrant sonic environment, I will focus on three acoustic atmospheres created and sensed in specific locations of the city. My understanding of atmospheres is informed by the philosophical thinking of Gernot Böhme. In his work, *Atmospheric Architectures: The Aesthetics of Felt Space* (2017), Böhme discusses atmospheres as "emanating from and produced by things, people or their constellations."[7] In this understanding, atmospheres are neither objective nor subjective, like demonstrations of a state of mind. They are object-like, as they belong to the things that create them—insofar as things articulate their spheres of presence through their qualities. And they are also subject-like, belonging to subjects insofar as they are sensed by humans in their bodily presence.[8] This sensing is simultaneously the subject's bodily-being located in space.[9]

With this theoretical underpinning in mind, I will examine the selected acoustic atmospheres as emerging from specific objects or people (and their qualities) in the city, and at the same time sensed by different Londoners on the streets. The atmospheres under examination are presented in the order encountered in the narrative. They are not equal in duration or impact, thus not equal in the length of the analysis I provide. I will demonstrate how these randomly created acoustic environments affect the characters' thoughts and attitude, and how these attitudes add further notes to the sonic atmospheres of each place. Woolf, in the novel, reflects the inner world of her characters as influenced by the city in almost every description of the urban environment and the events occurring in it.[10] She also portrays how this inner world reflects upon London, revealing alternative atmospheres and moods as the characters move along its streets.[11] This intrinsic characteristic—the rare capacity to capture this double interaction between place and users—renders the narratives extremely valuable for a spatial study on the topic.

The Chimes

The rhythmical ticking of London's numerous clocks—primarily Big Ben's—fill the novel's pages and the city's streets.[12] "Shredding and slicing, dividing and subdividing, the clocks (…) nibbled at the June day."[13] Clarissa Dalloway is the most appropriate character to examine the embodied interaction with this sonorous urban presence:

> For having lived in Westminster—how many years now? over twenty,—one feels even in the midst of the traffic, or walking at night, Clarissa was positive, a particular hush, or solemnity; an indescribable pause; a suspense (…) before Big Ben strikes. There! Out it boomed. First a warning, musical; then the hours, irrevocable. The leaden circles dissolved in the air.[14]

The excerpt provides a most enticing account of the ringing sound emanating from Big Ben's bells, spreading over the city's air and creating a unique acoustic atmosphere. The impressive tower's vibrant capacity provides for a strong literary image. The waves of the clock's musical and rhythmical chimes are described as leaden circles that dissolve in the air. The word "leaden" refers to the sound's material source: Big Ben's cast-iron. By the time the novel was written the clock featured four, seven-meter diameter, dials.[15] The word "circles" touches on the qualities of sound itself, as it travels through rippling waves. The literary image also captures the sound's path in the city: the sound ripples around the circular bells, concentrically expanding in all directions. The literary description concludes with the fact that the further away from their source the sound waves reach (with the inevitable passing of time), the more they open up and disappear, and along with them disappears the sound and acoustic atmosphere they create.

"The leaden circles dissolved in the air" initiate the first acoustic atmosphere. The physical movement and material qualities of the bells and the air belong to the qualities of the thing as Böhme argues. The sound atmosphere is thus object-like, but also subject-like as sensed by Mrs. Dalloway in her bodily presence, in the middle of the street. When the leaden circles surround her, she is about to enter Saint James Park, just a few minutes' walk from Big Ben. Woolf records a peculiar embodied effect that the repeated and rhythmical experience of the booming sound has on the protagonist and the inhabitants of the city. Subjected multiple times a day to the acoustic atmosphere of the leaden circles, and knowing that the chimes are about to be heard, a unique embodied sensation is created. It is a pause, a suspense, a solemnity in anticipation of the periodic and rhythmic strikes. Woolf suggests that this is a feeling sensed even when someone is surrounded by the midst of the traffic. The expectation for the booming sound makes Londoners feel an excitement, even a feeling of dignity. And then the chimes sound, spread through the noise or the quietness, and touch them as "sound is always a touch and its quality depends on space."[16]

Sound can dominate and transform the existing atmosphere of a place—in the case of the excerpt, Big Ben's chimes create a shared rhythmicality in London. As participants of a given atmosphere though—and given how the act of hearing works— we can tune out particular sounds and prioritize others. We can engage with sound through "selective listening," one of the four modes of listening as defined by Pierre Schaeffer's "Quatre Ecoutes" theory.[17] Clarissa feels even in the midst of traffic, which is admittedly a noisy urban condition, a solemnity and a hush: a pause of all other sounds, a quietness. It is an embodied possibility of the subject-like part of a sound atmosphere, reminding us of our capacity to focus on given sounds, favoring them over the general hubbub of a place.

The Explosion

The second acoustic atmosphere I discuss in this article creates a pause even stronger than the chimes of Big Ben; it seizes momentarily the activities of the street and engages the passersby in a commonly shared feeling. While reminiscent of the sound of a pistol shot, it is actually a motor car catching a flat tire that creates this second sonic environment:

> The violent explosion that made Mrs. Dalloway jump and Miss Pym go to the window and apologise came from a motor car which had drawn to the side of the pavement (…). Passers-by, who, of course, stopped and stared, had just time to see a face of the very greatest importance against the dove-grey upholstery, before a male hand drew the blind and there was nothing to be seen except a square of dove grey. Yet rumours were at once in circulation from the middle of Bond Street to Oxford Street on one side, to Atkinson's scent shop on the other, passing invisibly, inaudibly, like a cloud, swift, veil-like upon hills, falling indeed with something of a cloud's sudden sobriety and stillness upon faces which a second before had been

utterly disorderly. But now mystery had brushed them with her wing; they had heard the voice of authority; the spirit of religion was abroad with her eyes bandaged tight and her lips gaping wide. But nobody knew whose face had been seen. Was it the Prince of Wales's, the Queen's, the Prime Minister's? Whose face was it? Nobody knew.[18]

The rubber of a motor car's wheel, the air it contains, and a failure of its materiality against the asphalt of the street, create the explosive sound of a flat tire. In the streets of London, in 1920s, this was actually not an uncommon occurrence.[19] Passersby walking on the street and people in nearby shops, jump, look outside windows, and stop. The embodied perception of the sound is strikingly sharp, shared and common. To this initial urban acoustic atmosphere, another sound is added, emerging from the curiosity prevalent on the street. The sound emerges this time from the passersby themselves, who spread rumors, vocalizing their speculations on whom they thought they saw at the back window of the motor car. The explosion provokes their murmuring—whispering sound of words—that spreads from one street to the next, tuning all the attendants in a shared mood of sobriety, stillness and order.

What is particularly fascinating in this literary image is that the rumors move from passerby to passerby so discreetly, so subtly, that Woolf describes them as inaudible and illegible. She does not even need to describe the sound of the rumors in order to record the atmosphere they create. Like a fast-moving cloud that can easily dissolve into vapor or rain, a transparent and airy veil, the rumors fall on the faces of the crowd. It is the visible facial changes that loudly prove the sound's embodied affect. To further reveal this affect, Woolf even introduces a metaphorical reference to sound: "the voice of authority." Although no other sounds than the explosion and the rumors prevail on the air, people seem to feel that an official command has been announced, has been heard, and that they need to conform. The flat tire of a car transporting possibly a figure of authority and the speculative rumors that circulated along the sidewalks, create an acoustic atmosphere that attunes people to the feeling of a shared national identity, as defined by political and religious beliefs. A patriotic sense is transmitted in the street, a sense of belonging, a sense of meaning, that "is beyond the control of one person and draws in each new participant like a raindrop into a hurricane," an intrinsic characteristic of atmospheres according to Heidegger.[20] In Arendt's terminology, the acoustic atmosphere under examination creates also a "space of appearance." Political consciousness emerges indeed for a few seconds and fails to survive the actuality of the movement that brings it into being, disappearing with the dispersal of men and the arrest of the activities themselves.[21] The fact, moreover that this acoustic atmosphere and a shared political sentiment emerge because of a technological break, the flat tire, even reminds us the characteristics of a "focal event."[22] As philosopher Albert Borgmann has argued, we live our lives in the midst of the technological devices, but, every now and then, the holding sway of technology breaks down, and we feel our lives to be full of meaning.[23] Indeed, this sense of existential meaning is further observed on the people in the street, as:

> at once they stood even straighter, and removed their hands, and seemed ready to attend their Sovereign, if need be, to the cannon's mouth, as their ancestors had done before them. The white busts and the little tables in the background covered with copies of the *Tatler* and bottles of soda water seemed to approve; seemed to indicate the flowing corn and the manor houses of England; and to return the frail hum of the motor wheels as the walls of a whispering gallery return a single voice expanded and made sonorous by the might of a whole cathedral.[24]

The frail hum emanating from the car, enhances further the prevailing atmosphere in terms of sound and participants. Elements of London's immaterial world are also driven into the commonly shared atmosphere. Busts, tables, newspapers and glasses, not only appear to approve people's active engagement with the extant urban mood, they also seem to echo back the sound of the motor wheels and augment it. Indeed "as people act and develop in relation to things, the things themselves are also disclosed in their manifold depth," as philosopher David Strong argues.[25] The marble, copper, or metallic materiality of busts, the metallic or wooden materiality of the tables, the paper and glass nature of newspapers and soda containers, return the hum with the power of an acoustic gallery and a mighty cathedral.

Woolf provides for a strong acoustic metaphor. The way the frail hum of the motor wheels is received and returned back to the city, by the surrounding objects, is reminiscent of the whispering gallery of Saint Paul's Cathedral: the circular walkway in the church's dome where whispers uttered in one part of the gallery can be heard clearly in other parts. Woolf adds to this acoustic effect the capacity of the cathedral's might to expand a single voice and make it sonorous, loud, imposing and impressive. The physical elements of the city—the commercial shops that define the limits of its streets, and the gentlemen's clubs—are in a dialogue with the passing car; they reproduce in the city a space similar to a cathedral. The smaller objects capture the hum, the car's whisper, and supported by the mighty presence of the whole city, echo back in a way that seems to approve of people's feelings, and intensify them. At the beginning of the 20th Century, in an age of growing secularism following the horror of World War I, the modern city, through its acoustic presence, undertakes the role of a cathedral itself. It becomes the place of transcendental experiences, the place offering guidance and consolation from mundane everyday reality, through the way sounds are transmitted, intensified, felt and heard by the citizens. With striking power, like that of an explosive sound, Woolf records how the acoustic atmospheres of London, deeply affect the consciousness and actions of the citizens, on both an unconscious and conscious level.

The Band Music

Another character in the narrative that gets carried away by the city, and decides to walk for the first time in unfamiliar streets, is Elizabeth Dalloway, Clarissa's young daughter. Her spontaneous afternoon walk offers the reader a unique glimpse of the Charing Cross area, south of Trafalgar Square. The young woman decides to leave behind the areas of West End, Westminster and the strict confines of Victorian houses, and wander in parts of the city her family does not usually frequent. She thus proceeds with confidence to navigate the Strand and Cornhill,[26] a newly booming center of commercial and professional life in the 1920s.[27]

The last sound related atmosphere I examine in this article, combines feelings of joy and sorrow in a most interconnected way. Walking on Strand Street:

> she penetrated a little further into the direction of St. Paul's. She liked the geniality, sisterhood, motherhood, brotherhood of this uproar. It seemed to her good. The noise was tremendous; and suddenly there were trumpets (the unemployed) blaring, rattling about in the uproar; military music; as if people were marching; yet had they been dying—had some woman breathed her last and whoever was watching, opening the window of the room where she had just brought off that act of supreme dignity, looked down on Fleet Street, that uproar, that military music would have come triumphing up to him, consolatory, indifferent.[28]

The acoustic atmosphere that captures Elizabeth is initially that of an uproar, a loud and impassioned noise. It comes from the busy, crowded streets of this specific part of the city. This tremendous urban noise is boosted with the sounds and vibrations of the loud military music, which Elizabeth hears as she continues to walk towards Saint Paul's Cathedral. Unemployed musicians fill the air with the sound of trumpets, which due to the instruments' brass materiality spread vibrations of metallic tone. The rhythm is that of a military beat, although the literary image of trumpets blaring, as Woolf writes, denotes harsh, insistent and usually discordant sounds. Despite the lack in harmony, the loud musical atmosphere prevails upon the urban uproar, giving the impression that a marching crowd is about to appear. The military music appears triumphant in the city, encompassing all bystanders, communicating joy but also consolatory feelings even to someone who might have just faced death, might have just stood next to someone who breathed their last breath. The acoustic urban atmosphere can draw them in, and despite their sorrow or fear, console and encompass them.

Conclusion

I wish to argue that the novel is of particular importance to architects and urban planners. The evocative descriptions that Woolf's novel provides, prove a valuable resource to grasp, understand, and study acoustic atmospheres, both in regard to how they can be created through the materiality of the urban objects, but mostly in relation to how they are embodied. The literary descriptions can even evoke a reader's emotional understanding of these atmospheres, drawing them in. This is an approach to place that differs loudly from the dry look that maps, diagrams, or statistics on urban noise and soundscapes provide. Woolf's literary work can record the double nature of acoustic atmospheres, their object-like and subject-like nature, as defined by Böhme, revealing them in all their complexity.

These urban atmospheres are ephemeral and triggered by momentary events and sounds, offering an equally ephemeral image of the physical urban environment, and Woolf thought them to be in accordance with London's modern architectural conditions. In the essay "Oxford Street Tide," she comments on the modern materials prevalent in the city, like glass and plaster, and observes that the ephemeral nature of these new materials resembles the ephemeral character of people's desires in the city:

> The charm of modern London is that it is not built to last; it is built to pass. Its glassiness, its transparency, its surging waves of coloured plaster give a different pleasure and achieve a different end from that which was desired and attempted by the old builders and their patrons, the nobility of England. Their pride required the illusion of permanence. Ours, on the contrary, seems to delight in proving that we can make stone and brick as transitory as our own desires. We do not build for our descendants, who may live up in the clouds or down the earth, but for ourselves and our own needs. We knock down and rebuild as we expect to be knocked down and rebuilt.[29]

Almost a century after Woolf wrote *Mrs. Dalloway*, architects and urban planners knock down and rebuild more than ever. Moreover, when people engage with a city, they even carry their own sound elements—their music through their headphones or their conversations on their portable devices. How could designers look at the urban environment and study a city's specific sound atmospheres, as they relate to cultural, political, and social elements, in order to add their notes in the given polyphony? How could their architecture become acoustically either an interlocutor or a loud opposer to the voice of the city, through its materiality and the way it can echo back like a whispering gallery? Could architects look into words and authors' literary images in order to search for sound characteristics unique to specific places so that they can knock down and rebuild accordingly? A literary turn in architecture, could actually foreground the existential and deeply human side of place, and address questions of affect and emotional belonging, which are much needed in current global conditions. A careful study of literary descriptions that capture interactions between place and users can reveal paramount acoustic elements specific to given urban spaces and tune architectural production to the loud, noisy, never quiet cities of our times.

Notes

1. Carl Woodring, *Virginia Woolf, Columbia Essays on Modern Writers* (New York; London: Columbia University Press, 1966), 42.
2. David Dowling, *Mrs. Dalloway, Mapping Streams of Consciousness* (Boston: Twayne Publishers, 1991),17.
3. Susan M. Squier, *Virginia Woolf and London, The Sexual Politics of the City* (Chapel Hill: University of North Carolina, 1985), 95.
4. Tamar Katz, "Pausing, Waiting, Repeating: Urban Temporality in *Mrs. Dalloway* and *The Years*," in *Woolf and the City, Selected Papers from the Nineteenth Annual Conference on Virginia Woolf*, ed. Elizabeth F. Evans, Sarah E. Cornish (Clemson: Clemson University Digital Press, 2010), 58.
5. Margaret Church, "Joycean Structure in *Jacob's Room* and *Mrs. Dalloway*," International Fiction Review 4 (1977): 108, as quoted in Dowling, *Mrs. Dalloway, Mapping Streams of Consciousness*, 11.
6. Virginia Woolf, *Mrs. Dalloway*, edited by David Bradshaw (New York: Oxford University Press, 2000), 4.
7. This is a position that opposes older beliefs regarding the creation of atmospheres, like Hermann Schmitz's thesis that atmospheres are free floating. Gernot Böhme, *Atmospheric Architectures: The Aesthetics of Felt Spaces*, edited and translated by A.-Chr. Engels-Schwarzpaul (New York: Bloomsbury Academic, 2017), 23.
8. Ibid.
9. Ibid.
10. Jean Moorcroft Wilson, *Virginia Woolf, Life and London; A Biography of Place* (London: Cecil Woolf, 1987), 12.
11. Ibid.
12. David Dowling argues that Woolf got the idea of a city novel organized around the principles of chiming hours from Joyce's *Ulysses*, which she was reading in 1922. (Dowling, *Mrs. Dalloway, Mapping the Stream of Consciousness*, 11.)
13. Woolf, *Mrs. Dalloway*, 87.
14. Ibid., 4.

15.   David Bradshaw, "Introduction," in *Mrs. Dalloway*, xl.

16.   As quoted in Angela Leighton, *Hearing Things: The Work of Sound in Literature* (Cambridge, Mass.: Belknap Press, 2018) 7.

17.   For more see: Pierre Schaffer, *Treatise on Musical Objects: An Essay across Disciplines*, trans. Christine North and John Dack (Oackland: University of California Presss, 2017).

18.   Woolf, *Mrs. Dalloway*, 14.

19.   Ibid.

20.   Martin Heidegger, *The Fundamental Concepts of Metaphysics: Word, Finitude, Solitude*, as quoted in Hubert L. Dreyfus, "Why the Mood *in* the Room and the Mood *of* the Room Should be Important to Architects," in *From The Things Themselves: Architecture and Phenomenology*, ed. Jacquet Benoit and Vincent Giraud (Kyoto: Kyoto University Press, 2013), 27.

21.   Hanna Arendt, *The Human Condition* (Chicago: Chicago University Press, 1958), 199.

22.   Albert Borgmann, *Technology and the Character of Contemporary Life. A Philosophical Inquiry* (Chicago and London: The University of Chicago Press, 1987), 3.

23.   Albert Borgmann, ibid., as quoted in Pekka Passinmäki, "Technology, Focality and Place: On the Means and Goals of Architecture," in *Understanding and Designing Place: Considerations on Architecture and Philosophy*, ed. Pekka Passinmäki and Klaske Havik (Tampere: Tamper University, 2019), 72.

24.   Woolf, *Mrs. Dalloway*, 18.

25.   David Strong, "Philosophy in the Service of Things", in *Technology and the Good Life?*, ed. Eric Higgs, Andrew Light and David Strong (Chicago; London: The University of Chicago Press, 2000), 332.

26.   Deborah Epstein Nord, *Walking the Victorian Streets: Women, Representation, and the City* (Ithaca: Cornell University Press, 1995), 247.

27.   Susan M. Squier, *Virginia Woolf and London*, 102.

28.   Woolf, *Mrs. Dalloway*, 138.

29.   Virginia Woolf, "Oxford Street Tides," in *Virginia Woolf Selected Essays*, ed. David Bradshaw (Oxford: Oxford University Press, 2008), 201.

14.

Lacrimae Rerum and Tears of Memory: Sonic Encounters in the Public Realm

Karen Van Lengen

In the art world, the phrase "sound art" has been coined to describe work that uses sound as a major component of a piece. This term, however, is somewhat problematic as a meaningful category, for it tends to bracket artists and designers who may use sound within their work but are exploring very different themes and ideas. Sound, just like visual perception, can act and generate different channels of spatial engagement and provoke a variety of reactions depending on the context and the concept of the piece.

In the 1970s, when the art world was expanding beyond the boundaries of traditional galleries and art museums, public installation art began to emerge and became an area of increasing experimentation for artists and musicians. This kind of artistic endeavor opened up the possibility for provocative site-specific pieces that were intended to intersect with the general public rather than an elite museum-going population. Many of these public installations incorporated sound as a primary element to develop the themes of the work. They were also site-specific, transforming the experience of a particular place in the public realm. Salome Voegelin, an artist and scholar of the sonic arts, has written:

> Sound as a concept invites us into the materiality of things, not to deny the visual but to augment how we might see; and it transgresses the boundaries between the object, the thing looked at, and the space and context of its appreciation, introducing a sense of simultaneity instead of pre-existence, and promoting the reading and experiencing of things as agitational, interventionist, multisensory and capacious.[1]

A sound-generated installation demands that visitors stop and change their sensorial attention to the ear. This engagement with sound is temporal and fleeting and it requires a different kind of concentration. The attention given to something unexpected may be disruptive, but when one gives into it, it can offer an imaginative flowering of new associations. This individual engagement with the piece/site can also spark a collective reaction as people share their newly discovered experiences with others. This activation of the public realm is a highly valued attribute of these installations, especially in a cultural period in which so much of our public life has turned inward to private networks, headphones and digital landscapes. If we consider sound to be the agent in this relationship to a site, we can also say that this agent is helping to expose something, to call attention to a particular idea, or to alter our experience of that place. In that sonic alteration there is a change in the atmosphere of the urban condition that creates an associative memory specific to that location. In many cases that new memory remains as an active participant in that public space, long after the sound has gone.

Sound has the emotive potential to invite us to feel a place, a memory or an event in a new way. It is an inward experience that is grounded within our bodies and helps us to renegotiate our own personal engagement with a particular place and/or event located in that space. This experience opens up the potential for a richer and more nuanced understanding of our public realm and its multiple histories. Kate Lacey, a scholar of media history and theory, refers to this listening as "imaginative visiting," a level of engagement "that involves the imagination in travelling across boundaries physical, personal, social and temporal…"[2] This "imaginative" listening can develop into layers of historical memories, that are both individual and collective. These are the qualities that give public spaces their character.

This essay examines three different sound installation projects that effectively communicate emotive aspects of historical events and sites through the use of sound, supported by inventive installation strategies. These projects were created to explore significant world events with the potential to deeply influence our remembrance and personal engagement with them. This emergent listening can provoke a personal engagement that has the power to temporarily displace our everyday living patterns, allowing us to travel inside of that collective memory. It helps us to deeply consider important events and allows us to associate those memories with these sites. The three projects presented here are "Sound Island" by Bill Fontana, "Negative Memorial Aschrottbrunnen" by Horst Holheisel, and "Vatnajokull (the sound of)" by Katie Paterson. They use a diversity of means and methods to achieve an emotive connection for each event, but each project incorporates the sound of water as a primary component of their installation. These projects vary in size and dimension. "Sound Island" was a large non-permanent installation that included three different sound presentations all made in real time and located at one of Paris's iconic monuments.

The Aschrottbrunnne Memorial is a permanent installation located in the Courtyard of Honor in Kassel, Germany while the Vatnajokull (sound of), a limited time installation, was located in a remote landscape in Iceland but became sonically accessible through iphones worldwide. As it pertains to each example, I will discuss how the sound of water signifies very different associations within the context of each piece. When we think of the many fountains and water features found in our public parks and urban environments, we often associate the sound of water with peaceful, calming spaces or with playful gathering spots. Yet water can be a terrifying, violent and ominous force and in the following examples the sound of water is the substance of such acoustic experiences; it is the agent of the transformation of memory.

Turbulent Waters

"Sound Island", created by Bill Fontana in 1994, commemorated the 50th anniversary of D-Day, when the Allied Forces invaded the Normandy beaches in northern France during World War II. This commemorative installation was located at the *Arc de Triomphe* in Paris, one of the city's most important monumental spaces. "Sound Island" was a powerful transformational piece made to honor this pivotal battle, one that changed the course of the War and consequently the future of western European history. On June 14, 1944, the British, American, Canadian, and Norwegian armed forces staged a surprise landing on five beaches located along the Nazi-occupied Normandy coast of France. More than 155,000 troops arrived by ship and air with the ambition to gain control of northern France. Many of the troops landed in the water, facing heavy gunfire as they moved to take over the beaches. Over 10,000 Allied troops were killed in these battles, while the German forces lost between 4,000 and 9,000 soldiers.[3] The successful advance would eventually force the German army out of France and mark the beginning of Germany's retreat and their surrender the following year. Every year, thousands of tourists visit the Normandy beaches to imagine the day of that invasion, accompanied by stories and memorabilia associated with this famous maneuver.

On the 50th Anniversary of D-Day, June 14, 1994, Bill Fontana opened the "Sound Island" installation at the *Arc de Triomphe*. The *Arc* itself is layered with history from many different battles and wars. It was built by Napoleon to commemorate the 1805 Battle of Austerlitz, and in 1921, the Tomb of the Unknown Soldier was added to the space underneath the *Arc* to honor French soldiers who had died in World War I. It was also from this monument that the Nazis flew their flag in June of 1940 to signify that Paris was under Nazi control. Finally, it was to the *Arc* that Parisians stormed to celebrate the end of World War II on May 8, 1945 (Figure 1). Yet Parisians know the *Arc* as much for its status as a historical landmark as for its urban significance as

Figure 1: Liberation of Paris on August 25, 1944 (LOC). Open Source. (Plate 11, p. 297)

a primary focal point in the public works program of Georges-Eugène Haussmann, who redesigned the urban infrastructure of 19th-century Paris. Today the *Arc* is one of the busiest traffic intersections in the city, as its circular form is the genesis of twelve streets that radiate outwards to the various neighborhoods of the city.

Fontana's project at the *Arc* was comprised of three different installations: one at street level, one in the tunnel under the street, and one at the top of the monument. Each one provoked a different emotive connection to the events of D-Day. On the street level of the monument, Fontana had set up a system that transmitted the sounds from the shores of the Normandy beaches and sent them directly to speakers that washed the walls of the monument with these oceanic sounds. From this level, visitors standing under and along the façade of the monument could hear the waves crashing along the Normandy shores located 175 miles away. This real-time transfer of sounds displaced the normal traffic noises at this busy intersection and transported the listeners to another landscape. The sound of beach waves, a sound we often associate with pleasure, was in this case representative of the sonic background for cacophonous gunfire and other sounds of battle. Those waves were the water of terror that day. While the visitor heard only the sound of waves, as they might have sounded minutes before the invasion began, in this act of listening, they could share in the anticipation of what was about to occur on June 14, 1944. Through this kind of imaginative listening the audience could engage in a shared atmospheric memory of the past, one that connected this particular urban site to the Normandy shore and to the angst of so many soldiers that battled their way to the shore.

The second part of the installation, located in the tunnel under the street, played underwater sounds coming from microphones installed on a bouy in the English Channel. Fontana installed these hydrophones in the Channel waters and sent these recordings, again in real-time, to the speakers located within the tunnel space. The sonic quality of the tunnel, as an enclosed arched space, already has a specific acoustical signature, one that has a long reverberation time due to its contained and arched interior shape. The addition of these underwater sounds to that tunnel created an all-encompassing sonic effect. These sounds were reminiscent of what Allied soldiers would have heard that day as they fell into this water of terror, where so many men would drown. Walking through this enclosed tunnel had the overwhelming aspect of fright as it transported the listener directly into those waters.

The third part of the installation was located at the top of the *Arc*, where one can clearly feel the centrality of this monument as the source of those twelve streets radiating out to various Parisian neighborhoods. From a height of 164 feet, or 16 stories, one has an unobstructed view to these very neighborhoods, which can be normally seen but not heard. On this day, Fontana located microphones in these neighborhoods to be played back to the rooftop speakers. Suddenly the visual connections to these places came alive with the real-time sounds, creating a unique connection to these distant views. This kind of urban eavesdropping gave the visitor an intimate connection to the real life of these neighborhoods: to the traffic, the voices, the conversations, the animal sounds, and to other everyday sonic features of urban life. As Fontana has proclaimed, " I explored the idea of hearing as far as one can see."[4] This aural connection gave an assurance of the liveliness of these communities that had survived and flourished since the end of the War. These recordings, 50 years later, sonically confirmed the continuing life force that grew out of the end of the occupation of Paris.

Taken together, all three aspects of this commemorative piece delivered the opportunity for emotive remembrance and sharing, by the precise displacement of site-specific sounds overlaid onto one of Paris's most historic monuments. The real-time aspect is particularly important here because it created a stronger connection to being at the sites of D-Day, affording an immediacy of that experience. It demanded the visitor's presence and encouraged an imaginative transfer to the place and the event. It was not only a great tribute to those who lost their lives that day, but a different kind of personal connection to European history. The emotive aspects of this installation project did not replace the written commemorative pieces of D-Day, but they augmented one's perception of the events. The sense of "being there," if only for a few moments, altered the personal memory of this historic day and provided opportunities for public engagement in the celebration of its 50-year anniversary.

Reflective Waters

Negative Memorial Aschrottbrunnen (Kassel 1986/87) is a permanent Holocaust memorial located in Kassel, Germany, and designed by Horst Hoheisel. It is unique among Holocaust memorials as it presents itself as the "anti-memorial," so named by its creator. Most of the Holocaust memorials of the past 70 years have included the names of victims, as well as artifacts and stories intended to bring these events into our consciousness. The Kassel monument is purposely different. Its emptiness first begs us to remember a time in German history when Kassel was an open and vibrant city in which many cultural groups thrived. Located in the Courtyard of Honor at the City Hall of Kassel, the space had once included a fountain built in 1908 at the behest of a Jewish entrepreneur, Sigmund Aschrott, to celebrate the City and its life within. Children often played in the water, located at the base of the fountain, and their joyful voices gave a sonic liveliness to the Courtyard space. The original sandstone obelisk and surrounding fountain, designed by Karl Roth, were destroyed by the Nazis in 1939 because its original patron had been Jewish. In the 1940s, the Nazis then planted the empty stone base with flowers, camouflaging the ruin of the first monument. In 1963, the *Aschrottbrunnen* was rebuilt and the fountain was restored to its former state with a replica of Karl Roth's 1908 design. As many noted, however, this restoration back to the pre-war original did not tell the full story of the fountain. The artist Horst Hoheisel, who would go on to design the new monument, advocated to replace the restored fountain with a different kind of memorial that he termed a "negative memorial." Hoheisel has been an important voice in redefining the concept of memorial architecture in Germany, advocating for a more personal engagement with artifacts of memory so that people are obliged to consider past events in the course of their everyday lives. As he recollected:

> During my childhood in Kassel, there were no signs to remind us either of the obelisk designed by Karl Roth or of its founder, Sigmund Aschrott. In Kassel, no one wished to be reminded of the victims of National Socialism, of their own guilt, turning to look in the other direction while crimes were being committed. The fountain had become a symbol of memories repressed, the desire to forget.[5]

Figure 2: Fuente Invertida de Aschcott, Kassel, Germany. Photographer: Simenon. Open source. (Plate 12, p. 297)

The memorial that Hoheisel designed is constructed as a sunken fountain, one that has been turned upside down and lodged into the ground. The upside-down obelisk, a replica of the original, has a thin tall profile with a pointed top, which when plunged into the ground brings forth the idea of a deep wound in this urban landscape, a wound of past events and lost lives. What is now visible (Figure 2) is only the outline of the original base configuration of the first fountain. Around that base configuration is a thin open border that reveals glimpses of the underground space where the fountain now hangs in its inverted position. A visitor walking into the square does not see the monument but can only see the beginning of small canals of water designed and constructed at the edge of the space, that send the moving water to the site of the monument in the middle of the square. At the edges of this public space one can hear that water begins its travel to the location of the fountain. Standing directly over the footprint of the former base, visitors can clearly hear the sound of the churning waters below. It is this turbulent sound of water that causes the visitors to stop and listen, to inquire, to find out what lies below this surface. This reaction is made possible by the emptiness of the space and the fullness of the sound of the water below, heard but not seen. This is not a quiet water, but water in motion, churning and seemingly washing the monument below as it rushes around its perimter. To understand it one must excavate the meaning of the water under this site. The visual emptiness of the statue base demands that one finds out what is below the surface and only then does

the full story of the fountain and its destruction become apparent. Only then is one
challenged to listen to the past. At the 1987 opening of the new memorial, Hoheisel
commented:

> A simple counter-question is my way of meeting the never-ending stream of at-
> tempts to interpret the Shoah.[6] The form that Germans destroyed between 1933
> and 1945 can no longer be grasped, either mentally or physically. The destruction
> of the sandstone form, an 'architectural folly' as the architect of City Hall then
> termed it, was followed by the destruction of the human form. The only way I
> know to make this loss visible is through a perceptibly empty space, representing
> the space once occupied. Instead of continuously searching for yet another expla-
> nation or interpretation of that which has been lost, I prefer facing the loss as a
> vanished form. A reflective listening into the void, into the negative of an irretriev-
> able form, where the memory of that which has been lost resounds, is preferable
> to a mere numb endurance of the facts.[7]

James Young, the founding Director of the Institute for Holocaust, Genocide and
Memory Studies has written about this project and gives a poignant account of visiting the memorial:

> As we enter the square, we watch as water fills narrow canals at our feet before
> rushing into a great underground hollow, which grows louder and louder until
> we finally stand over the "Aschrott Brunnen." Only the sound of gushing water
> suggests the depth of an otherwise invisible memorial, an inverted palimpsest that
> demands the visitor's reflection. Through an iron grate and thick glass windows,
> we peer into the depths.[8]

Reflective listening is the central and key aspect of this project. Without the sounds
of water, a visitor would not know that the obelisk lies below the surface. A fountain
turned upside down is not something that can be seen, but in this memorial the sound
of water draws us closer to what lies below. Like the Fontana piece at the *Arc de Tri-
omph*, the sound of water is not soothing, a quality that we often associate with it, but
rather it is churning around an artifact of history, trying to wash something away that
can never be washed away, thus forcing one to confront the memory and losses associated with this historical period. "With the running water," Hoheisel suggests, "our
thoughts can be drawn into the depths of history, and there perhaps we will encounter
feelings of loss, of a disturbed place, of lost form." The emptiness of this monument in
this important urban space is powerful and made more so by the sonic quality that is
the agent of its memory. Both the "Sound Island" and the Aschrott Fountain projects
effectively use sound to create that emotive connection to the past.

Destructive Waters

The last project, "Vatnajökull (the sound of)," was designed in 2007-8 by Katie Patterson, a Scottish artist whose work addresses geological changes over time and is effective in creating poetic dialogues between nature and culture, between the intimate process of change and the global ramifications of climate change. In 2007 she visited the Jokulsarlon Lagoon, near the town of Vatnajökull in Iceland, to record the sounds of the melting glacier. She then set up a telephone line from which callers could listen to the melting sounds of the glacier in real-time. One could dial the number 0 7 7 5 7 0 0 1 1 2 2 from anywhere in the world to connect to the recording device. The connection was made possible by the use of a satellite network, and once connected, the caller heard the sound of water dripping, slowly and consistently. After a few minutes of listening to the sound of the glacier melting, there was a feeling of relentlessness and helplessness as callers heard the inevitable melting but could not turn the dripping off. Even when the cell phone connection was no longer there, one imagined that this melting sound would not stop until all the ice was gone. While many people have recorded the sounds of glaciers melting and one can find these recordings on the internet, they do not have the real-time immediacy that this piece had, which is what made it so significant. The dripping signified physical loss and the listener experienced that loss directly. Every drop marked a new dimension of the diminishing iceberg, a process that cannot reverse itself under current climatic conditions associated with our international global habits. The piece was a dramatic and a powerful reminder of what we are losing. Here again, the water was not a calm agent but instead a relentless force. However, the force was heard and imagined not as an overpowering waterfall, for example, but as one single drop, after another drop, after another drop and so on. It was the sound of one drip at a time that we know will continue unabated. The piece demanded that we confront the meaning of this situation, not by listening to scientific projections and reviewing data collections, but by the emotional atmosphere that these continuous drips describe. These water drops are the lost tears, the crying of a far away landscape (Figure 3).

Unlike the previous examples in Paris and Kassel, this piece was not located in a specific urban setting. A person could access this sound from any place in the world using their cell phones and internet connections. This meant that the site associated with the listening to this piece had the potential for a new memory located within the Jokulsarlon Lagoon. Imagine, for example, that a person dialed this number while having a waterfront drink in Venice. It would be hard to forget this association after it had been made, because this recorded sound of water is in the act of changing the relation of this waterfront to the lagoon around Venice. The damaging effects of sea level rise shall be felt first by Venice and the many other coastal cities and landscapes around the world. This emotive catalyst that delivered this information would have

Figure 3: Jokulsarlon glacier lagoon, Iceland. Photographer: Giuseppi Milo. Open source.

been hard to forget. In this installation one could understand memory in its most im-mediate condition. Every drip was a memory. Every drip was in the process of creat-ing global environmental history. So this piece had the dual agency of listening to the memory of an iceberg that is in the process of melting and also forcasting an ominous future world that will be created by this melting condition.

Conclusion

In thinking about these three examples one might ask if the use of sound is a more effective generator of remembrance than a visual presentation of the same historical events. Would a person who read about D-Day or saw historic photographs about the invasion be equally moved by its visual documentation? Facts and photographs are always important, as they place these events in their proper context. But sounds, without the visuals, require more of our imagination, of what it might have been like that day on the Normandy beaches. Was it cold or foggy, did the journey through the water seem heavy with the weight of all the equipment and weapons, did soldiers look straight ahead or look to their comrades for reassurance? In Kassel, we can imagine the sounds of children who once played in the fountain while their parents went about their business in or near Kassel's Town Hall. Did they know what would happen here and what their future would hold once this fountain was destroyed? And the drip of the glacier melting brought forth the anguish of regional and consequent wildlife lost, of the immediacy of sea level rising and of the terrifying possibilities of world changes that accompany this warning. It is this pure sound, without images, which creates the background for one's imagination and for a deeply personal connection to this ongo-ing event. Sound can augment what we know by creating that emotional overlay. As one considers all three installations, it is possible to understand how powerful sound can be in the activation of memory and how it can shift our intimacy with history. The development of new technologies to record and transfer sound has indeed pro-moted many of these effective projects and affords artists the opportunities to create many new sound-driven installations. They are the songs of a different kind of infor-mation that we experience from the inside, and they allow us to form new knowledge about places and new personal memories of what we thought we already knew.

Notes

1. Salome Voegelin, *The Political Possibility of Sound,* (London: Bloomsbury Academic Press, 2019), 47.

2. Kate Lacey, *Listening Publics,* (Cambridge, UK: Polity Press, 2013), 91.

3. "National World War II Museum", Accessed on February 19, 2020, https://www. nationalww2museum.org/sites/default/files/2019-03/D-Day-75-Fact-Sheet_0.pdf

4. Bill Fontana, " Sound Island", *Resoundings,* accessed on August 27, 2020, https://echo-sounddesign.com/media/Paris.mov,

5. James E. Young, "Memory and Counter-Memory", in *Harvard Design Magazine, Constructions of Memory: on Monuments Old and New*, no. 9 (1999).

6. Shoah is the Hebrew word for "catastrophe" specifically related to the 6 million Jews that died under the Nazi regime in Europe.

7. Horst Hoheisel, "Aschrottfountain(Kassel 1985)", *Hoheisel & Knutz,* accessed on March 7, 2020, http://www.knitz.net/index.php?option=com_content&task=view&id=3 0&Itemid=32&lang=en

8. Young, "Memory and Counter Memory".

15.

The Border between Sound and Silence: Sonic Preservation at the Berlin Wall

Pamela Jordan

On February 8, 2018, the Berlin Wall passed the milestone of being dismantled as long as it once stood—10,316 days. An entire generation of Berliners has grown up solely in the political and architectural aftermath of reunification, engaging with the city long after the concrete barrier slabs were drawn away. Yet the Wall is still a presence in the cultural and physical experience of the city, down to the sonic infrastructure its presence created. This is nowhere more patently true than at the Berlin Wall Memorial. Today, the sonic relationships inscribed by the Wall's military landscape are still accessible in the 200 ft long section of the wall at *Bernauer Straße* (Bernauer Street) in downtown Berlin, scene to the greatest number of fatal casualties of any section of the Wall[1] as well as street protests, soldier defections, and media attention. Its transition into a national monument created a national locus of remembrance of divided Berlin and the victims of GDR repression during the Wall's 26-year stance.

Manufacturing an acoustic environment was a vital part of the engine of control and intimidation designed by the GDR's military forces. Sound and silence were weaponized and used progressively to demarcate a territory of surveillance and hostile power. For example, Dolff-Bonekämper explains that "[a] lurking silence reigned, stifling for observers in the West, threatening for residents to the east of the death-strip."[2] Visitors to the Memorial today experience a version of this silence alongside a variety of sonic atmospheres corresponding to different architectural and political conditions in the past.[3] The Memorial's success in relating this past to hundreds of thousands of visitors a year, many of whom have no direct memory or experience of the site while militarized, seems to rely in part on this acoustic layer of embodied sensorial experience. A thorough understanding of the Berlin Wall Memorial's success as a conserved monument and interpretive pedagogical space is incomplete without a consideration of its historically constructed soundscape.

The consideration of sound's impact on heritage has emerged only recently and often requires pooling contributions from multiple disciplines. Affective heritage is perhaps the most recent field of inquiry to emerge that carries direct implications for sonic consideration.[4] Important reference points are also found in architectural phenomenology,[5] affective theory,[6] sensory studies,[7] music and sound archaeology,[8] and wider archaeological investigation via embodied research and sensory archaeology.[9] Recent studies have attempted to expand the understanding of place through sensed experience and phenomenology from both heritage and tourism perspectives as well.[10] The shift towards considering sound *as* heritage has also advanced: for example, in the context of natural landscapes,[11] the expanding field of soundscape study,[12] urban studies,[13] and European cultural heritage,[14] among others. Meanwhile, widely recognized heritage definitions continue to undergo significant expansions towards including more diversified perspectives, all of which carry potential sonic components; these include the greater recognition of intangible heritage,[15] values-based and participatory practices aimed at more inclusive representation in preservation,[16] and expanded confines of heritage.[17]

Sonic Evolution: 1961-1990

Tracing the changing sonic forms of the Wall's architectural space requires understanding its various aural pasts *as they were experienced at the time.* The source for such insights comes from a collection of living witness interviews held in the Berlin Wall Foundation as well as visual and textual information contained in the Foundation's archives. The records begin with the sudden construction of the Berlin Wall on the night of August 13, 1961, when a roll of barbed wire fencing was stretched by GDR guards along the boundary between Soviet-controlled Berlin and the sectors controlled by the US, UK, and French authorities. The Wall started out quite permeable, sonically and otherwise—Berliners on both sides came out to see the proceedings, meet family and friends now on the 'other' side, perhaps attempt to hop over or under when the guards were occupied. Along Bernauer Straße, the border fell exactly on the exterior facades of many residential buildings, meaning that residents could live in the Soviet sector but open their front doors into the Western sector. These doors were now forcibly locked. People started to jump out of their windows to defect.

Over the coming days and weeks, this border was gradually solidified, expanded, and made more complex through the addition of low brick walls, concrete blocks, guarded checkpoints, and further barbed wire fencing. Along Bernauer Straße, doors and windows were bricked in floor by floor, forcing defectors to jump out of ever-higher windows and rooftops. Fire brigades started to coordinate clandestinely, announcing their plans to be below a certain building at a set time and then setting up

Figure 1: Border strip with house facades serving as the western border wall at Bernauer Straße, 1963-66. BWM image F-020564. (Plate 13, p. 298)

rescue nets at night to catch jumping residents. One anonymous Western resident remembers this as a time when gunshots were fired every day. As he describes:

> (W)e couldn't see Bernauer Straße. We could only hear it and would … go down to the street to see what was going on. Our police officers were standing down there with pistols drawn to give cover for people who were coming out [of their windows].[18]

What had been a residential street was now filled with Wall construction, military patrols on either side by day, and a steady pace of escape attempts, gunshots, and protests at night.

In 1962, the first Wall infrastructure was offset by another, this one positioned about 10 meters to the east. The contents within this ring encircling western Berlin were gradually razed, including buildings, trees, even burial sites. Thus, the border strip of no-man's-land, what became known later as the death strip, was created through indiscriminate erasure. Along Bernauer Straße, a form of façadism gave shape to the western Wall's appearance for many years; the original residential buildings were demolished save for their bricked-in first floor street-fronts (Figure 1).

Even as the Wall hardened in form and expanded in breadth, even as the phone lines were cut, sound continued to transcend its physical limits as Berliners found ways to communicate. Sister Hanna Alm, who lived and worked at the Lazarus Hospital across from the Wall on Bernauer Straße, recounted an improvised call-and-response that developed between separated family members. A cemetery bell first would ring from the East as a signal to family members waiting on the West; in response, a trombone choir in the West would play so as to be heard by those on the East.[19] A more militant form of communication also developed: the loudspeaker war, where groups on the East and West would project messages, news, and music over the Wall as loudly as possible using large speakers—loud enough to penetrate buildings and disrupt daily life (Figure 2).[20] Cars on the West would honk their horns in counter-protest, creating a constant din, while the US set up radio stations that would broadcast directly to East Berlin residents.[21] A tourist industry had grown out of the initial year of protests from intense media scrutiny. Most visitors would attempt to see over the Wall by climbing platforms erected along the street;[22] some would even join residents in shouting taunts at the Eastern guards.[23] As Grünter Malchow (who also worked in the hospital) described it:

> Bernauer Straße was livelier than *Kurfürstendamm* [ed: a lively shopping district in West Berlin]. Particularly on weekends it was such that the street was entirely a tourist mile. Everything that came streaming into Berlin made an obligatory visit to Bernauer Straße. Every car, every bus and bus company drove through Bernauer Straße. The car horn choruses were awful. People would beep well into the night as a form of protest. For the locals who lived here and for the patients that I dealt with, it was, of course, catastrophic.[24]

Eventually in 1980, the last building vestiges along Bernauer Straße were replaced by taller concrete barriers and the death strip was fortified, sometimes extending to 40m wide with multiple intermediary walls.[25] The death strip was populated with surveillance towers, patrol roads and barking guard dogs on wires. It stretched belowground with electrical wires, tunnels, and sonar detection, and was equipped with various defensive mechanisms, including anti-tank barriers, 12.5 cm spikes hidden in the sand, and trip wires connected to sirens and flares.

With this visible infrastructural shift, a new phase of the sonic atmosphere in the neighborhood was also solidified. Direct sonic contact between East and West became all but impossible; the border strip now absorbed the constant verbal abuse and car horns from Western residents and maintained silence on the East through the constant patrols of GDR guards. Any activity near the Eastern Wall was suspicious and monitored, even from those citizens who lived nearby, so silence prevailed as Eastern residents kept away as much as possible. It was a silence so profound, in

Figure 2: Untitled. Loudspeakers mounted to vehicle during the loudspeaker war, July 1962.
BWM image F-020974.

fact, that the nuns running Lazarus hospital recalled the resurgence of nightingales in a cemetery now isolated behind the Wall, where the bell and trombones had earlier exchanged messages.[26] On the East, it was a thick silence, a monitored and enforced state of control, the breaking of which could always be ruptured in a split-second by a distant gun shot or a siren from the death strip.

Memorial Sounds

When the Wall finally fell in 1989, the imposing silent landscape did not disappear overnight. At first, its relationship with the city inverted both spatially and acoustically: residents flooded the initial openings in the wall and walked along the patrol road of the border strip; school trips became common and flocks of tourists returned,

Figure 3: Ebertstraße, wall-peckers at work, February 1990. BWM image F-015772. (Plate 14, p. 298)

this time tracing the path of the Wall from within a unified Berlin. For months, the constant "dry, irregular rattling and knocking" of "wall-peckers" could be heard as people chipped away at the concrete for souvenirs,[27] a slow-motion de-construction that left the structural rebar of the Wall sections exposed and rusting before their eventual removal altogether (Figure 3).

The complex physical history of the Wall along Bernauer Straße can seem particularly distant when contrasted with the groomed, park-like landscape of today. But the materials that so effectively stage the Wall fragments also conveniently support a series of acoustic atmospheres in different parts of the memorialized territory. The memorial intervention was originally designed as a block-long conserved portion of the entire Wall apparatus, including original walls, no-man's-land, and smaller artifacts like functioning light-posts, all blocked off at either longitudinal end with a substantially taller metal wall.[28]

No visitor may enter this memorial core. It is flanked on its longitudinal ends by grassy landscapes containing various artifacts of the Wall, demolished buildings, informational stations, and a new memorial chapel where a 19th-century church was razed during German division.[29] Within this ensemble of elements, a number of distinct acoustic zones can be identified corresponding to material remains and intervention designs. These often contain subtle signals that function both visually and acoustically

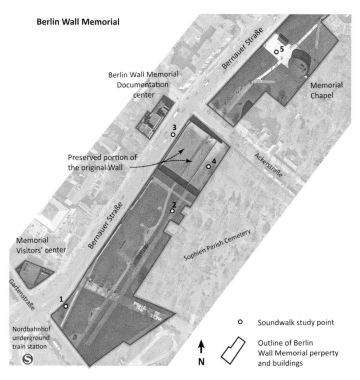

Figure 4: Diagrammatic plan of the Berlin Wall Memorial, with preserved portion of the Wall and death strip in the center. © the author. (Plate 15, p. 299)

to connect visitors with past conditions. These zones are anchored by five elements: the conserved West Wall, the rehabilitated western face of the preserved swath of the Wall; the adjoining East Wall, a reconstructed eastern face of the preserved swath of the Wall; the patrol road landscape where the Wall is present but not conserved;[30] the patrol road landscape where the Wall is absent and visually reinterpreted instead; and the Chapel of Reconciliation grounds and historic church bell enclosure, which are contemporary architectural features that also house historic artifacts (Figure 4).

In order to study these zones beyond personal observations, a series of public soundwalks and surveys were developed by the author to understand how various user groups experienced them as well. Twenty-seven individuals responded to an open call, including original witnesses, new visitors, and memorial staff. They were asked to share their impressions at each of the five points listed above: first without any contextual information, and then again after sharing relevant details about the historic soundscape from primary sources.

Figure 5: Photos of the western and eastern sides of the preserved Wall (left and right images respectively.) A sound level analysis showed that measured dB(A) values vary by as much as 20 dB(A) on either side. © the author.

The most apparent sonic zones to visitors were the conserved West Wall and the reconstructed East Wall, which together contain the preserved death strip. It is here that the sonic realities of the past have been preserved most starkly, where the sheer difference in loudness and sonic character marks a conspicuous contrast. The physical sound conditions throughout the memorial were documented by the author through a week-long binaural recording study of characteristics such as measured dB levels and psychoacoustic metrics such as perceived sharpness.[31] Entering the West Wall zone, one experiences a dense sonic compression or 'room' formed by the Wall, a tall building across busy Bernauer Straße, and stone sidewalks on either side of the asphalt pavement. The abundance of highly reflective surfaces means that the full range of sounds from vehicles, public trams, and frequent tour buses are reflected numerous times before they dissipate. No space or accommodation was added that might encourage a moment of pause by passersby. The resulting reverberation chamber is thus one of anonymity and transit by all users that is often described as unpleasant or uncomfortable while also being highly evocative of a chaotic, noisy, tourist-filled historic condition (Figure 5).

Most tourists pass through this western zone before circling around to the eastern portion of the memorial. The entry sequence is vital to understanding the contrast between the two—visitors can only enter the East Wall area from a small plaza between the street and imposing metal wall, then through a much smaller open passageway between new walls—a more intimate compression this time—before opening into the gravel-floored expanse of the East Wall observation area. The density of activity and population on the West is immediately rendered distant, with occasional traffic sounds reverberating into the East. The relative quietness of the East is reinforced by the choice of loose gravel underfoot, which accentuates one's personal movements and their echoed consequence within the closed-off space, speckled occasionally with birdsong from the adjacent cemetery. Visitors invariably modulate their speaking volume when entering the area. Their heightened self-awareness is reinforced when the new viewing platform is noticed towering over the Wall in the West, where visitors crowd to observe and take pictures of the death strip from above. What begins as a feeling of contemplation in this zone often transitions into a sense of isolation and hovering scrutiny for many visitors, again a condition highly reminiscent of historic realties on the eastern side of the Wall.

Moments of reflection are partially choreographed through similar material choices elsewhere. Gravel is also deployed around the chapel roughly where the original church stood. The gravel extends from the chapel forward to the street, where, to one side, the original church bells were reinstalled at ground-level in a simple open-slatted wooden shelter. The gravel forms an open plaza, demarcating a different zone within the surrounding parklands that again emphasizes one's personal movements and those of people nearby. It serves as a transitional space into the practically silent haybale chapel itself while also helping to accentuate the sound of the bells when rung (in contrast to the nearby absorbent grass).[32] Elsewhere, the gravel creates directed pathways between and around interpretive stations, continuing the subtle reinforcement of personal experience in areas of historic contemplation. This relationship is only apparent in spaces of relative quiet however, underscoring how sonic cues can function as a morphing and informative layer to visitor experience (Figure 6).

As a last consideration, the sonic environment of the Berlin Wall Memorial also bears separate significances for residents, caretakers, and historic witnesses at different timescales than tourists will often apprehend. The entire site returns to a calmer state outside of the summer tourist season, with school groups and small clutches of tourists dominating visitation next to residents walking their dogs. Traffic density eases, and clear differences between day and evening soundscapes emerge. The historic bells are rung by hand every day to announce a memorial service in the chapel; this sound reverberates down through the conserved memorial and into the death strip landscape beyond, connecting the entire landscape in remembrance. On weekends, this ringing also coincides with the tolling of bells at other nearby churches, effectively reconnecting the chapel within an historic sonic network that predated the Wall's construction entirely.

The implications of these sonic gestures can be profound when considered in the context of the Berlin Wall Memorial's mission to both convey historic realities and commemorate lost individuals. Many original relationships between people and place are mirrored in the conditions that remain today, though they may not appear precisely as they did in the past: the density of tourists and traffic, the solitude and feeling

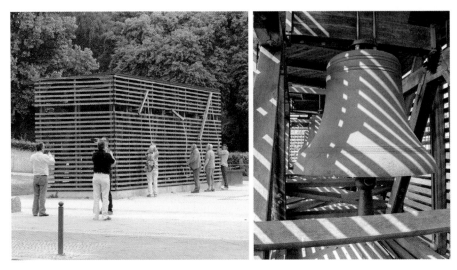

Figure 6: Photos of the contemporary wooden shelter in a gravel plaza, in which the original church bells are suspended. Image at left shows local volunteers ringing the bells before a memorial service held in the adjacent chapel; image at right shows the three bells. © the author.

of imposed quiet, the church bells rendered visible but silent, and multiple moments of hearing the street noise modulated in some way by the Wall in the East are all parallels between the past and today. Many participants in the study described a strong contrast in their experiences with the addition of sonic awareness. A member of the memorial staff described that "[t]here's a gap between my acoustic imagination (gun shots, church bells, protests…) and the actual sounds I can hear. The combination is interesting." A visitor became aware of the Wall's presence in a new way, stating that "[t]he wall is silent; the wall produces silence in passersby. It is a powerful thing to sense the wall in such proximity. It is unsettling that it still shapes the space in such powerful ways." Another staff member saw an opportunity for future programming at the memorial: "This is very intense. I need to implement a listening step into my guided tours to evoke concentrated listening and allow the group to focus."

The study revealed that gaining access to the sonic layer of history added a meaningful element to study participants' understanding of place and historic reality along Bernauer Straße. Results from the study suggest the importance of considering sound and silence as vital and contributing forces in heritage management plans. It is also worth challenging the premise that demanding or uncomfortable acoustic conditions are a problem to be solved— historic value can be embedded in uncomfortable situations, which can allow a meaningful connection between visitors and past actors. In the case of the Berlin Wall Memorial, finding meaning in sound was possible by allowing visitors time to listen deeply to the environment and reinforce their experience through detailed primary source accounts in situ.

The Berlin Wall Memorial renders the internationally-permeated history into its local and lived meanings. The echoes of these moments and memories reverberate still, making it difficult for some German colleagues to even visit the Memorial let alone participate in a soundwalk there. And it is through simple moves of conservation that those who did not grow up in Berlin can reach back and understand the profound effect such sonic atmospheres had. Disregarding this acoustic layer of historic places jeopardizes the possibility of direct, sensorial connection with the past, and, to borrow from Jonathan Bach, ignores the potential for turning the invisible into something sensate.[33]

Acknowledgments

Research of the historic soundscape of the Berlin Wall was funded by the Alexander von Humboldt Foundation and the HEAD Genuit Foundation. The author wishes to thank the Berlin Wall Foundation and Berlin Wall Memorial for research and support assistance, particularly Mrs. Lydia Dollmann, Prof. Dr. Axel Klausmeier, and Dr. Manfred Wichmann. Translation and research assistance were provided by Ms. Tessa Smith. Prof. Dr. Brigitte Schulte-Fortkamp and Dr. André Fiebig provided essential suggestions for soundscape analysis. Lastly, the anonymous participants and their dedicated interest throughout each soundwalk made the research both possible and consistently rewarding, for which the author is especially grateful.

Notes

1.   Dirk Verheyen, *United City, Divided Memories?* (Lanham, MD: Lexington Books, 2008), 224.

2.   Ibid, 224.

3.   Brian Ladd provides a useful background of the many readings of the Wall as a historic physical and intellectual reality as well as an evolving preserved memory for Berliners [Brian Ladd, *The Ghosts of Berlin* (Chicago: University of Chicago Press, 2018), chap. 1].

4.   A thorough summary of affective heritage theory origins and practices can be found in: Margaret Wetherell, Laurajane Smith, and Gary Campbell, "Introduction: Affective Heritage Practices," in *Emotion, Affective Practices, and the Past in the Present*, ed. Laurajane Smith, Margaret Wetherell, and Gary Campbell (New York City: Routledge, 2018), 1–17.

5.   Christian Norberg-Schulz, *Genius Loci: Towards a Phenomenology of Architecture* (New York City: Rizzoli, 1980).

6.   Laurajane Smith and Gary Campbell, "The Elephant in the Room," in *A Companion to Heritage Studies*, ed. William Logan, Máiréad Nic Craith, and Ullrich Kockel (Hoboken, NJ: John Wiley & Sons, Inc, 2015), 443–60.

7.   Duane Jethro, *Aesthetics of Power: Heritage Formation and the Senses in Post Apartheid South Africa* (London: Bloomsbury, 2019).

8.   John Schofield, "The Archaeology of Sound and Music," *World Archaeology* 46, no. 3 (May 2014): 289–291; Rupert Till, "Sound Archaeology: Terminology, Palaeolithic Cave Art and the Soundscape," *World Archaeology* 46, no. 3 (May 2014): 292–304.

9.   Jo Day, ed., *Making Senses of the Past: Toward a Sensory Archaeology* (Carbondale: Southern Illinois University Press, 2013); Shane Butler and Sarah Nooter, eds., *Sound and the Ancient Senses* (London: Routledge, 2019).

10.   Tomas Pernecky and Tazim Jamal, "(Hermeneutic) Phenomenology in Tourism Studies," *Annals of Tourism Research* 37, no. 4 (October 2010): 1055–75; Barbara A. Masberg and Lois H. Silverman, "Visitor Experiences at Heritage Sites: A Phenomenological Approach," *Journal of Travel Research* 34, no. 4 (April 18, 1996): 20–25.

11.   *Protecting National Park Soundscapes* (Washington: National Academies Press, 2013).

12.   R. Murray. Schafer, *The Soundscape: Our Sonic Environment and the Tuning of the World*, *The Soundscape: Our Sonic Environment and the Tuning of the World* (Rochester: Destiny Books, 1994); Barry Truax, "World Soundscape Project and Database," accessed March 13, 2019, https://www.sfu.ca/sonic-studio/worldsoundscaperoject.html

13.   Karin Bijsterveld, ed., *Soundscapes of the Urban Past: Staged Sound as Mediated Cultural Heritage* (Bielefeld: transcript Verlag, 2013).

14.   Meri Kytö, Nicolas Remy, and Heikki Uimonen, eds., *European Acoustic Heritage* (Grenoble: Tampere University of Applied Sciences, 2012).

15.   Laurajane Smith and Emma Waterton, "The Envy of the World?," in *Intangible Heritage*, ed. Laurajane Smith and Natsuko Akagawa (London: Routledge, 2009), 289–302; Pinar Yelmi, "Protecting Contemporary Cultural Soundscapes as Intangible Cultural Heritage: Sounds of Istanbul," *International Journal of Heritage Studies* 22, no. 4 (April 2016): 302–311.

16.   Marta De La Torre, "Values and Heritage Conservation," *Heritage & Society* 6, no. 2 (2013): 155–66; Henriette Roued-Cunliffe and Andrea Copeland, eds., *Participatory Heritage* (London: Facet Publishing, 2017).

17.   Gustavo Araoz, "Conservation Philosophy and Its Development: Changing Understandings of Authenticity and Significance," *Heritage & Society* 6, no. 2 (2013): 144–54; Jukka Jokilehto, "Considerations on Authenticity and Integrity in World Heritage Context," *City & Time* 2, no. 1 (2006): 1–16.

18.   Interview with Mr. K. De, page 18, interviewed 10/15/02 by M. Nooke, translated by T. Smith, Zeitzeuge Collection, Berlin Wall Foundation (BWF).

19.   Interview with Sister Hanna Alm, page 5, interviewed 1/18/2001 by M. Nooke, translated by T. Smith, Zeitzeuge Collection, BWF.

20. Interview with Sisters Margarete Umlandt, Sophie Herrmann, and Jutta Lenk, page
     10–11, interviewed 1/17/01 by M. Nooke, translated by T. Smith, Zeitzeuge Collection,
     BWF.

21. Nicholas J. Schlosser, *Cold War on the Airwaves: The Radio Propaganda War against East
     Germany* (Urbana: University of Illinois Press, 2015).

22. Joachim Schloer, "'It has to go away, but at the same time it has to be kept': the Berlin
     Wall and the making of an urban icon," *Urban History* 33, no. 1 (2006): 98.

23. Interview with B. Seschwind, page 45, interviewed on 07/23/07 by L. Dollmann, trans-
     lated by T. Smith, Zeitzeuge Collection, BWF.

24. Interview with G. Malchow, page 1.f, interviewed on 04/07/99 by M. Nooke, translated
     by T. Smith, Zeitzeuge Collection, BWF.

25. See Frederick Baker, "The Berlin Wall: Production, Preservation and Consumption
     of a 20th-Century Monument," *Antiquity* 67, no. 257 (December 2, 1993): 709–33;
     Verheyen, *United City, Divided Memories?*, chap. 11, for thorough summaries of the con-
     struction phases of the Wall, its surveillance elements, and social and political contexts
     throughout its militarized use.

26. Interview with G. Malchow, page 25, interviewed on 04/07/99 by M. Nooke, translated
     by T. Smith, Zeitzeuge Collection, BWF.

27. Interview with H. Gissler, page 14, interviewed on 10/14/05 by M. Nooke, translated
     by T. Smith, Zeitzeuge Collection, BWF.

28. Kohlhoff & Kohlhoff Architects completed the initial memorial design after a public
     competition in 1994. This was later expanded to encapsulate the grounds to either side,
     a new observation deck, a visitor center, and a documentation center, among others.
     For effective summaries of the memorial's construction influences, its physical forms,
     and its evolving socio-political interpretations, see for instance Gerd Knischewski and
     Ulla Spittler, "Remembering the Berlin Wall: The Wall Memorial Ensembles Ber-
     nauer Struass," *German Life and Letters* 59, no. 2 (2006): 280–93; Verheyen, *United City,
     Divided Memories?*, chap. 12.

29. Designed by Sassenroth and Reitermann using earthen construction mixed with
     original church fragments instead of concrete [Knischewski and Spittler, "Remember-
     ing the Berlin Wall: The Wall Memorial Ensembles Bernauer Struass," 282, 283; Axel
     Klausmeier, *The Berlin Wall* (Berlin: Christoph Links Verlag, 2015), 306.

30. See D. Sandler's pertinent discussion on 'counterpreservation' in Berlin since 1989
     through the phenomenological experience of visible decay, particularly the discussion
     on the Berlin Wall Memorial [Daniela Sandler, *Counterpreservation: Architectural Decay in
     Berlin Since 1989* (Ithaca: Cornell University Press, 2016), 217–30].

31. Pamela Jordan, "Historic Approaches to Sonic Encounter at the Berlin Wall Memo-
     rial," *Acoustics* 1, no. 3 (2019): 517–537; Pamela Jordan and André Fiebig, "COVID-19
     Impacts on Historic Soundscape Perception and Site Usage," *Acoustics* 3, no. 3 (2021):
     594–610.

32. The original church grounds were returned to the parish long before the memorial was designed around it, leading both the memorial and chapel forms to evolve independently before their eventual merging. Yet both centered themselves in the concept of a silent core, perhaps in part deriving from the district assembly's direction that "[t]he future memorial site was to be a 'place of quiet, reflection, and commemoration'" [Verheyen, *United City, Divided Memories?*, 225]. As Mr. Rainer Just explained about the chapel's design as early as 1996, "…it was supposed to be a place of silence…" ("…es sollte ein Ort der Stille sein…") ["Ein Ort Der Stille Auf Dem Ehemaligen Todestreifen: Interview Mit Rainer Just," Earth Kultur, 2013, accessed March 13, 2019, http://www.earthkultur.com/rainer-just-germany_de/]. The commissioned organ within is itself quite symbolic as well and is only played on infrequent occasions ["Klänge Zur Versöhnung; Kapelle an Der Bernauer Straße Erhält Eine Neue Orgel" in *Berliner Zeitung*, September 29, 2017].

33. Jonathan Bach, "The Berlin Wall after the Berlin Wall: Site into Sight," *Memory Studies* 9, no. 1 (2016): 53.

16.

Listen and Write! Addressing Urban Sound-scapes in Architectural Education

Klaske Havik and Michael de Beer

"Listen," he said. There was no loud or distinct sound. It was an intricate curtain of muffled ringing tones. The city's church bells chiming the sun to rest. "The key they are tuned to becomes the tonic in a major or minor triad. An overtone, which is an octave plus a minor or a major third, varies along with the tonic. The city is a sound map. Grundtvig Church. Tuned in D. And above that, the F-sharp is heard just as strongly. The church has only the one huge bell. Its chimes could never be confused with those of the Church of Our Saviour. Each is unique in its own way. So if you talk on the phone at sunset, and listen beyond the voice and compensate for the flat sound picture, you get an impression where the person at the other end is located on the sound map."[1]

This literary fragment, describing the acoustic presence of the city of Copenhagen in Peter Høeg's novel *The Quiet Girl* (2006), suggests that places are tuned in particular tonalities and people can orient themselves in a city based upon its particular sound map. The capacity to understand space through listening can be an important and meaningful skill for architects and urbanists, who respond to and intervene in urban soundscapes through their work. In 1959, Danish architect Steen Eiler Rasmussen drew attention to the sonic experience of urban spaces that were defined both by the size, shape, materiality and dimensions of the space as well as by the activities they host.[2] However, in today's architectural practice and education, there seems to be a lack of attention to the auditory qualities of space. Finnish architect and theorist Juhani Pallasmaa criticized the hegemony of the eye in his seminal essay, *The Eyes of the Skin* (1996), stating that "A space is conceived through its echo as much as through its visual shape, but the acoustic percept usually remains an unconscious background experience."[3] Harry F. Mallgrave emphasized, "sounds play an extraordinary important role in how we perceive a room, a space, an urban environment."[4] Examining the acoustic quality of churches as examples, Mallgrave suggests that historically, there was more attention to sound in architecture, while today, sound is a "neglected element in our sensory life."[5] To focus architects' attention on the role of sound in urban situations, we will look at how architects are taught and discuss the topic of sound in relation to architectural pedagogy.

In architectural education, acoustics as a design parameter generally comes to the fore in design studios focusing on concert halls, music venues and dance theatres, architectural typologies in which sound indeed plays a major role. However, the sound of the everyday urban environments is less discussed. In design studios, site analysis and design exercises are often conducted in spatial, material, and social terms, but the ways these characteristics play a role in the acoustic atmosphere of a site and the respective architectural proposal is seldomly part of the discussion. Nevertheless, in spatial terms, conditions like distance, dimension, enclose, and curvature have their impact on the way sound is heard and perceived. In material terms, sound may be absorbed or reflected, it may dampen or echo depending on the sonic properties of materials. In social terms, different rhythms and tonalities are produced by varying activities, movements, and voices. As Pallasmaa argues, the way we perceive sound has to do with a sense of embeddedness, of connectedness and collectiveness: "sight is the sense of the solitary observer, whereas hearing creates a sense of connection and solidarity."[6] This phenomenon has to do with the directionality of vision and the omnidirectional character of sound. Indeed, our visual gaze is generally focused on what appears in front of us, while sound can reach us from behind, beside, above or below; therefore, "sight isolates, whereas sound incorporates."[7]

If we acknowledge that sound is intrinsically related to architectural experience in spatial, material and social terms, we alight with the perspectives of Pnina Avidar, Raviv Granchrow and Julia Kursell, who "consider sound as an equal component [compared to the visual], an overall spatial atmosphere that is inseparable from the dimensions and tectonics within which it resides."[8] Recent reflections from philosophers, such as Tonino Griffero and Gernot Böhme to architect Peter Zumthor and artist Olafur Eliasson, also stress the multisensory character of atmospheres.[9] It is this notion of sound being intricately related to the experience of urban atmospheres, that we plea should be more present in architectural education.

The relative lack of emphasis on sound and sound studies in architectural education may be related to the tools that architects use, which are mainly visually oriented: drawings, maps, models, and computer-aided image processing tools. In this article, we explore how the educational and architectural tools we have at our disposal could be adjusted or expanded to allow for the study of sound, and subsequently how students can be stimulated to take the sonic characteristics of place and architecture into consideration. In order to move away from the predominance of visual tools in architectural education, we suggest the use of writing as a complementary educational tool. In this article, we will stress the significance of teaching students to *listen* and to *write*, as it is through narrative, rather than drawing, that architectural soundscapes can be best expressed, evoked and imagined. We will highlight some exercises and studio work which took place at Delft University of Technology as examples that explicitly address the sonic characteristics of space. Through these pedagogical experiences, we will convey how honing student skills in listening and writing can incorporate the topic of sound to help analysis and design in architectural education.

Evoking Sonic Awareness through Writing

Writing, compared to drawing or visual arts, allows for other senses, besides sight, to emerge as prominently. Even a novel completely about smell is imaginable, such as Patrick Süsskind's well-known work *Perfume: The Story of a Murderer* (1985).[10] Some authors have focused specifically on sound, especially in the literary experiments of Oulipo, a French writers collective in the mid-20th century, with members such as Italo Calvino, Georges Perec and Raymond Queneau. In his *Exercises of Style* (1947), Queneau wrote multiple variations on one very short story, about an encounter in a Parisian bus (line S) between the narrator and a young man—but the story itself is less relevant than the 99 stylistic variations in which Queneau has re-written it: as a dream, as a hesitation, as an official letter, as a sonnet, or as a description focused on one of the senses.

> Auditory: Quacking and letting off, the S came rasping to a halt alongside the silent pavement. The sun's trombone flattened the midday note. The pedestrians, bawling bagpipes, shouted out their numbers. Some went up a semitone, which sufficed to carry them off towards the Porte Champerret with its chanting arcades. Among the panting elite was a clarinet tube to whom the untowardness of the times had given human form, and the perversity of a hatmaker had given to wear on the coconut an instrument which resembled a guitar that might perhaps have plaited its strings together to make a girdle. Suddenly in the middle of some minor arrangements between enterprising passengers and consenting passengeresses and of bleating tremolos from the covetous conductor, a ludicrous cacophony broke out in which the fury of the double bass was blended with the irritation of the trumpet and the jitters of the bassoon.
> Then, after sigh, silence, pause and double pause, there rang forth the triumphant melody of a button in the process and going up an octave.[11]

In the book *Under the Jaguar Sun* (1986),[12] Italo Calvino offers a series of short stories that each focus on one particular sense, such as sound, smell or taste. The story focused on sound describes the space of a castle in terms of its acoustic characteristics and the sounds of activities taking place there. These somewhat forced exercises in which sound is isolated from other senses may not result in the most subtle literary descriptions of architectural perception, but they do offer a very useful format for exercises in architectural education. Following the examples by Queneau and Calvino, a very simple writing exercise for architecture students is this: *Describe your route from home to the Faculty of Architecture, only by means of sound.* At first, students may be slightly puzzled, as they are usually not very aware of the soundscape of their daily commute, but once asked to write down their memories of this trajectory, their route appears to be full of sounds: the sound of their feet on the staircase, the door closing in its lock, the wheels of their bike on the uneven stones, the church bells, the slow traffic, the wind playing with the water on the canals, or with the leaves in the trees. It only takes attention to become aware of the richness of our urban soundscapes. For readers, the soundscape of the historical Dutch city of Delft may have resonated in this given list of possible auditory experiences. Through writing, it becomes apparent to the students that each city, each urban space, has its own soundscape, and that we are able to communicate this by our evocative descriptions of the sound of our routes.

The seminar course, "Readings on the Public Realm," a 10-weeks elective at the level of the first year of the Master of Architecture, explored literary methods and approaches in order to "read" the public realm. The Dutch west coast was the subject for experimentation with writing and visualization explorations of landscape, urban space and architecture. As a theoretical basis, the course provided key texts regarding spatial practices by Henri Lefebvre and Michel de Certeau as well as more literary readings of the public realm by writers such as Italo Calvino, Walter Benjamin and Dutch authors. Through exercises pairing creative writing with visualization, students were challenged to become aware of site-specific perceptions.

As a first task, the students were asked to visit the Dutch coast and describe in writing their sensory experiences of the landscape. Attention was paid to haptic experiences and sounds, their feet sinking in sand at the low tide, hearing the sound of approaching waves at high tide. One student listened to the forces of flood: "The water roars, hisses and gurgles. Again and again it takes off, hits the coast ... The waves whine while they thunder over their predecessors, before they, again, withdraw—much to the pleasure of the seagulls who cheer them, screaming from above."[13]

The next set of writing exercises asked the students to describe the everyday use of space through the perspective of the inhabitants of the harbor town. Writing from the perspective of particular characters also offers potential if we wish to explore how the world is experienced without the dominance of sight: a student might turn to the perspective of a character who is visually impaired or blind. Indeed, as architect

Sarah Robinson states: "Blind people are connoisseurs of sound and echo. Designing with an awareness of their refined spatial awareness would open a new dimension of architectural space for sighted people, as well."[14]

It was exactly this premise that led Mike Schäfer to graduate with a research driven design project that took the spatial experience of blind people as point of departure.[15] In order to focus on other senses than sight, Schäfer turned to literary description as a tool to explore the experience of space, and to include it within the design process. For this purpose, a number of literary references were employed, such as the novel *Ruw* (2009), by Belgian author Marie Kessels,[16] which is written from the perspective of a blind character. The descriptions in the novel helped Schäfer to understand how a blind person navigates urban space, particularly aided by the sense of hearing. For the design of a training center for blind people in the countryside of the Netherlands, he produced a sound map of the site, and developed the architectural design by means of multiple models, with close attention to the sonic properties of spaces and materials.

Rhythms, Noises, Voices: Punctuations in Urban Space

The two following projects we will discuss in more detail have been conducted within in the graduation studio "Positions in Practice" offered by the Chair of Methods & Analysis at the Department of Architecture in Delft. This graduation studio, which runs for two semesters, aims to attain and test instruments and methods for the analysis of and design for a complex, contemporary urban condition. Studio discussions are situated at the crossing point of urban studies, literary studies and architecture. The studio seeks to establish a relationship between personal observation of place and the acknowledgement of social practices that inform design students about the identity, history and conditions of specific sites.

In 2018-2019, the studio focused on the Teusaquillo neighborhood in Bogotá and started with a workshop that was developed in collaboration with the Department of Design at the Universidad de los Andes.[17] During this workshop, titled "Thinking Through Things," students were asked to explore Teusaquillo through domestic items, such as a cup, a candle, a hairbrush or scissors. The objects' form, use or material properties allowed the students to engage with the neighborhood in new and unexpected ways. Alexander Petrounine, for instance, immersed himself in the soundscape of the neighborhood by using a simple metallic teaspoon to test rhythms, materials and resonances of different sites in the neighborhood (Figure 1). The spoon, due to its materiality and shape, facilitated musical-percussive interactions with the surroundings. In his experience, tapping every object in the neighborhood with the spoon "transformed into a means of urban exploration. The fences, the walls, the

Figure 1: Alexander Petrounine using a spoon to explore soundscapes of Bogotá. Still from video, "Thinking through Things," https://www.tudelft.nl/index.php?id=45168. (Plate 16, p. 300)

streets, turned into a found musical instrument."[18] Indeed, people and even animals responded to the sound by talking, singing or barking. The experiment was documented through the use of video. Through montage, Petrounine edited the information which he captured, revealing the way local inhabitants react to the acoustic conditions of the site.

Based upon their investigations in Teusaquillo (of which the domestic object exercise was but one), the group of students compiled a book as a collection of their findings. This format paired their writing (mixed academic reflection with instances of narrative and poetry) with their visual representation. They presented their observations, conceptually, as a set of punctuation marks:

> The comma, then, denotes a pause within the constructive whole, the question mark investigates the unexpected. Periods are seen as obstructions in the city, while semi-colons give stage to research of affordances. A singular angle bracket marks a hierarchy between two things and suggests an investigation of societal hierarchies of the built environment. The space in between two brackets can include additional layers of sensory information... Punctuation marks are an integral part of any written text, serving as tools to set the pace, tone and focus.[19]

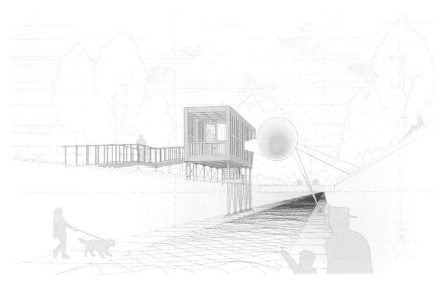

Figure 2: Alexander Petrounine, Design for a sound pavilion at the Rio Arzobispo, Bogotá.
(Plate 17, p. 300)

Indeed, if punctuation offers a set of devices to read a text, it may as well help us to 'read' an urban neighborhood. We may also think of punctuation in sonic terms: as indications to stop, pause, move forward. The initial exercise with the spoon led Petrounine to an even deeper exploration of sound in the urban environment of Bogotá—a city with nine million inhabitants, and problems of urban density and traffic congestion. Rather than being disturbed by the noise of the city, Petrounine took the opportunity to listen to the urban sounds attentively, inspired by John Cage's observation that "Wherever we are, what we hear is mostly noise. When we ignore it, it disturbs us. When we listen to it, we find it fascinating."[20] In particular, he explored how the soundscape of the city challenges the boundaries of space, indicating sonic boundaries by documenting changes in intensity of urban noise.

Based upon his recordings and maps, Petrounine identified a number of spaces in the neighborhood suitable for urban sound pavilions, and he set for himself the task to create architectural interventions that separate, abstract and re-organize the myriad of sounds of the environment, which otherwise end up heard as a cacophony. As a design task, he developed sound pavilions for a number of these urban spaces, which allowed particular urban sounds to become more apparent to inhabitants through architectural form. The intervention consisted of a sounding box, built in wood and designed with a strong attention to tectonics, and a listening device or 'ear' with strong plastic properties (Figure 2). In this design, the sounds of the surroundings were captured and amplified; the harvested sounds conjured up a new acoustic environment. One could both receive the sounds of the surrounding space and create new sounds by using the pavilions as performance spaces. The idea was for these structures to be accessible to the public, with the ability to reveal the specific sounds of the city in different situations. This way, the installations created awareness for the specific soundscapes of the neighborhood, and offered the citizens the agency to alter them.

Listening to Valparaíso: Soundscape and Topography

In the academic year 2017–2018 the same graduation studio focused on the Chilean city Valparaíso.[21] Due to its particular topography of deep cut valleys (*quebradas*) connecting the mountaintop to the idyllic bay and harbor front at its feet, the city performs spatially and socially as an amphitheatre (Figure 3). The rapid change in elevation is mirrored in the city activities; the bustling urban centre straddles the bay while the residential neighborhoods slowly climb up the spurs between the valleys. The difference of topography is so extreme that it forms strong physical separations between neighborhoods and has stimulated unique ecosystems of growth and social connections.

Michael de Beer graduated from this studio in 2018. In his theoretical explorations of sound, he referred to Pallasmaa, who described the ability of sound to orientate and situate. This suggestion inspired de Beer to focus on sound's particular spatial significance. At a conference dedicated to urban sounds, Pallasmaa highlighted how in the dark, the dripping of water carves out a void in our imagination.[22] Sound's quality to situate and trigger our imagination led de Beer to explore sonic research techniques and investigate how sound could be utilized in understanding the spaces we inhabit. He turned to sonic tools and methods of representation that would uncover spatial and atmospheric qualities to inform his design.

De Beer conducted a thorough investigation of Valparaíso's soundscape for the design of a school on one of the city's hills. He broke the research into two stages: recording and synthesizing spatial and sonic information. The first stage, recording, explored the city's soundscapes using an omnidirectional microphone,[23] writing narrative descriptions of sonic spaces, and sketching these spaces. Although sound recordings are a powerful tool, it was evident that forms of mapping and modelling would be required for the second stage: synthesizing the spatial and sonic information into an understandable and communicable form.

During recoding, de Beer methodically identified places and found situations within the city that would offer a diverse collection of sounds. The intention was to build a sonic profile of the city. The methods of documenting soundscapes formed a sound diary which also included an annotated diagrammatic sound-score (Figure 4).

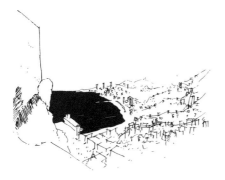

Figure 3: Michael de Beer, Sketch of Valparaíso from the high hills.

Viewing Point

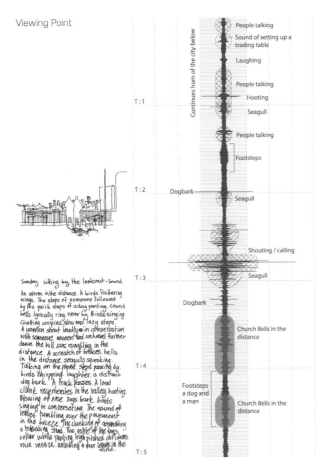

People talking

Sound of setting up a trading table

Laughing

People talking

Hooting

Seagull

People talking

Footsteps

Continues hum of the city below

T : 1

T : 2   Dogbark   Seagull

Shouting / calling

T : 3   Seagull

Dogbark

Church Bells in the distance

T : 4

Footsteps a dog and a man

Church Bells in the distance

T : 5

Sunday sitting by the lookout - Sound.

An alarm in the distance. A birds fluttering wings. The steps of someone followed by the quick steps of a dog panting. Church bells lyrically ring near by. Birds singing. Chatting couples, slow and lazy steps. A woman shout loudly is in conversation with someone unseen and unheard further down the hill. cars rumbling in the distance. A screatch of brakes. bells in the distance. seagulls squaking. Talking on the phone. steps passing by. birds chirpping. laughter. a distant dog bark. A truck passes. A loud clink reverberates in the valley. hooting. Blowing of nose. Dogs bark. birds singing in conversation. The sound of leaves tumbling over the pavement in the breeze. the clunking of assembling a trebading stand. The raffle of the dogs collar while panting. high pitched children voice. sneeze. unlocking a door. leaves in the wind.

Figure 4: Michael de Beer, Soundscape analysis of Valparaíso, description, sketch and diagram.

(Plate 18, p. 301)

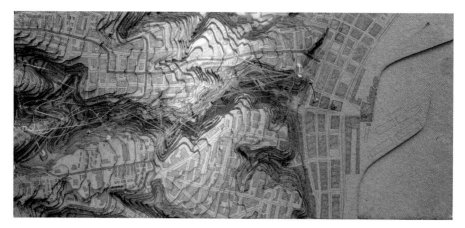

Figure 5: Michael de Beer, Model of Valparaíso valley and sound study of varying conditions.
(Plate 19, p. 302)

To identify the sound configurations of spaces, recordings were coupled with written observations, which carefully described how people were (inter-)acting. These narratives, accompanied by site sketches, conveyed a sense of place and atmosphere. Like Pallasmaa's dripping of water, descriptive encounters trigger a situational awareness. Narrative made the following primary research not only accessible but also relatable:

> Cemetery. Through the threshold. Gravel under foot. Birds singing. Silence. Rustling bushes. Leaves. Whistling. Moving toward the threshold the hum of the city comes into earshot. A distant rumble, hoot, screeching. The hum of many tiny people below. Birds singing. Wind rustling over foliage. A buzzing bee. A truck huffing and heaving up the hill. Music traveling in the wind becomes clear for just a moment. The hum of the city is broken by the discussion of an approaching couple, who drown-out the quite respite. Through the threshold the city disappears. Silence, leaves, birds and wind whistling through the graves. The crunch of gravel. A distant bark. Leaves rustling and bees buzzing.[24]

Through sound, the study uncovered specific rhythms, activities and atmospheres. These acoustic qualities and characteristics would not have been evident had other techniques and tools been used. For example, along the contour road Avenida Alemania, which acts as a spine connecting the neighborhoods on the hills, the sound recordings highlighted the ebb and flow of activity created by the regular buses moving along the route. A particular insight was that this ebb and flow was uniquely possible because one is distinctly aware of the proximity of the bus due to the nature of the topography—one can hear its slow and distant approach as it winds through the valley.

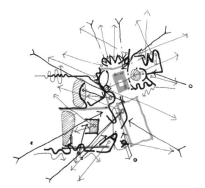

Figure 6: Michael de Beer, Synthesis of form and experience. (Plate 20, p. 302)

The investigation revealed spatial qualities inherent in the hills and an intimate urban community life. Hawkers shouting, music blaring, dogs barking and crowds chatting loudly were starkly contrasted by the sound of the distant harbor, birds singing and intimate conversations amongst friends traversing the gravel pavement. These localities were in contrast to the valleys that intensified in sonic complexity as they led down to the bay, toward the city centre. This dialectic relationship between top and bottom was not only a physical environmental boundary, but also one of activity and atmosphere. Inspired by inhabitants shouting across the valley from hill to hill, another acoustic study explored how sound would travel through a valley. Using a physical model of the topography and strings to represent the path of sound, the research mapped how sound traveled through the valley. The exercise created a three-dimensional spatial map of the sonic environments and how they interacted (Figure 5).

This study informed the choice of a site location for the design assignment by way of defining the acoustic thresholds within the city. The model highlighted crossover points between hill and valley and illustrated sonic relationships with squares, churches and roads. It also revealed isolated zones. De Beer discovered a precipice at the beginning of the valley, an exposed site on a cliff adjacent to Valparaíso's central urban square that provided vantage points offering noisy interactions with the city at some locations and tranquil spots in others. The site's potential paralleled the sensory experience of Cementerio N° 1 de Valparaíso. De Beer set out to design a school, including both indoor and outdoor spaces, making use of the diverse sound conditions of the site (Figure 6).

The site-specific findings were analysed and documented in the form of section and model. Sections showed the sonic relationship that the site has with its environment—emphasising sonic connections and sound generators within the city.[25] This two-dimensional information was then translated into a three-dimensional model at

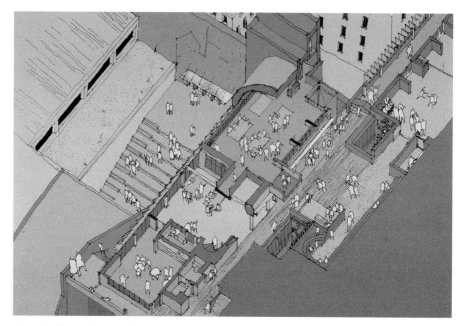

Figure 7: Michael de Beer, School design in Valparaíso, indicating different sonic zones.
(Plate 21, p. 303)

1:200 scale, showing the sources of sounds and their interaction with the large site that climbed from valley floor to hilltop. Based on this model, the design could account for the way in which the sound moves in the unique topography of Valparaíso. Classrooms and the library of the proposed school were conceived as sonically protected spaces, hidden behind walls shielding the space from the city noise. The outdoor paths and courtyards captured the sounds of the environment, while offering a view of the ocean below (Figure 7).

For the final presentation, de Beer created a sonic experience of walking through the site based on the sounds one might hear. It was a hypothetical atmospheric soundtrack. The compilation demonstrated the diversity of sonic environments that were synthesized in the project. Doing so he created an immersive experience of the new design. He also wrote and recited a poem, "Perpetually afoot" (2018), which presented the architectural environment. The writing combined sonic and atmospheric qualities and expressed a sense of place and atmosphere—communicating the proposed experience directly to the imagination.

Listen and Respond

In this contribution, we have explored writing as tool for the documentation and analysis of sound and sonic spaces, complementary to varied techniques more commonly employed such as mapping, sketching and modelling. We conclude by stating how these exercises not only lead to a more sonic spatial awareness, but also allow to bring such an awareness forward in design. We have shown how creative writing exercises help students to convey their perceptual focus. We have seen students use the empathic powers of fiction to try to understand how the world is experienced by a visually impaired or blind person that relies on senses other than sight, specifically sound.

While encouraging students to explore their own and imagined embodied perceptions of urban space, the studio exercises also set out to understand the social conditions of sites, thus moving from individual perception to the collective. The study of sound offers unexpected ways to achieve a deeper understanding of how communities relate to their environment. The exercises in Bogotá informed the students how locals both perceived and produced sounds in the studied neighborhood. These interactions provided valuable information about domestic and commercial practices as well as about the boundaries between these practices—which appeared in the sound maps of Petrounine. In the Valparaíso studio, the observed sounds were closely connected to the rhythm of everyday life that was strongly influenced by the specific topography of the city.

We have explored how metaphorical literary devices, such as the 'reading' of an urban area through punctuation can raise design awareness of phenomenological and social considerations related to the sonic experience of the lived environment. Such attentiveness to sonic landscapes draws forward an alternative approach to spatial practice that is innately site-specific and situational. Moving from analysis to design, we have seen how the organization and amplification of particular urban sounds, or the building of a programmatic sonic pallet, may offer alternative approaches to site selection. By curating how spaces ought to be experienced or performed, designers can connect tectonic intentions with wider compositional and situational questions, uncovering otherwise unrelated environmental qualities.

In the investigations of Petrounine and De Beer, listening and making noise were both considered as an act. Taken for granted, these acts are fundamental to how we navigate the world socially: to walk softly in a library, or scream at the top of one's voice in protest, to change the way one talks in a crowded elevator. These actions seem natural because they are so intertwined to behavior in social and environmental circumstances. When navigating our interaction with society, we readily adjust the tone and level of our voice, or the manner in which we listen, according to the situation. To make a sound is to alter the soundscape and denote one's existence—and so does architecture. Every piece of architecture—through its very presence, shape, surface, materiality, composition and dimensions—intervenes in a soundscape and alters it.

We hope that the pedagogical explorations brought to the fore in this article help future architecture students to develop a sensitivity to urban soundscapes, to listen to them, to write them, and to respond to them in meaningful ways.

Notes

1. Peter Høeg, *The Quiet Girl* (New York: Picador, 2009), 39.
2. Steen Eiler Rasmussen, *Experiencing Architecture* (Cambridge, MA: MIT Press, 1993 [1959]).
3. Juhani Pallasmaa, *The Eyes of the Skin: Architecture and the Senses* (London: Academy Editions, Polemics, 1996), 35.
4. Harry F. Mallgrave, *From Object to Experience. The New Culture of Architectural Design*, (London: Bloomsbury, 2018), 84.
5. Ibid., 82.
6. Juhani Pallasmaa, *The Eyes of the Skin,* 35.
7. Ibid, 34.
8. Pnina Avidar, Raviv Granchrow, Julia Kursell, editorial, *OASE, Journal For Architecture* 78 *Immersed, Sound and Architecture,* (2009):4
9. See for instance Tonino Griffero, *Atmospheres: Aesthetics of Emotional Spaces.* (London: Routledge, 2016); Christian Borch (ed) *Architectural Atmopsheres. On the Experience and Politics of Architecture,* (Basel: Birkhauser 2014); Klaske Havik, Gus Tielens, and Hans Teerds (eds), *OASE, Journal for Architecture* 91 *Building Atmosphere with Juhani Pallasma and Peter Zumthor,* (2013).
10. Patrick Süskind, *Perfume: Story of a Murderder* (London: Penguin Books, 2007). Originally published as *Das Parfum. Die Geschichte eines Mörders* (Zürich: Diogenes, 1985).
11. Raymond Queneau, *Exercises of Style*, Barbara Wright (tr.), (New York: New Direction Books 2012), 82. Originally published as: Raymond Queneau, *Exercises de style,* (Paris: Gallimard Editions, 1947).
12. Italo Calvino, *Under the Jaguar Sun* (London: Vintage, 1993), originally published as: *Sotto il sole giaguaro* (Milan: Garzanti, 1986).
13. Msc2 Seminar "Readings on the Public Realm," taught by Klaske Havik and Hans Teerds, TU Delft 2012. The work of the students was collected and presented at a symposium entitled *The Story of the Netherlands,* in Amsterdam Oct 20, 2010, and appeared for that occasion in: *Writingplace. The Story of the Netherlands: Landscape,* (Delft: TU Delft / Writingplace 2012), 30.
14. Sarah Robinson, "Nested Bodies" in: Sarah Robinson and Juhani Pallasmaa (eds.) *Mind in Architecture. Neuroscience, Embodiment, and the Future of Design* (Cambridge, Mass.: MIT Press, 2015), 137–159, citation p. 144.

15. Mike Schäfer, "Descriptive Designing: A search for awareness of space and experiences in architecture," Graduation project ExploreLab TU Delft 2009–2010, Tutors Klaske Havik, Patrick Healy, Elise van Dooren.

16. Marie Kessels, *Ruw* (Amsterdam/Antwerpen: De Bezige Bij, 2009).

17. Departemiento de Disegno, Universidad de los Andes, Bogotá: tutors Christaan Job Nieman and Daniel Nadal, Department of Architecture, chair of Methods&Analysis TU Delft: tutors Alberto Altés, Klaske Havik and Jorge Mejía Hernández.

18. The graduation project of Alexander Petrounine is available at https://repository. tudelft.nl/islandora/object/uuid%3A0d42bf77-4530-4cf1-8998-14fb78194ab1?collection=education

19. Chair of Methods&Analysis, Studio Positions in Practice 2018–2019, *Punctuations in Teusaquillo* (Delft: TU Delft 2019), 7. Participating students and authors of the collective book: Ksymena Borcynska, Ege Cakir, Emilia Golebiewska, Iris van de Heide, Danlei Huang, Hsuan-Ya Kao, Hiu Ching Debby Lam, Silvia Leone, Cherk Ga Leung, Ilianne Logotheti, Rebecca Lopes Cardozo, Agnieszka Panasiuk, Miguel Peluffo, Alexander Petrounine, Elena Rossoni, Julia Slopnicka, Robert Stubbs, Isabel Ulrich.

20. John Cage, *The Future of Music: Credo*, Lecture given in Seattle, in 1937, in: John Cage, *Silence. Lectures and Writings*. (London: Marion Boyars 1978), 3.

21. Graduation studio Methods&Analysis, Positions in Practice Valparaíso, Chile, 2017-18. Tutors Óscar Andrade Castro, Klaske Havik, Pierre Jennen. Graduation project Michael de Beer: "A Sonic Designing with Sound Acts."

22. Juhani Pallasmaa, "Invisible Spaces: Touching the World," lecture at the conference *Invisible Places. Sound, Urbanism and Sense of Place*, April 7–9, 2017 Azores, Portugal, accessed on 25-11-2017 https://www.youtube.com/watch?v=eksSydf--fk

23. Omnidirectional microphones pick up sound from all directions and do not prioritize one sound over another. With the focus on sonic environments, such a microphone enables recording of atmospheric qualities.

24. Sonic description of Cementerio N° 1 de Valparaíso, Michael de Beer, 2017.

25. Sound generators are places, things and events that actively inform the sonic environment.

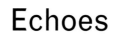
Echoes

On Atmospheres and Other Difficulties: A Conversation with Alberto Pérez-Gómez

Angeliki Sioli

This interview was conducted in May 2020 online, taking place between Montreal (Canada) and Delft (the Netherlands) with a time difference of six hours.

Angeliki Sioli: In your article, "Architecture as Musical Atmosphere" (2019), you explain how meaningful architecture was understood historically to be connected to harmonious musical atmospheres.[1] You trace this tradition from Vitruvius to the Renaissance and conclude with the Romantic theory of the 18th Century (e.g., the notion of *Stimmung*), when the conversation about musical atmospheres becomes more focused. However, this connection of meaningful architecture to musical harmony and musical ratios (like the Pythagorean numbers, for example) is always presented and understood as a theoretical argument. When Palladio uses such musical ratios in his architecture, he is clearly not actually interested in how music resonates in his buildings, nor does he focus on the sound that the materiality of his buildings will create. He trusts that by following the musical ratios and by translating them into space, the result will be by default harmonious. So, it seems to me that in that sense, the connection between architecture and music is not literal.

Alberto Pérez-Gómez: It is indeed expressed as a theoretical connection, yet one that has always been supported by Western culture's appreciation of the healing capacity of music in general. We actually do not know a great deal about how actual music sounded, for example, in ancient Greece. We know though, from the philosophical writings of the time and all the literature that surrounds this issue, that the experience of music was central in the way the Greeks articulated their language, for instance, with general ramifications for culture. In that way we know that people experienced the articulation of music as something felt. They valorized it as literally healing, and they connected the kind of articulation that the music expresses with the activity that took place in conjunction with its performance. For example, soldiers would go into battle with Dorian music, which was a particular articulation of the diatonic scale, different from other "modes."

Although we do not know how music really sounded in the buildings or the open air (people have tried to reconstruct it), we know that from the beginning of the Western tradition, music was a central experience that stood for an articulated environment—something that made you feel well and that was appropriate to what you were doing. It could be dance music, funerary music, dramatic music – accompanying classical plays, or religious music, for example, but not music for the sake of music itself; so, in this respect, understanding that music was "functional," we could argue that there was a literal connection. Later developments in relation to *Stimmung* in the late 18th and early 19th Century, furthermore, are different and must be qualified. On the one hand, starting with the questioning of classical theory's assumptions in the work of Claude Perrault, the connection between musical harmony and architectural beauty could no longer be taken for granted. Perrault actually postulated that beauty in architecture has nothing to do with the mathematics ruling the heavens and its harmonious ratios. But, on the other hand, and almost at the same time, music performance became much more important socially. Compared to the Renaissance or even to the 17th Century, people in the 18th Century really listened to much more music, yet another literal connection between architecture and music.

Angeliki Sioli: They did listen to music more in social situations, but this listening was not understood as an aesthetic phenomenon, like it is understood now, correct?

Alberto Pérez-Gómez: Yes, exactly. The aesthetization of music happens in the 19th Century, when people start to play and listen to music in public concert hall settings. In the 18th Century, music is still connected more tangibly to specific human actions. Think for example about Georg Philipp Telemann's music (*Tafelmusic*) to accompany dinners or meals of all types. But we have evidence that Europeans in general started to listen to much more music than before, and this music was explicitly connected to functions in everyday life. In contrast, up until the 10th Century music was performed in churches, occasionally in palaces and castles or rich people's living rooms, but not really for the people. This starts to change dramatically in the 18th Century. More to what you were asking, when Palladio thinks about the harmony in his buildings, he does not think about how music will sound well, or in relation to any kind of acoustic properties. But on the other hand, for example, when Vitruvius talks about it in the chapter on the theater, he is indeed evoking an acoustic experience. In Vitruvius the theater really appears as some kind of musical instrument, because that's where you have performance. So, as you may appreciate, while we can state the centrality of music in European culture since the Greeks, the nature of its connections to other cultural manifestations is real, yet anything but straightforward. Understanding the true nature of perception through phenomenology sheds light as to why this is so.

Angeliki Sioli: In the 18th Century, do we have any architectural treatises in which there is more interest—from the side of the architect—in how acoustics work or music is heard in space? With the writings of Nicolas Le Camus de Mézières, for example, it seems that this connection for the first time becomes more literal, as he really cares about how music is heard in the different rooms of a building.

Alberto Pérez-Gómez: I think you are probably right. Generally, though, where this appears very clearly is in 18th Century books by architects on theaters, like in Pierre Patte's writings.[2] The topic of acoustics interested him a lot, starting with the problem first stated by Vitruvius, but understood by Patte in more practical terms, certainly more similar to our discussions.

Angeliki Sioli: Again referring to your article, you write that like other sensorial stimuli, music qualifies our experience of place. You even discuss, as an example, the experience of walking in a city with our headphones on, listening to our own music. It is "a powerful instance of the true dimension of the present moment," you argue. Isn't it also the case that music can completely override place? For example, it is very common in open space offices, where the acoustic qualities of the rooms have not been considered properly, for people to put their headphones on in order to override both the bad acoustics and the lack of privacy, so as to concentrate, feel comfortable and work. In this case music does not qualify the true dimension of place, but overrides place, and I wonder whether this is actually a problem or not when it comes to design.

Alberto Pérez-Gómez: Well, I think this is similar to the question of whether the experience of being invested in a screen overrides your experience of place. Does it really completely override it, though? I don't think it does. Merleau-Ponty would actually say that it absolutely does not. It doesn't override your experience of place, because you know what is actually primary, you know, perhaps not through your representational consciousness, but you know. On that front, Merleau-Ponty offers a beautiful and funny example from the experience of being in the cinema. When we do not like something that is happening in the movie, let's say it is a scene of horror, we hide our eyes with our hands or we turn our heads so we do not look at the screen. What does that mean? It means that there is a primacy to the situated bodily experience. Our body knows we are safe. The screen does not override the place. So, I think, I would not agree that wearing headphones overrides the experience of an office. Absolutely not! It qualifies it and you can choose to give all your attention to your headphones, but if someone pulls your chair away, while you are listening to your music, you know what is primary and your body reacts to it. That's the real phenomenological contribution to this argument, that deeply contradicts the tendency we have in our culture of cybernetics to believe that music or screens override place and architecture.

Angeliki Sioli: There are theoretical voices arguing that a phenomenology of sound still needs to be developed, as a special kind of approach within phenomenology. Do you believe that it should indeed be a separate category for studying sound? Doesn't that contradict the whole idea of phenomenology?

Alberto Pérez-Gómez: It does indeed contradict it, and I certainly do not believe that we need a phenomenology of sound – though of course, even the way the term phenomenology is used is often vague, and it may be hard to grasp what is meant. Phenomenology basically argues that what we miss is the way that the sensory experience is cross-modal, it crosses over the different senses. That is the crux of Merleau-Ponty's critique of older psychological models of perception, recovered more recently by enactive cognitive scientists. So, of course we can talk about listening, because it is one of our senses, we can identify the category, but I think fundamentally what phenomenology would argue is that listening is not an emancipated mechanist condition. Rather we listen really through the vibrations that we feel in our body, something which by the way is really complicated when the issue is the representation of voice or sound. Maybe there is more work to be done on what it means to listen, though. David Michael Levin has a wonderful book on listening and hearing. It's called *The Listening Self: Personal Growth, Social Change and the Closure of Metaphysics* (2020). He uses the vocabulary of phenomenological psychology to distinguish four processes of listening and brings out related developments for music, psychotherapy, ethics, politics and ecology. This analysis substantiates his claim that the development of our listening capacity is a process that forms our characters as social beings and agents. Our self-development as auditory beings is necessary for the achievement of a just and democratic society, because, as he argues, ethical ideas and political principles require the realization of a communicative potential.[3] Anyway… what I am trying to say, when I say that there is more work to be done on what it means to listen, is that we do not really pay attention to what we listen to. We are always ahead of ourselves and we may choose to pay attention to something we listen or not.

Angeliki Sioli: Selectiveness is indeed a particularity of listening and hearing. You can tune in and out of a given acoustic context. You can literally be having dinner at a restaurant, completely unaware of what the person next to you says, because you focus let's say on the music (or the other way around). Hearing in that sense is very unique. Of course, somebody could say that in a similar way you can also direct your eyes towards one view or another but with hearing you do not even need to direct your ears necessarily to tune in and out of a sound condition.

Alberto Pérez-Gómez: It is indeed unique because you cannot shut down your hearing. And the hearing is not only the ears, it is also the body. That's why it is different to hear music performance live from hearing it through your headphones, or your audio system at home. The experiences are qualitatively distinct in emotional and cognitive range, and that's why we go to concerts. I think the real challenge in architecture is to understand this interwoven condition of all acoustic experience.

Angeliki Sioli: Speaking of this interwoven condition, have you been to places that have been purposefully designed to work with sound, like a concert hall, in which the experience was disappointing or even unexpectedly surprising? Have you visited buildings (outside the theater of Epidaurus, which I know you have) where the sound was very unique for you?

Alberto Pérez-Gómez: Yes, I definitely have. I think one of my most interesting experiences has been in Hans Scharoun's Berlin Philharmonic. Because I think there—and I experienced a concert in the building—if you close your eyes, you almost have the sense that you are, how can I put this, that you are in the countryside, that somehow the sound comes from everywhere. Although the orchestra is in the middle and the seating is all around, somehow the sound does not feel directional. It is like an expansive sound that reminds us of an outdoors condition. I do not know why, but this was the impression that I got, and that was quite unique. And I don't know how Hans Scharoun actually designed that. I know that it was not a totally rational operation, but it is absolutely remarkable. There are two concert halls in the building, a smaller and a bigger one. One is for chamber music and the bigger one is for symphony. It's the same principle for both of them, with the orchestra in the middle and the seating all around. Frank Ghery tried to follow the same spatial configuration in Los Angeles, but I have never experienced his building, and I have no idea whether Ghery's is equally good. I know that in other theatres emulating this "informal" seating arrangement surrounding the orchestra, the acoustics are problematic. It is a very tricky spatial problem because the orchestra has an orientation already; the first violins are on the left, the second violins are on the right, etc., and this is the organization that the composers base their work on. So, it's a tricky thing with the seating. Scharoun's philharmonic works in a magical way… I don't know how it works… I am not an expert. But that was truly my experience of that place.

Angeliki Sioli: To conclude, I wanted to ask you something not necessarily about sound and music but about atmospheres, more generally, because you have taught generations of designers at different Schools of Architecture. How do you guide students towards the creation of meaningful atmospheres (acoustic or not)? I am not looking for a recipe, of course, but I wonder how you approach the question of atmospheres with students.

Alberto Pérez-Gómez: The truth is that when it comes to design teaching, I usually supervise students that have their own agendas and interests, since they are Masters-level students working on their graduation theses. So, I need to guide them following what they wish to do. It is thus not always the case that the students bring to the table something that is amenable to these kinds of conversations. When the question of atmospheres does show up though, I try to make them pay attention to what we call program, whatever this program might be in relation to what they wish to design. I try to make them understand program through human situations, as potentially poetic moments than can then be articulated in words or through some kind of atmospheric sketches. From these points of departure, I attempt to move them in whatever direction they are seeking, by incorporating more concretely into the design some of these initial reflections. I have never run a full studio project emerging from these questions, but if I had the chance to do so, this is what I would do. Rather than exercises into the creation of form I would try to invite students imagine the situations that their projects would eventually frame, and discuss appropriate atmospheres related to these situations. One more thing that would be prominent, would also be an actual engagement with the materiality of the design itself, through making. I truly think that this is an important issue. The "material imagination" that Bachelard talks about, and how to get through the material to specific atmospheres, can only be achieved by "getting your hands dirty" as a student, by working at the woodshop, or the metal shop, creating artifacts with your hands, the materiality of which informs deeply the design process.

Angeliki Sioli: Such approach towards materiality would be particularly helpful for studying acoustic atmospheres in design studios as well. Sound atmospheres are not often addressed in architectural education; maybe they are topics discussed in specialized workshops but not in regular design studios usually. But by "getting your hands dirty," as you suggest, and engaging with the materiality, you can definitely approach aspects of the project's acoustic nature. Unfortunately, even when (in architectural education) we talk about atmospheres, we focus on visual atmospheres mainly, through renderings and drawings. Though, through models, or writing assignments, a student could evoke the sound of the imagined project.

Alberto Pérez-Gómez: I think the question of materiality is indeed key when it comes to architectural education (or even practice) and acoustic atmospheres. Because if you look at music just through rhythms, it becomes just a formal analogy. People have tried that a lot. But when we say a musical or acoustical atmosphere, what do we mean? It is really a complicated issue, because today it is mainly understood as acoustic efficiency—that as long as you can hear well the issue is resolved. While on the contrary the issue is always qualitative. The Roman Pantheon has a kind of musicality, for example, which has nothing to do with hearing well what other people around you are saying. It is a musicality that has to do with the reverberation of the place itself, which is of course a fundamental part of the whole atmosphere and the embodied experience of the building.

Angeliki Sioli: I agree. If we talk about the ancient theater of Epidaurous, for example, there is the technical fact that a voice, without the use of a microphone, can be heard across the theater and 10.000 people in the audience can hear the actors very clearly. But the actual embodied experience is so much more connected with the atmosphere of a performance and the place itself, than just this technical factor.

Alberto Pérez-Gómez: Precisely. It is the quality of the experience that makes the atmospheres, not just the fact that you need no amplification. The place adds inherent qualities to the music and the voices of actors performed and experienced, and ultimately, I would argue, a good writer can always describe the experience better than probably traditional forms of architectural representation can.

Notes

1. Alberto Pérez-Gómez, "Architecture as Musical Atmosphere," in *Atmosphere and Aesthetics, A Plural Perspective*, edited by T. Griffero and M. Tedeschini (London: Palgrave Macmillan, 2019).
2. For example: *Essay on Theatrical Architecture* (Paris, 1782) or *From the most Advantageous Ordinance to a Performance Hall, Relative to the Principles of Optics and Acoustics* (Paris, 1782).
3. David Michael Levin, *The Listening Self: Personal Growth, Social Change and the Closure of Metaphysics* (London; New York: Routledge, 2020).

18.

Places where Silence
is Eloquent

Ricardo L. Castro

This narrative emerges from personal experiences, which took place distant from each other, both in time and geography. They happened at different times of my life; nonetheless they are closely intertwined and clearly speak of silence, sound, and architecture.

In the early 1990s, I had the opportunity of visiting with some students, the Tairona area of the Sierra Nevada in northern Colombia. This is a mountainous region that has been, since times immemorial, the habitat for several indigenous groups— Tairona, Kogi, and Arhuaco among them. As my students and I were walking along the ancient path, which connects the coastal Tairona Eco-hab area with Pueblito, an archeological village nested in the Sierra, we came across some unusual features along the path:

> Tunneled passages through large rock formations are common along the paths... Often, specific segments of the path are paved with large slabs that are perfectly balanced and permit a slight tilting and repositioning. The weight of an individual walking on them is sufficient to cause them to tilt and hit a strategically placed supporting slab. The distinct sound that is produced resonates audibly throughout the thick tropical forest.[1]

Apparently, the purpose of this lithic sound-making device was to warn the arrival of intruders. Sound and architecture, or to be more precise landscaped infrastructure, as it were, became evident here at an acoustic and spatial scale penetrating the dense jungle. The echo of those lithic sounds still reverberates in recondite parts of my memory.

Ten years later, I had a similar experience while travelling in Japan. This time it took place indoors, in the Himeji Castle, a hilltop majestic complex situated in the city of the same name in the Hyōgo Prefecture, west of Osaka. There, I encountered for the first time a cunning strategy conceived by the fortification architects to announce the arrival of intruders: the Nightingale floor—as it is called. Located in the access halls of the castle, it consists of wooden planks that bend, producing a loud squeak under the weight of someone walking on them. They work in the same manner as the slabs in the Tairona path. The Himeji's Nightingale floors, as well as those in several other Japanese feudal castles, were elements, as I discovered later, of sophisticated ways, which Japanese have used to deal with sound, silence, and space. This is also clearly evident in Japanese traditional music which utilizes a variety of devices —percussion, wind, and strings— to penetrate the silence in rooms, courtyards, temples, and gardens. This preoccupation with silence and sound seems to prevail in many aspects of Japanese life. Expressed, for instance, in the believers' ritual short clapping, at the entrance of the main building in a Shinto shrine, when they begin praying to call the "Kami" or divinity, and also to ward off evil spirits.

I had a memorable experience of this condition when I saw and heard for the first time, a Japanese sound machine called "Sōzou." It is basically a garden water fountain consisting of a bamboo rocker arm, which collects water from a stream and hits a rock through the process of filling and emptying water. The one I experienced in operation was located in the garden of the main Zen temple complex of Shisen-dō in Kyoto. The sound of the bamboo cylinder hitting a rock every time the water discharges is conceived to ward off animals but, undoubtedly, it is directly related to the concept of "ma," (間), silence or interval between notes.[2] I often experience this when listening to a concert trying to concentrate in the caesura moments, which reminds me of architectural galleries, where columns and their in-between spaces create the whole, reinforcing thus the thought that music is made by both the notes played and the silence in between.[3]

Some 20 years ago, I had the opportunity of travelling to Peru to visit some of the Inca architecture along the short stretch of the Inca trail (a two-day hike) near Cusco, and in the surrounding areas, particularly the Sacred Valley of the Incas. One of the places I visited, Tipon, left me with a deep impression. This is an extraordinary landscape dating from the 15th Century when the Inca consolidated their power. The site comprises of "a set of 13 large, integrated, central terraces that stair-step down a former ravine, the terraces formed by handsome, carefully designed stone walls that are judged to be among the finest in all Peru."[4] Evident throughout is the extraordinary hydraulic complex of stone fountains, a main canal, and smaller canals that served to irrigate the agricultural fields. When I visited the site, I had the privilege of being the only visitor—today it has, no doubt, become more touristy—although I hope, it is still not along the beaten path of tours. The sound of the water falling in the stone fountains, moving along the stone canals, delicately breaks, in many different places, the silence of the enclosed ravine where the terraces are tucked in.

Related to my experience in Tipon was my annual visits from 2006 to 2016 to one of the most secluded parts of the Boboli Garden in Florence, the Fountain of the Mo-

Figure 1: Detail (left) and upper section (right) of the Mostaccini Fountain in the Boboli Gardens, Florence, Courtesy: Ricardo L. Castro. ©RLC-2008. (Plate 22, p. 304)

staccini, (literally, Fountain of the Little Ugly Faces).[5] The fountain, dating from the early 17th Century, is basically a canal that runs on top of a stair stepped wall along 16 contiguous sections, which run the entire length of an ample gravel alley.[6] Each one of the sections was designed as a watering trough for birds, ending in a bestiary head, which functions as a spitter, letting the rainwater gush through its mouth, into a small basin, and down the next trough, to the next spitting head (Figure 1).

As one walks up or down the graveled alley, each sculpted mustached face of the water work, helps to control the flow and sound of the water, contributing to the aural and kinetic experience of a memorable place. Each section of the waterworks, seems to serve as a phrase of a sound score, which is accompanied by the melodic sound of crushed gravel under the weight of steps, varying in intensity depending on one's tread. The whole acts as a memory connector. It helps me recall that the etymology of melody refers to the ancient Greek word for limb, "melos" (μέλος). It also brings together similar memories of other places, which rush to my conscious imagination and lead me to think of the "crush" sound I have heard while walking in baroque gardens and public parks.

There are many onomatopoeias, for instance the squeak sounds of climbing wooden stairs, which surface in my mind to attempt describing what I heard when walking over many of the surfaces that I have experienced and described in this coda. The repertoire can be easily enlarged as memory helps new places to emerge. In all these cases, the interval, the emptiness, occupied by silence, acquires eloquence as it becomes the necessary backdrop for sound to achieve a unique and memorable spatial presence.

Notes

1.   Richardo L.Castro, "Sounding the Path: Dwelling and Dreaming.", in Alberto Pérez-Gómez and Stephen Parcell (eds.), *Chora Three: Intervals in the Philosophy of Architecture* (Montreal: McGill University Press, 1999), 39–40.

2.   See Donald Richie, *Viewed Sideways Writings on Culture and Style in Contemporary Japan.* (Berkeley: Stone Bridge Press, 2011), Kindle Edition.

3.   Gunter Nitschke, "MA: Place, Space, Void", at *Kyoto Journal*. May 16, 2018, https://www.kyotojournal.org/culture-arts/ma-place-space-void/ accessed May 20, 2020.

4.   Kenneth R. Wright with Gordon McEwan and Ruth M. Wright, *Tipon: Water Engineering Masterpiece of the Inca Empire* (Reston: American Society of Civil Engineers, 2006), 1. This is a definitive treatise, amply illustrated, on the hydraulic complex of Tipon.

5.   Susan Mahr, "Giardino di Boboli (Boboli Gardens), Florence, Italy" at *Wisconsin Master Gardener* website, February 27, 2017. https://mastergardener.extension.wisc.edu/files/2017/02/BoboliGardens.pdf Accessed July 21, 2020.

6.   The alley where the fountain is located defines part of the southern limit of the garden and runs East to West almost parallel to the main axis of the garden, called the Vittolone (Cyprus Road).

About the Editors

Angeliki Sioli, PhD is an assistant professor of architecture at the Chair of Methods of Analysis and Imagination, TU Delft, where she was awarded the 2021 Comenius Teaching Fellowship by the Dutch Ministry of Education, Culture and Science. She obtained a professional degree in architecture from the University of Thessaly, Greece and was granted a post-professional master's degree in architectural theory and history from the National Technical University of Athens. She completed her Doctor of Philosophy in the history and theory of architecture at McGill University. She is a registered architect and has worked on projects ranging from residential and office buildings to the design of small-scale objects and books. Her research seeks connections between architecture and literature in the public realm of the city, focusing on aspects of atmospheres and embodied perception of place in the urban environment. She has edited the collected volume *Reading Architecture: Literary Imagination and Architectural Experience* (Routledge, 2018). Before joining TU Delft, Sioli taught both undergraduate and graduate courses at McGill University, in Canada; Tec de Monterrey, in Mexico; and Louisiana State University in the US.

Elisavet Kiourtsoglou (1981) holds a diploma of Architecture (University of Thessaly, Greece), a post-professional master's degree in architectural theory and history from the National Technical University of Athens and a PhD in Architecture (Université Paris 8). Her thesis on the relation of music to architecture in Iannis Xenakis' work has been awarded the *Prix de la Recherche de l'Académie d'Architecture* (Paris, 2017). Her research interests focus on the analogy of music and sound to space. She prepares a monograph on rythme of music and architecture in Xenakis' work (Athens: Nefeli, 2022). She has tought in Schools of Architecture in France ENSA Paris-Malaquais, ENSA Versailles and ENSA de Strasbourg. Currently she is assistant professor at the Departement of Culture, Creative Media and Industries of University of Thessaly, Greece and a post-doc fellow of the Greek State Scholarships Foundation (IKY) for a research on the relations of theory of music harmony and architectural treatises.

About the Authors

Anna Ulrikke Andersen is a Norwegian architectural historian and filmmaker, currently a postdoctoral researcher on *Disobedient Buildings* at the University of Oxford. She holds a PhD in architecture from the Bartlett School of Architecture, where she focused on a series of windows, literal and figurative, in the life and work of Christian Norberg-Schulz. Her book *Christian Norberg-Schulz: An Architectural History through the Essay film* (2022) was published with Bloomsbury Press. In 2018/2019 she held a Fellowship at Harvard Film Study Center, where she began exploring filmmaking, sculpture, and essay writing as methods to investigate the architecture experienced by people living with chronic illness. She continues exploring these ideas as a 2021 Fellow of Future Architecture, the European Architecture Programme.

Timothy Carey is a designer and musician working at the intersections of architecture and the performing arts. He earned a Bachelor of Arts in Music and the History of Art and Architecture from Brown University and subsequently completed a Master of Architecture at Harvard University, with coursework in acoustics and sound studies at the Massachusetts Institute of Technology. His graduate thesis, focused on the relationships between concert hall design and recording studio design, was published in *Platform*, a publication of the Harvard Graduate School of Design. Timothy has worked most recently in the offices of Selldorf Architects, REX, and Maryann Thompson Architects, focused on the design of innovative spaces for art, music, theater, and dance. He is also active as an orchestral clarinetist in New York City.

Ricardo L. Castro, RCA, FRAIC, received the degree of Arquitecto from Universidad de Los Andes, Bogotá as well as an M.A. in Art History and an M.Arch at the University of Oregon. He has taught at the Universidad de Los Andes, Bogotá, the University of Oregon, Kansas State University and l'Université Laval, where he received the equivalence of a doctorate in 1977. He is currently an Associate Professor of Architecture (Post-Retirement) at McGill University in Montreal, where he has taught since 1982. He has participated in photographic exhibitions in Canada, Colombia, and the United States. He contributes criticism and photographs to local and international architectural publications and is the author of numerous articles and three books: Rogelio Salmona (1998), Arthur Erickson: Critical Works (2006), co-authored with Nicholas Olsberg, and Rogelio Salmona: A Tribute (2008). He was inducted into the Royal Canadian Academy of Arts in 2015.

Joseph L. Clarke is an assistant professor of art history at the University of Toronto and the author of *Echo's Chambers: Architecture and the Idea of Acoustic Space* (2021). Clarke has held visiting fellowships at the Max Planck Institute for the History of Science in Berlin and the Canadian Centre for Architecture in Montreal. He is licensed as an architect in the United States and has worked at Eisenman Architects and Skidmore, Owings & Merrill.

Carlotta Darò holds a PhD in art history (Università di Roma La Sapienza, University of Paris 1 Panthéon-Sorbonne), is associate professor at ENSA Paris-Malaquais, and member of the Laboratoire Infrastructure Architecture Territoire. Her research explores the impact of sound technologies, telecommunications infrastructure and media on architectural and urban culture in the 19th and 20th Centuries. She is the author of the books *Avant-gardes sonores en architecture* (Presses du réel, 2013) and *Les murs du son: le Poème électronique au Pavillon Philips* (B2, 2015), and has published several articles. In 2016 Darò organized an international conference entitled *Architectural Acoustics: theories, practices, cultures* (Centre Pompidou, Paris).

Michael de Beer is a multidisciplinary designer and an aspiring storyteller who believes in building commonality (Ubuntu philosophy, "I am because we are"). To recognize our common humanity is to be able to explore alternative ways of seeing and discovering the possibilities that bind us. Notable achievements include: being a key designer of the DNK (by West 8), a commercial and residential district vision in Amsterdam, awarded the ARC2020 stedenbouwkundig award for best urban design project of the year; having served as a steering committee member for the Urban Design Institute of South Africa; and having successfully organized talks, workshops and conferences on public space, architecture and cities; as well as having been a co-editor for Atlantis magazine, a POSAD publication. Michael is committed to enabling a better future.

James Deaville teaches Music in the School for Studies in Art and Culture at Carleton University, Ottawa. He edited *Music in Television* (Routledge, 2011), with Christina Baade co-edited *Music and the Broadcast Experience* (Oxford, 2016), and co-edited *The Oxford Handbook on Music and Advertising* (2021). His publications have appeared in the *Journal of the American Musicological Society, Journal of the Society for American Music, American Music, Sound and the Moving Image*, and *Music and Politics*, and he has contributed to books published by Oxford, Cambridge, Routledge, Chicago and Yale, among others. Among other articles, he published "Le Chant du désert: The

Arab-Islamic World in Late Nineteenth-Century French Chansons and Piano Music" in *Music in Art* (2017), a study of Orientalist representation in sheet music.

Ross K. Elfline is an art and architectural historian whose work on radical architectural practices in the 1960s and 70s concentrates on the architectural implications of non-tectonic mediums. He has published widely on the Italian group Superstudio, the Viennese collective Haus-Rucker-Co., and other counterculture designers. He was a lead consultant on the acclaimed Walker Art Center exhibition Hippie Modernism. Currently, he is at work on a book focusing on the intersection of architecture and performance in the United States circa 1970 that considers how urban streets became contested sites through which to agitate for a sense of the common good amid rampant privatization. He is Associate Professor of Art History at Carleton College, where he offers courses on the history, theory, and criticism of art and architecture since 1945.

Clemens Finkelstein is a doctoral candidate at Princeton University. His work explores the History and Theory of Architecture at the field's junction with Media Studies and the History and Philosophy of Science and Technology. His dissertation investigates the *phenomenotechnique* of vibration as an epistemic thing between 188x-194x, tracing its formative impact on art and architectural space theories, planetary ecologies of the built/natural environments, and the conception of atmospheric control through modern design. A complimentary project examines the cybernetics of operative ambience and sensory substitution design in the total environment of vibe, 195x-197x. His articles and reviews have appeared in several edited volumes and journals, including *Iconology of Abstraction: The Language of Non-Figurative Images* (Routledge, 2020). He is a Fulbright scholar, received scholarships from Harvard University (2015-2017), Princeton University's Lowell M. Palmer Fellowship (2018-2019), support from the Princeton-Mellon Initiative in Architecture, Urbanism & the Humanities, and the History of Science Society.

Federica Goffi is Interim Director, Professor of Architecture, and Co-Chair of the PhD and MAS Program in Architecture at the Azrieli School of Architecture and Urbanism at Carleton University, Ottawa, Canada. Her book, *Time Matter[s]: Invention and Re-imagination in Built Conservation: The Unfinished Drawing and Building of St. Peter's in the Vatican,* was published by Ashgate in 2013. Her recent edited volumes include *Marco Frascari's Dream House: A Theory of Imagination* (Routledge 2017); *InterVIEWS: Insights and Introspection in Doctoral Research in Architecture* (Routledge 2019), and the co-edited *Ceilings and Dreams: The Architecture of Levity* (Routledge 2019). She is the editor of a special issue of *Architecture and Culture*, titled, *And Yet It Moves: Ethics, Power, and Politics in the Stories of Collecting, Archiving and Displaying of Drawings* *and Models* (Routledge 2021) and *The Routledge Companion to Architectural Drawings and Models: From Translating to Archiving, Collecting and Displaying* (Routledge, 2022). She holds a PhD in Architecture and Design Research (Virginia Tech), a *Dottore in Architettura* (University of Genoa), and she is a licensed architect in her native country, Italy.

Klaske Havik is Professor of *Methods of Analysis and Imagination* at Delft University of Technology. She relates architectural and urban questions about the use, experience and imagination of place to literary language in her book *Urban Literacy: Reading and Writing Architecture* (2014). Other publications include *Writingplace, Investigations in Architecture and Literature* (2016) and *Architectural Positions: Architecture, Modernity and the Public Sphere* (2009, co-edited with Tom Avermaete and Hans Teerds). Klaske Havik initiated the platform *Writingplace* and organized the international conference on architecture and fiction: *Writingplace: Literary Methods in Architectural Research and Design* (2013). For architecture journal OASE she edited, among other issues, OASE#98 *Narrating Urban Landscapes* (2018), OASE#91 *Building Atmosphere* (2013), *OASE#85, Productive Uncertainty,* (2011) and OASE 70 *Architecture and Literature* (2007). Havik's literary work appeared in Dutch poetry collections and literary magazines. Havik is editor of the *Writingplace Journal*, and chair of the EU Cost Action *Writing Urban Places*.

Paul Holmquist is assistant professor of Architecture at Louisiana State University whose research and teaching focus on the interrelationship of architecture, political theory and theory of technology, particularly in terms of conceptions and experience of the public realm. He holds a Doctor of Philosophy in Architectural History and Theory from McGill University where his dissertation examined Claude-Nicolas Ledoux's architectural theory in relation to the moral and political philosophy of Jean-Jacques Rousseau. Paul has taught architectural history, theory and design at universities in the United States and Canada, and his research has been published in *Chora 7: Intervals in the Philosophy of Architecture, Reading Architecture: Literary Imagination and Architectural Experience,* and *The Figure of Knowledge: Conditioning Architectural Theory, 1960s-1990s.*

Pamela Jordan is a licensed architect (USA, LEED AP) who uses sound-based methodologies to analyse historic built environments, including ancient sanctuaries, places of worship, military installations, infrastructural ruins, and cultural landscapes. Her work is grounded in independent research, institutional affiliations and collaborations based in architecture, acoustics, heritage, art, and psychoacoustics. The results of her research have featured in academic, peer-reviewed publications, applied research studies, and contemporary art spaces and exhibitions. She is also the guest-editor of "Sounding Heritage", issue 9.2 of *Change Over Time* (2021, University of Pennsylvania Press). Her research has been supported by the Alexander von Humboldt Foundation (DE), the HEAD Genuit Foundation (DE), the Netherlands Organization for Scientific Research (NL), and the Society of Architectural Historians (USA). Pamela holds master's degrees in architecture and historic preservation from the University of Pennsylvania and is a doctoral candidate at the University of Amsterdam's Centre for Ancient Studies and Archaeology.

Alberto Pérez-Gómez was born in Mexico City in 1949, where he studied architecture and practiced. In 1983 he became Director of Carleton University's School of Architecture. From January 1987 until his retirement in 2020, he occupied the Bronfman Chair of Architectural History at McGill University, where he founded the History and Theory Master's and Doctoral Programs (https://www.mcgill.ca/architecture/events/introduction). He has lectured extensively around the world and is the author of numerous articles and books. His *Architecture and the Crisis of Modern Science* (MIT Press, 1983) won the Hitchcock Award. Later books include *Polyphilo* (MIT Press, 1992), *Architectural Representation and the Perspective Hinge* (MIT Press, 1997), *Built upon Love* (MIT Press, 2006), and more recently *Timely Meditations* (RightAngle, 2016), a two-volume collection of essays, and *Attunement* (MIT Press, 2016), examining the centrality of atmosphere in architecture through history, neurophenomenology and narrative language. Pérez-Gómez was also co-editor of a seven-volume series of books entitled *CHORA: Intervals in the Philosophy of Architecture*. He is currently working on an *Alliterative Lexicon of Architectural Memories*.

Cécile Regnault is an architect and designer of sound environments. She is Professor in the School of Architecture of Lyon, reseacher at EVSLAURe, UMR 5600 CNRS, University of Lyon, chair of the Master's degree program. She is the founder of Collaborative Experiments field of study. Her main research concerns the sensible experiences of the atmospheres, as well as the representations of space focusing on the sense of hearing. Her PhD thesis focused on the visual representations of the sound phenomena and their applications in urban design projects. She closely follows the emergence of the new professions as sound or light designer in these projects. She leads in parallel sound experiments in the public place and since 2007 is the director of Aciréne (Studio of cultural and aesthetic Treatment of sound environment). She promotes sound culture and good practices in urban planning by leading actions during the Sound Week (La semaine du Son), under the auspices of UNESCO.

Karen Van Lengen, FAIA, is the Kenan Professor of Architecture at the University of Virginia. She is a designer that champions the collaboration of the visual and aural attributes of space to effectively create more sensorial places in our private and public realms. She has emphasized the importance of communicative architecture as a means of social and political engagement. Her sound animations, (with Jim Welty), and speculative design projects (with Joel Sanders) have been exhibited and collected in major national and international museums. She is also the author of several publications on aural architecture, and public "sound art". Van Lengen was Dean of the Architecture School from 1999-2009, following her Directorship of the Department of Architecture at Parsons New School University in New York City. Van Lengen began her professional career as an Associate at IM Pei & Partners, before founding her own award-winning design firm in New York City. She received her B.A. from Vassar College, and her MArch from Columbia University.

Michael Windover is associate professor of Art and Architectural History and Assistant Director of the School for Studies in Art and Culture at Carleton University in Ottawa. He is cross-appointed to the Institute for Comparative Studies in Literature, Art and Culture and the School of Industrial Design at Carleton and is adjunct curator of design at Ingenium: Canada's Museums of Science and Innovation. A historian of modern architecture and design, he is author of *Art Deco: A Mode of Mobility* (Presses de l'Université du Québec, 2012) and co-editor with Bridget Elliott of *The Routledge Research Companion to Art Deco* (2019). He is also co-author with Anne MacLennan of *Seeing, Selling, and Situating Radio in Canada, 1922-1956* (Dalhousie Architectural Press, 2017). His research has appeared in *The Journal of the Society for the Study of Architecture in Canada, Architectural History, RACAR, Buildings & Landscapes*, and *The Journal of Architecture*.

List of illustrations

Bibliography

[Anonymous]. "A Teetotal Nightclub Where Personal Experience is All." *Life* (April 4, 1969): 28–29.

Andersen, Anna Ulrikke "The Death of the Chemist: the role of sound in the life and work of Christian Norberg-Schulz explored through the essay form in film and writing" in *InForma Journal,* no. 12 (2019):176–187.

Araoz, Gustavo. "Conservation Philosophy and Its Development: Changing Understandings of Authenticity and Significance." *Heritage & Society* 6, no. 2 (2013): 144–54.

Arendt, Hannah. *The Human Condition*. Chicago: Chicago University Press, 1958.

Augoyard, Jean-François. *"Éléments pour une théorie des ambiances architecturales et urbaines"*. In *Les Cahiers de la recherche architecturale*, nos 42/43, (1998): 13–23.

Augoyard, Jean-François. "L'environnement sensible et les ambiances architecturales." In *L'espace géographique* no. 4 (1995): 302–317.

Augoyard, Jean-François. "Les qualités sonores de la territorialité humaine." In *Architecture & Comportement*, no. 7 (1991): 13–24.

Augoyard, Jean-François. "Un instrumentarium urbain." In *Urbanités sonores*, Michel Grosjean and Isaac Joseph, (1989), 14. https://hal.archives-ouvertes.fr/hal-02104257

Auret, Hendrik Andries. "Care, Place and Architecture: a critical reading of Christian Norberg-Schulz's architectural interpretation of Martin Heidegger's philosophy," PhD thesis, the University of the Free State, 2015.

Bach, Jonathan. "The Berlin Wall after the Berlin Wall: Site into Sight." *Memory Studies* 9, no. 1 (2016): 48–62.

Bacon, Mardges. *Le Corbusier in America: Travels in the Land of the Timid*. Cambridge: MIT Press, 2001.

Baker, Frederick. "The Berlin Wall: Production, Preservation and Consumption of a 20th-Century Monument." *Antiquity* 67, no. 257 (December 2, 1993): 709–33.

Barnett, Kyle. "Furniture Music: The Phonograph as Furniture, 1900–1930." *Journal of Popular Music Studies* 18, no. 3 (2006): 301–324.

Barron, Michael. *Auditorium Acoustics and Architectural Design*. London/New York: Spon Press, 2010 [1993].

Barthélémy, Jean-Hugues. "Fifty Key Terms in the Work of Gilbert Simondon." Translated by Arne De Boever. In: *Gilbert Simondon: Being and Technology*. Eds. Arne De Boever, Alex Murray, Jon Roffe, and Ashley Woodward. Edinburgh: Edinburgh University Press, 2012.

Bégout, Bruce. *Le concept d'ambiance*. Paris: Seuil, 2020.

Benton, Tim. "The Sacred and the Search for Myths." In *Le Corbusier Architect of the Century*, 238–49. London: Arts Council of Great Britain, 1987.

Biennial Census of Manufactures: 1921. Washington, DC: Government Printing Office, 1924.

Bienz, Peter. *Le Corbusier und die Musik*. Wiesbaden: Vieweg, 1999.

Bijsterveld, Karin, ed. *Soundscapes of the Urban Past : Staged Sound as Mediated Cultural Heritage*. Bielefeld: transcript Verlag, 2013.

Bijsterveld, Karin. *Sonic Skills: Listening for Knowledge in Science, Medicine and Engineering (1920s–Present)*. London: Palgrave Macmillan, 2019.

Birksted, Jan Kenneth. *Le Corbusier and the Occult*. Cambridge, MA: MIT Press, 2009.

Böhme, Gernot. *Atmospheric Architectures: The Aesthetics of Felt Spaces*. Edited and translated by A.-Chr. Engels-Schwarzpaul. New York: Bloomsbury Academic, 2017.

Böhme, Gernot. "Atmosphere as a Fundamental Concept of a New Aesthetics." In *Thesis Eleven*, 36, 1993.

Borch, Christian. ed. *Architectural Atmospheres: On the Experience and Politics of Architecture* Basel: Birkhäuser, 2014.

Borgmann Albert, *Technology and the Character of Contemporary Life. A Philosophical Inquiry*. Chicago and London: The University of Chicago Press, 1987/1984.

Bowman, Rob. *Soulsville U.S.A.: The Story of Stax Records*. New York: Schirmer, 1997.

Brandon W. Joseph. "The Tower and the Line: Toward a Genealogy of Minimalism," in *Grey Room* no. 27 (2007): 58–81.

Broad, Stephen. "Messiaen and *Art Sacré*." In *Messiaen Perspectives 1: Sources and Influences*, edited by Christopher Dingle and Robert Fallon, 269–78. Burlington, VT: Ashgate, 2013.

Brown, Adrienne. *The Black Skyscraper: Architecture and the Perception of Race*. Baltimore: Johns Hopkins University Press, 2017.

Burbank, Emily. *Be Your Own Decorator*. New York: Dodd, Mead and Company, 1923.

Burd, Alexander. "Acoustic Modelling—Design Tool or Research Project?". In *Auditorium Acoustics: The Proceedings of an International Symposium on Architectural Acoustics*, edited by Robin MacKenzie, 73–85. London: Applied Science Publishers, 1975.

Buskin, Richard. "Classic Tracks: The Ronettes 'Be My Baby'". *Sound on Sound* 22, no. 6 (2007): 104–113.

Butler, Shane, and Sarah Nooter, eds. *Sound and the Ancient Senses*. London: Routledge, 2019.

Caleb Kelly, ed. *Sound,* London; Cambridge, Mass.: Whitechapel Art Gallery and The MIT Press, 2011.

Carpo, Mario. *The Second Digital Turn: Design Beyond Intelligence*. Cambridge: MIT Press, 2017.

Chanan, Michael. *Repeated Takes: A Short History of Recording and Its Effects on Music.* New York: Verso, 1995.

Clark, Bruce. *Neocybernetics and Narrative.* Minneapolis: University of Minnesota Press, 2014.

Clarke, Joseph. "Iannis Xenakis and the Philips Pavilion". *The Journal of Architecture*; 17, no 2, (2012): 213–229.

Cogan, Jim and William Clark. *Temples of Sound: Inside the Great Recording Studios.* San Francisco: Chronicle Books, 2003.

Corbin, Alain. *Time, Desire and Horror: Towards a History of the Senses.* 1991. Translated by Jean Birrell. Cambridge, UK: Polity, 1995.

Covell, Alwyn T. "Music in the Home: What Modern Furniture Offers to the Music Lover." *Style in Home Furnishing* (February 1916): 2–5.

Cox, Christoph. "Von Musik zum Klang: Sein als Zeit in der Klangunst," in *Sonambiente Berlin: Klang Kunst/Sound Art.* Edited by Helga de la Morte-Haber, et al. Heidelberg: Kehrer Verlag, 2006.

Crary, Jonathan. *Techniques of the Observer: On Vision and Modernity in the Nineteenth Century.* Cambridge: MIT Press, 1992.

Cremer, Lothar. "Reichardt, Walter 1903–1985." *The Journal of the Acoustical Society of America* 78, no. 5 (1985): 1915.

Dan Lander and Micah Lexier, eds. *Sound by Artists.* Toronto: Art Metropole, 1990.

Darò Carlotta. *Les Murs du Son.* Paris : Editions B2, 2015.

Darò, Carlotta. "Lines for Listening: On Gustave Lyon's Geometrical Approach to Acoustics." *The Journal of Architecture* 23, no. 6 (2018): 881–902, special issue: *Sound Modernities: Histories of Media and Modern Architecture*, edited by Sabine von Fischer and Olga Touloumi.

Daston, Lorraine and Peter Galison. *Objectivity.* New York, NY: Zone Books, 2007.

Day, Brian F. "A Tenth-scale Model Audience." *Applied Acoustics* 1, no. 2 (April 1968): 121–35.

Day, Jo, ed. *Making Senses of the Past: Toward a Sensory Archaeology.* Carbondale, IL: Southern Illinois University Press, 2013.

Day, Timothy. *A Century of Recorded Music: Listening to Musical History.* New Haven: Yale University Press, 2000.

De Boever, Arne, Alex Murray, Jon Roffe, and Ashley Woodward (Eds.). *Gilbert Simondon: Being and Technology.* Edinburgh: Edinburgh University Press, 2012.

De Heer Jean, Tazelaar Kees. *From Harmony to Haos. Le Corbusier, Varèse, Xenakis and Le Poème Electronique.* Amsterdam : Duizend en Een Uitgeverij, 2017.

De Wolfe, Elsie. *The House in Good Taste.* New York: The Century Co., 1913.

Deaville, James. "The Well-Mannered Auditor: Zones of Attention and the Imposition of Silence in the Domestic Public Sphere of the 19th Century." In *Oxford Handbook of Music Listening in the 19th & 20th Centuries*, edited by Christian Thorau and Hansjakob Ziemer, 55–75. New York: Oxford University Press, 2019.

Delalande François. *"Il faut être constamment un immigré", Entretiens avec Xenakis.* Paris: Buchet/ Chastel-INA, 1997.

Douglas, Paul H. "Wages and Hours of Labor in 1919." *Journal of Political Economy* 29, no. 1 (January 1921): 78–80.

Dowling, David. *Mrs. Dalloway, Mapping Streams of Consciousness.* Boston, CA: Twayne Publishers, 1991.

Dreyfus L. Hubert in "Why the Mood *in* the Room and the Mood *of* the Room Should be Important to Architects," in *From The Things Themselves: Architecture and Phenomenology*, edited by Jacquet Benoit and Vincent Giraud, 23–39. Kyoto: Kyoto University Press, 2013.

Dunlap, Richard Stockton. "Reassessing Ronchamp: The Historical Context, Architectural Discourse and Design Development of Le Corbusier's Chapel Notre Dame-du-Haut." Ph.D. dissertation, London School of Economic and Political Science, 2014.

Earth Kultur. "Ein Ort Der Stille Auf Dem Ehemaligen Todesstreifen: Interview Mit Rainer Just," 2013.

Elie, Paul. "30 Variations and a Microphone". *The New York Times*, 7 Sept 2012.

Ellsworth, Therese and Susan Wollenberg, eds. *The Piano in Nineteenth-Century British Culture: Instruments, Performers and Repertoire.* Aldershot, UK: Ashgate, 2007.

Erhorn, Philip C. "Audio Console Design Notes". *Journal of the Audio Engineering Society*, 4 no. 2 (Apr. 1956): 65–71.

Evans, Robin. *The Projective Cast: Architecture and Its Three Geometries.* Cambridge, MA: MIT Press, 1995.

Feather, Leonard. *Encyclopedia of Jazz.* New York: Horizon, 1960.

Fechner, Gustav Theodor. *Elemente der Psychophysik.* Leipzig: Breitkopf & Härtel, 1860.

Fischer, Sabine von. "A Visual Imprint of Moving Air: Methods, Models, and Media in Architectural Sound Photography, ca. 1930." *Journal of the Society of Architectural Historians* 76, no. 3 (September 2017): 326–48.

French, Lillie Hamilton. *Homes and their Decoration.* New York: Dodd, Mead and Company, 1903.

Fuhrmann, Wolfgang. "The Intimate Art of Listening: Music in the Private Sphere During the Nineteenth Century" In *Oxford Handbook of Music Listening in the 19th & 20th Centuries*, edited by Christian Thorau and Hansjakob Ziemer, 277–311. New York: Oxford University Press, 2019.

Furlong, William. ed. *Audio Arts: Discourse and Practice in Contemporary Art.* London: Academy Editions, 1994.

Furuhata, Yuriko. "The Fog Medium: Visualizing and Engineering the Atmosphere" in *Screening Genealogies: From Optical Device to Environmental Medium*, edited by Craig Buckley, Rüdiger Campe, and Francesco Casetti, 187–213. Amsterdam: Amsterdam University Press, 2019.

Fuss, Diana. *The sense of an Interior: Four Writers and the Rooms that Shaped Them*. New York; London: Routledge, 2015.

Gilroy, Paul. *The Black Atlantic: Modernity and Double Consciousness*. Cambridge, MA: Harvard University Press, 1993.

Godwin, Jocelyn. *Athanasius Kircher: un homme de la Renaissance à la quête du savoir perdu*. Paris: Homes ad Hudson, 1980. (trad. S. Matton, J.-J. Pauvert).

Godwin, Jocelyn. *Théâtre du monde*. Paris: Actes Sud, 2009.

Goodman, Steve. *Sonic Warfare: Sound, Affect, and the Ecology of Fear*. Cambridge, MA: The MIT Press, 2010.

Gorrell, Lorraine. *The Nineteenth-Century German Lied*. Portland, OR: Amadeus, 1993.

Granata, Charles. *Wouldn't It Be Nice: Brian Wilson and the Making of the Beach Boys' Pet Sounds*. Chicago: Chicago Review Press, 2016.

Grietzer, Peli. "A Theory of Vibe," *Glass–Bead Journal, Site 1: Logic Gate, the Politics of the Artifactual Mind* (2017).

Grietzer, Peli. "Ambient Meaning: Mood, Vibe, System." Ph.D. dissertation, Harvard University, Cambridge, MA, 2018.

Hal Foster. *The Art – Architecture Complex*. London: Verso, 2013.

Halttunen, Karen. "From Parlor to Living Room: Domestic Space, Interior Decoration, and the Culture of Personality." In *Consuming Visions: Accumulation and Display of Goods in America 1880–1920*, edited by Simon J. Bronner, 157–189. New York: Norton, 1989.

Harris, Dianne. "A Tiny Orchestra in the Living Room: High-Fidelity Sound, Stereo Systems, and the Postwar House." In *Making Suburbia: New Histories of Everyday America*, edited by John Archer, Paul J. P. Sandul and Katherine Solomonson, 305–328. Minneapolis: University of Minnesota Press, 2015.

Hayburn, Robert F. *Papal Legislation on Sacred Music: 95 AD to 1977 AD*. Collegeville, MN: Liturgical Press, 1979.

Heatley, Michael. *Jimi Hendrix Gear: The Guitars, Amps & Effects that Revolutionized Rock 'n' Roll*. Minneapolis, MN: Voyageur Press, 2009.

Helmholtz, Hermann von. *Die Lehre von den Tonempfindungen als physiologische Grundlage für die Theorie der Musik*. Heidelberg, 1863.

Hendrix, Jimi. The Jimi Hendrix Experience. *Electric Ladyland*. Reprise Records, 2RS6307, 2 x Vinyl LP, 1968.

Hermann, Thomas, Andy Hunt, John G. Neuhoff (Eds.). *The Sonification Handbook*. Berlin: Logos, 2011.

Heynen, Hilde. *Architecture and Modernity: A Critique*. Cambridge, Mass: MIT, 1999.

Higgs Eric, Andrew Light and David Strong. *Technology and the Good Life?* Chicago; London: The University of Chicago Press, 2000.

Høeg, Jan and Ola Rypdal, *Ris kirke 1932–2007*. Oslo: Ris Menighetsråd, 2007.

Hvattum, Mari et.al. eds, *An Eye for Place: Christian Norberg-Schulz: Architect, Historian and Editor*. Oslo: Akademisk publisering, 2009.

Izzo Leo. "La Genesi compositiva del "Poème Electronique" di Edgard Varèse". *Il Saggiatore musicale*, 22, no. 1 (2015): 61–96.

Jethro, Duane. *Aesthetics of Power: Heritage Formation and the Senses in Post Apartheid South Africa*. London: Bloomsbury, 2019.

Johanna Burton, ed. *Mel Bochner: Language, 1966–2006*. Chicago: Art Institute of Chicago, 2007.

Jokilehto, Jukka. "Considerations on Authenticity and Integrity in World Heritage Context." *City & Time* 2, no. 1 (2006): 1–16.

Jordan, Pamela. "Historic Approaches to Sonic Encounter at the Berlin Wall Memorial." *Acoustics*, 2019.

Jordan, Vilhelm Lassen. "Acoustical Criteria for Auditoriums and Their Relation to Model Techniques." *The Journal of the Acoustical Society of America* 47, no. 2 (1970), 408–12.

Jordan, Vilhelm Lassen. "Acoustical Design Considerations of the Sydney Opera House." *Journal and Proceedings of The Royal Society of New South Wales* 106, pts. 1–2 (November 21, 1973): 33–53.

Kahn, Ashley. *Kind of Blue: The Making of the Miles Davis Masterpiece*. Cambridge, MA: Da Capo Press, 2000.

Kalins, Dorothy. "Here's Looking at You: Voyeurism in New York." *New York Magazine* (March 3, 1969): 34–40.

Kaufman, David. *Ridiculous! The Theatrical Life and Times of Charles Ludlam*. New York: Applause Theatre & Cinema Books, 2002.

Kaye, Nick. *Site-Specific Art: Performance, Place, and Documentation*. London: Routledge, 2000.

Kazdin, Andrew. *Glenn Gould At Work: Creative Lying*. New York: E.P. Dutton, 1989.

Kelley, Robin D.G. *Thelonius Monk: The Life and Times of an American Original*. New York: Simon & Schuster, 2009.

Kelly, Wayne. *Downright Upright: A History of the Canadian Piano Industry*. Toronto: Natural Heritage/Natural History Inc., 1991.

Kircher, Athanasius. *Ars magna Lucis et Umbrae : in decem libros digesta*. Romae: Sumptibus Hermanni Scheus, 1646.

Kircher, Athanasius. *Musurgia Universalis*. Rome: Haeresdes Frangisci Corbellitti, 1650.

Kircher, Athanasius. *Phonurgia nova*. Kempten: R. Dreherr, 1673.

Klausmeier, Axel. *The Berlin Wall*. Berlin: Christoph Links Verlag, 2015.

Knischewski, Gerd, and Ulla Spittler. "Remembering the Berlin Wall: The Wall Memorial Ensembles Bernauer Struass." *German Life and Letters* 59, no. 2 (2006): 280–93.

Kramer, Eddie. Electric Lady Studios, "At Guitar Center." Interview. *YouTube*, https://www. youtube.com/watch?time_continue=127&v=MtOuQviX-UY. accessed May 10, 2018.

Kytö, Meri, Nicolas Remy, and Heikki Uimonen, eds. *European Acoustic Heritage*. Grenoble: Tampere University of Applied Sciences, 2012.

La Belle, Brandon and Ken Ehrlich, eds. *Surface Tension: Problematics of Site*, Los Angeles: Errant Bodies Press, 2003.

LaBelle, Brandon. *Background Noise: Perspectives on Sound Art*. London; New York: Bloomsbury, 2006.

LaBelle, Brandon. *Sonic Agency: Sound and Emergent Forms of Resistance*. London: Goldsmiths Press, 2018.

La Torre, Marta De. "Values and Heritage Conservation." *Heritage & Society* 6, no. 2 (2013): 155–66.

Lacroix, Laurier. "The Pursuit of Art and the Flourishing of Aestheticism Amidst the Everyday Affairs of Mankind." In *Artists, Architects & Artisans, Canadian Art 1890–1918*, edited by Charles C. Hill, 20–55. Ottawa: National Gallery of Canada, 2013.

Ladd, Brian. *The Ghosts of Berlin*. Chicago: University of Chicago Press, 2018.

Landy, Eugene E. *The Underground Dictionary*. New York: Simon and Schuster, 1971.

Latour, Bruno. "How to Be Iconophilic in Art, Science and Religion?" in *Picturing Science, Producing Art*, edited by Caroline A. Jones and Peter Galison, 418–40. London: Routledge, 1998.

Latour, Bruno. "Visualisation and Cognition: Thinking with Eyes and Hands." *Knowledge and Society: Studies in the Sociology of Culture Past and Present* 6 (1986): 1–40.

Latour, Bruno. *Enquêtes sur les modes d'existence : Une anthropologie des modernes*. Paris: La Découverte, 2012.

Lavin, Sylvia. *Flash in the Pan*. London: Architectural Association, 2014.

Lavin, Sylvia. *Kissing Architecture*, New York; Princeton, NJ: Princeton University Press, 2011.

Le Corbusier correspondence. Fondation Le Corbusier, Paris.

Le Corbusier. *Correspondance*, Vol. 3: *Lettres à la famille, 1947–1965*. Paris: Fondation Le Corbusier, 2016.

Le Corbusier. *Le Livre de Ronchamp*. Edited by Jean Petit. Paris: Cahiers Forces Vives/Editec, 1961.

Le Corbusier. *Journey to the East*. Edited and translated by Ivan Žaknić with John Gery and Nicole Pertuiset. Cambridge, MA: MIT Press, 2007.

Le Corbusier. *Oeuvre complete*. Edited by Willy Boesiger. 8 vols. Zurich: Les Éditions d'Architecture, 1929–70.

Le Corbusier. *Precisions on the Present State of Architecture and City Planning*. 1930. Translated by Edith Schreiber Aujame. Cambridge, MA: MIT Press, 1991.

Le Corbusier Sketchbooks. 4 vols. New York: Architectural History Foundation, 1981–2.

Le Corbusier. *Textes et dessins pour Ronchamp*. Paris: Editions Forces-Vives, 1965.

Le Corbusier. *When the Cathedrals Were White*. 1937. Translated by Francis E. Hyslop. New York: McGraw-Hill, 1947.

Leighton, Angela. *Hearing Things: The Work of Sound in Literature*. Cambridge, MA: Belknap Press, 2018.

Liénard, Pierre. *Petite histoire de l'acoustique. Bruits, sons et musique*. Paris: Lavoisier, 2001.

Loesser, Arthur. *Men, Women and Pianos: A Social History*. New York: Simon and Schuster, 1954. London: Academy Editions, 1980.

Louis Kalff papers. Getty Research Institute. Los Angeles, California.

Lucier, Alvin. *Reflections, Interviews, Scores, Writings*. Cologne: MusikTexte, 1995.

Lucretius. *On the Nature of Things*. Translated by Martin Ferguson Smith. Indianapolis: Hackett Publishing, 2001.

Marmorstein, Gary. *The Label: The Story of Columbia Records*. New York: Avalon, 2007.

Masberg, Barbara A., and Lois H. Silverman. "Visitor Experiences at Heritage Sites: A Phenomenological Approach." *Journal of Travel Research* 34, no. 4 (April 18, 1996): 20–25.

Matton, Sylvain. *Kircher Athanasius – (1602–1680)*. Encyclopædia Universalis [online], accessed October 20, 2019. http://www.universalis.fr/encyclopedie/athanasius-kircher/

McClung, Littell. "Player-Pianos for Piano-Players." *Lippincott's Monthly Magazine* 91 (January–June 1913): 248–249.

McClure, Marjorie Barkley. *High Fires*. Boston: Little, Brown, and Company, 1924.

McKinnon, John Love. *History of Walton County*. Atlanta, GA: The Byrd Printing Co., 1911.

McLuhan, Marshall. "Living in an Acoustic World." Lecture at University of South Florida,1970.

McLuhan, Marshall. *The Medium is the Massage*. New York: Penguin Books, 1967.

Meling, Lise Karin. "'The Lady at the Piano': From Innocent Pastime to Intimate Discourse." *Music & Practice* 5, 2018. Accessed September 29, 2020, https://www.musicandpractice.org/volume-5/the-lady-at-the-piano-from-innocent-pastime-to-intimate-discourse

Mellers, Wilfrid. *Music in a New Found Land: Themes and Developments in the History of American Music*. London: Barrie and Rockliff, 1964.

Messiaen, Olivier. "Autor d'une oeuvre d'orgue." *L'art sacré* 5.40 (April 1939): 123.

Meyer Felix, Zimmerann Heidy, ed. *Edgard Varèse, composer, sound sculptor, visionary*. Bâle : The Boydell Press, Paul Sacher Stiftung, 2006.

Milner, Greg. *Perfecting Sound Forever: An Aural History of Recorded Music*. New York: Farra, Straus & Giroux, 2009.

Miwon Kwon. *One Place After Another: Site-Specific Art and Locational Identity*. Cambridge, MA: The MIT press, 2002.

Moorefield, Virgil. *The Producer as Composer: Shaping the Sounds of Popular Music*. Cambridge: The MIT Press, 2010.

Morgan, Mary S. and Margaret Morrison. *Models as Mediators: Perspectives on Natural and Social Science*. Cambridge/New York/Melbourne: Cambridge University Press, 1999.

Morse, Philip M. *Vibration and Sound*. New York and London: McGraw-Hill, 1936.

Morse, Philip M., and K. Uno Ingard. *Theoretical Acoustics*. New York and London: McGraw-Hill, 1968.

Mouffe, Chantal *Agonistics: Thinking the World Politically*. London: Verso, 2013.

Murray, Peter. *The Saga of Sydney Opera House: The Dramatic Story of the Design and Construction of the Icon of Modern Australia*. London/New York: Spon Press, 2004.

Neiswander, Judy. *The Cosmopolitan Interior: Liberalism and the British Home, 1870–1914*. New Haven: Yale University Press for the Paul Mellon Centre for Studies in British Art, 2008.

New Galsworthy, John. *The Patrician*. New York: Scribners, 1911.

Norberg-Schulz, Christian. "Frossen musikk," In *Christian Norberg-Schulz: Et Festskrift På 70års Dagen*. Eds. Guttorm Fløistad, Thomas Thiis-Evensen, and Kjetil Moe, 8–15. Oslo: Norsk arkitekturforlag, 1996.

Norberg-Schulz, Christian. "Frossen musikk." In *Øye og Hånd: essays og artikler*. Ed. Gordon Hølmebakk, 40–48. Oslo: Gyldendal, 1997.

Norberg-Schulz, Chistian, *Genius Loci: Paesaggio, Ambiente, Architettura*. Milan: Electa editrice, 1979.

Norberg-Schulz, Christian. *Genius Loci: Towards a Phenomenology of Architecture*. London: Academy Editions, 1980.

Norberg-Schulz, Christian. *Intentions in Architecture*. Cambridge, MA: MIT press, 1963.

Norberg-Schulz, Christian. *Mellom jord og himmel: en bok om steder og hus*. Oslo: Universitetsforlaget, 1978.

Norberg-Schulz, Christian. *Nightlands: Nordic Building,* Translated by Thomas McQuillan. Cambridge, MA: London: MIT Press, 1996.

Nord, Epstein Deborah. *Walking the Victorian Streets: Women, Representation, and the City*. Ithaca, N.Y.: Cornell University Press, 1995.

Otero-Pailos, Jorge. "Norberg-Schulz' hus: en modern søken etter hjemmets visuelle mønstre» in *Arkitektur-N* (21 February 2017) https://arkitektur-n.no/artikler/norberg-schulz-hus. First published in *Arkitektur-N,* 7 (2006).

Otero-Pailos, Jorge. *Architecture's Historical Turn: Phenomenology and the Rise of the Postmodern*. Minneapolis: University of Minnesota Press, 2010.

Ouzounian Gascia. "Visualizing Acoustic Space". *Circuit : musiques contemporaines*, 17, no 3, (2007) : 45–56.

Page, Tim. *The Glenn Gould Reader*. New York: Random House, 1984.

Pallasmaa, Juhani. *The Eyes of the Skin: Architecture and the Senses*. Chichester, UK: John Wiley & Sons, Ltd., 2005.

Passinmäki, Pekka, "Technology, Focality and Place: On the Means and Goals of Architecture," in *Understanding and Designing Place: Considerations on Architecture and Philosophy*, ed. Pekka Passinmäki and Klaske Havikm Tampere: Tamper University, 2019.

Paul, Stephan. "Binaural Recording Technology: A Historical Review and Possible Future Developments." *Acta Acustica united with Acustica* 95 (2009): 767–88.

Pauly, Danièle. *Le Corbusier: The Chapel at Ronchamp*. Translated by Sarah Parsons. Basel: Birkhäuser, 2008.

Pearson, Christopher. "Le Corbusier and the Acoustical Trope: An Investigation of Its Origins." *Journal of the Society of Architectural Historians* 56 no. 2 (June 1997): 168–83.

Pernecky, Tomas, and Tazim Jamal. "(Hermeneutic) Phenomenology in Tourism Studies." *Annals of Tourism Research* 37, no. 4 (October 2010): 1055–75.

Peter, John. *The Oral History of Modern Architecture*. New York: Harry N. Abrams, 1994.

Petit Jean. *Le Poème Electronique*. Paris: Editions Vives, 1958.

Pevsner, Nikolaus. *An Outline of European Architecture*. 6th edition. Harmondsworth, UK: Penguin, 1960.

Philip, Robert. *Performing Music in the Age of Recording*. New Haven: Yale University Press, 2014.

Pippard, A. B. *The Physics of Vibration*. Cambridge: Cambridge University Press, 1989. *Postmodern*. Minneapolis; London: University of Minnesota Press, 2010.

Potter, Keith. *Four Musical Minimalists*. Cambridge, UK; New York: Cambridge University Press, 2000.

Raykoff, Ivan. *Dreams of Love: Playing the Romantic Pianist*. New York: Oxford University Press, 2014.

Read, Oliver and Walter T. Welch. *From Tin Foil to Stereo: Evolution of the Phonograph*. Howard W. Sams: New York, 1976.

Regnault, Cécile. "Les représentations visuelles des phénomènes sonores. Applications à l'urbanisme". PhD Thesis, Université de Nantes, 2001.

Rendell, Jane. *The Architecture of Psychoanalysis: Spaces of Transition*. London: Bloomsbury, 2017.

Renner, Claude. "Sur l'histoire des cornets acoustiques." In *Annales françaises d'Oto-rhino-laryngologie et de Pathologie Cervico-faciale*, 129. no.1 (2012): 75–81.

Ribowsky, Mark. *He's a Rebel: The Truth About Phil Spector – Rock and Roll's Legendary Madman*. New York: E.P. Dutton, 1989.

Rindel, Jens Holger. "Modelling in Auditorium Acoustics—From Ripple Tank and Scale Models to Computer Simulations." keynote lecture, Forum Acusticum, Sevilla, September 16–20, 2002.

Roell, Craig. *The Piano in America, 1890–1940*. Chapel Hill, NC: University of North Carolina Press, 1989.

Ross, Alex. *Listen to This*. New York: Farrar, Straus & Giroux, 2010.

Ross, James Andrew. "'Ye Olde Firme' Heintzman & Company, Ltd., 1885–1930: A Case Study in Canadian Piano Manufacturing." M.A. Thesis, University of Western Ontario, 1994.

Roued-Cunliffe, Henriette, and Andrea Copeland, eds. *Participatory Heritage*. London: Facet Publishing, 2017.

Sandler, Daniela. *Counterpreservation: Architectural Decay in Berlin Since 1989*. Ithaca, NY: Cornell University Press, 2016.

Scales, Rebecca P. *Radio and the Politics of Sound in Interwar France, 1921–1939*. Cambridge, UK: Cambridge University Press, 2016.

Schafer, R. Murray. *The Soundscape: Our Sonic Environment and the Tuning of the World. The Soundscape: Our Sonic Environment and the Tuning of the World*. Rochester, VT: Destiny Books, 1994.

Schaffer, Pierre. *Treatise on Musical Objects: An Essay across Disciplines*. Translated by Christine North and John Dack. Oackland: University of California Presss, 2017.

Schloer, Joachim. "'It has to go away, but at the same time it has to be kept': the Berlin Wall and the making of an urban icon," *Urban History* 33, no. 1 (2006): 85–105.

Schlosser, Nicholas J. *Cold War on the Airwaves: The Radio Propaganda War against East Germany*. Urbana: University of Illinois Press, 2015.

Schmarsow, August. "Über den Werth der Dimensionen im menschlichen Raumgebilde." In: *Berichte über die Verhandlungen der Königlich Sächsischen Gesellschaft der Wissenschaften zu Leipzig, Philologisch-Historische Klasse*, vol. 48 (1896): 44–61.

Schmarsow, August. *Das Wesen der architektonischen Schöpfung*. Leipzig: Karl W. Hiersemann, 1894.

Schmidt Horning, Susan. *Chasing Sound: Technology, Culture & the Art of Studio Recording from Edison to the LP*. Baltimore: Johns Hopkins University Press, 2013.

Schofield, John. "The Archaeology of Sound and Music." *World Archaeology* 46, no. 3 (May 2014): 289–291.

Sharr, Adam. *Heidegger's Hut*. Cambridge, MA: MIT Press, 2006.

Simondon, Gilbert. *Du mode d'existence des objets techniques*. Paris: Aubier, 1958.

Simondon, Gilbert. *L'individuation à la lumière des notions de forme et d'information*. Grenoble: Jérôme Millon, 2005.

Simondon, Gilbert. *On the Mode of Existence of Technical Objects*. Translated by Cecile Malaspina and John Rogove. Minneapolis, MN: Univocal, 2017.

Simons, David. *Studio Stories: How the Great New York Records Were Made: From Miles to Madonna, Sinatra to the Ramones*. San Francisco: Backbeat Books, 2004.

Smith, C. Ray. "Instant Interiors." *Progressive Architecture* 48, no. 6 (June 1967): 176–181.

Smith, C. Ray. "The New Interiors: Fad or Fact?." *Progressive Architecture* (October 1968): 150–159.

Smith, C. Ray. "The Permissiveness of Supermannerism." *Progressive Architecture* 48, no. 10 (October 1967): 169–173.

Smith, C. Ray. *Supermannerism: New Attitudes in Post-Modern Architecture*. New York: Dutton, 1977.

Smith, Laurajane, and Emma Waterton. "The Envy of the World?" In *Intangible Heritage*, edited by Laurajane Smith and Natsuko Akagawa, 289–302. London: Routledge, 2009.

Smith, Laurajane, and Gary Campbell. "The Elephant in the Room." In *A Companion to Heritage Studies*, edited by William Logan, Máiréad Nic Craith, and Ullrich Kockel, 443–60. Hoboken, NJ: John Wiley & Sons, Inc, 2015.

Smith, Patti. *Just Kids*. New York and London: Bloomsbury, 2010.

Solomos Makis. *De la musique au son. L'emergence du don dans la musique des XXe-XXie siècles*. Presses Universitaires de Rennes, 2013.

Sorkin, Michael. *Some Assembly Required.* Minneapolis: University of Minnesota Press, 2001.

Spandöck, Friedrich. "Akustische Modellversuche." *Annalen der Physik* 20, no. 4 (1934): 345–60.

Spigel, Lynn. *Make Room for TV: Television and the Family Ideal in Postwar America.* Chicago: University of Chicago Press, 1992.

Squier, Susan M. *Virginia Woolf and London, The Sexual Politics of the City.* Chapel Hill, NC; London: University of North Carolina Press, 1985

Sterken Sven. "Immersive Strategies in Iannis Xenakis' Polytopes". *Immersed. Sound and Architecture, OASE,* 78, (2009): 116–120.

Sterne, Jonathan. "Analog", in *Digital Keywords, a Vocabulary of Information Society and Culture,* edited by Benjamin Peters, 31–44. Princeton/Oxford : Princeton University Press.

Stirling, James. "Ronchamp: Le Corbusier's Chapel and the Crisis of Rationalism." *The Architectural Review.* March 1956. Reprinted in James Stirling, *Writings on Architecture,* edited by Robert Maxwell, 40–9. Milan: Skira, 1998.

Storyk. John. "Cerebrum, ELS, and the Acoustic Architecture of Vibe." Interview by Clemens Finkelstein. May 24, 2019.

Storyk. John. "Jimi's Vibe Infused in the Architecture of Electric Lady Studios." Interview by Clemens Finkelstein. March 31, 2019.

Strong, David. "Philosophy in the Service of Things," in *Technology and the Good Life?* ed. Eric Higgs, Andrew Light and David Strong, 316–338, Chicago; London: The University of Chicago Press, 2000.

Suderberg, Erika. ed. *Space, Site, Intervention: Situating Installation Art,* Minneapolis: University of Minnesota Press, 2000.

Sullivan, Dan. "Cerebrum: Club Seeking to Soothe the Mind—'Studio' Offers Trip for 'New Form of Communication.'" *The New York Times* (November 23, 1968): 62.

Tak William, "Les effets Sonores", *La Revue Technique Philips,* n°2/3, (1958): 47.

Tamar Katz, "Pausing, Waiting, Repeating: Urban Temporality in *Mrs. Dalloway* and *The Years,*" in *Woolf and the City, Selected Papers from the Nineteenth Annual Conference on Virginia Woolf,* edited by Elizabeth F. Evans and Sarah E. Cornish, 2–16. Clemson; SC: Clemson University Digital Press, 2010.

Tate, Greg. *Midnight Lightning: Jimi Hendrix and the Black Experience.* Chicago: Chicago Review Press, 2003.

Tazelaar Kees. *On the Threshold of Beauty. Philips and the Origins of Electronic Music in the Netherlands, 1925–1965.* Rotterdam: V2_Publications, 2013.

Thibaud, Jean-Paul. "Petite archéologie de la notion d'ambiance," In *Communications. Les bruits de la ville, 90* (2012): 155–174.

Thompson, Emily. *The Soundscape of Modernity: Architectural Acoustics and the Culture of Listening in America, 1900–1933.* Cambridge, MA: MIT Press, 2002.

Thompson, Marie. *Beyond Unwanted Sound: Noise, Affect and Aesthetic Moralism.* New York and London: Bloomsbury, 2017.

Till, Rupert. "Sound Archaeology: Terminology, Palaeolithic Cave Art and the Soundscape." *World Archaeology* 46, no. 3 (May 2014): 292–304.

Touzeau, Jeff. "Professional Sound: Electric Lady Studios—Historic Design, Modern Methodology." *WSDG Walters-Storyk Design Group*, https://wsdg.com/professional-sound-electric-lady-studios-historic-design-modern-methodology; accessed May 10, 2018. translated by A.-Chr. Engels-Schwarzpaul. London: Bloomsbury Press, 2017.

Treib Marc. *The Philips Pavilion. Space Calculated in Time.* Princeton New Jersey: Princeton University Press, 1996.

Truax, Barry. "World Soundscape Project and Database." Accessed March 13, 2019. https://www.sfu.ca/sonic-studio/worldsoundscaperoject.html.

Valle Andrea, Tazelaar, Kees, Lombardo, Vincenzo. "In a concrete space. Reconstructing the spatialization of Iannis Xenakis' Concret PH on a multichannel setup". *Proceedings of the 7th Sound and Music Computing Conference, SMC 2010.*

Van Drie, Melissa. "Hearing through the *théâtrophone*: Sonically Constructed Spaces and Embodied Listening in Late Nineteenth-century French Theatre." *Sound Effects: An Interdisciplinary Journal of Sound and Sound Experience* 5, no. 1 (2015): 73–90.

Verheyen, Dirk. *United City, Divided Memories?* Lanham, MD: Lexington Books, 2008.

Vincenzo Lombardo, Andrea Valle, John Fitch, Kees Tazelaar, Stefan Weinzierl, and Wojciech Borczyk. "A Virtual-Reality Reconstruction of Poème Electronique Based on Philological Research". *Computer Music Journal*, 33, no. 2, (2009): 24–47.

Vischer, Robert. *Über das optische Formgefühl: Ein Beitrag zu Ästhetik.* Leipzig: Hermann Credner, 1873.

Ward, Peter. *A History of Domestic Space: Privacy and the Canadian Home.* Vancouver: UBC Press, 1999.

Weber, Ernst Heinrich. *De Tactu (De Pulsu, Resorptione, Auditu et Tactu).* Leipzig: C. F. Koehler, 1834.

Weekes, Agnes Russell. *Yarborough the Premier.* New York: Harper & Brothers, 1904.

Wells, Jeremy. "Blackness 'Scuzed: Jimi Hendrix's (In)Visible Legacy in Heavy Metal." In *Race Consciousness: African-American Studies for the New Century.* Eds. Judith Jackson Fossett and Jeffrey A. Tucker. New York: New York University Press, 1997.

Wells, Matthew J. "Relations and Reflections to the Eye and Understanding: Architectural Models and the Rebuilding of the Royal Exchange, 1839–44." *Architectural History* 60 (2017): 219–41.

Wetherell, Margaret, Laurajane Smith, and Gary Campbell. "Introduction: Affective Heritage Practices." In *Emotion, Affective Practices, and the Past in the Present*, edited by Laurajane Smith, Margaret Wetherell, and Gary Campbell, 1–17. New York City: Routledge, 2018.

Wever Peter. *Inside Le Corbusier's Philips Pavilion. A multimedia Space at the 1958 Brussels World's Fair.* Rotterdam : nai010 Publishers, 2015.

Wilken, Rowan. "The Critical Reception of Christian Norberg-Schulz's Writings on Heidegger and Place" in *Architectural Theory Review,* 18: 3 (December 2013): 340–55.

Wilson, Jean Moorcroft. *Virginia Woolf, Life and London; A Biography of Place.* London: Cecil Woolf, 1987.

Windover, Michael and Anne MacLennan. *Seeing, Selling, and Situating Radio in Canada, 1922–1956.* Halifax, NS: Dalhousie Architectural Press, 2017.

Wogensky, André. *Le Corbusier's Hands.* Translated by Martina Millà Bernad. Cambridge, MA: MIT Press, 2006.

Wölfflin, Heinrich. *Prolegomena zu einer Psychologie der Architektur.* Munich, 1886.

Woodring Carl, *Virginia Woolf, Columbia Essays on Modern Writers.* New York, N.Y.: Columbia University Press, 1966.

Woolf, Virginia. *Mrs. Dalloway.* Edited by David Bradshaw. New York, N.Y.: Oxford University Press, 2000.

Woolf, Virginia. *Selected Essays.* Edited by David Bradshaw. New York, N.Y.: Oxford University Press, 2008.

Woudhuysen, Henry R. "Some Women Editors of Shakespeare: A Preliminary Sketch." In *Women Making Shakespeare: Text, Reception and Performance*, edited by Gordon McMullan, Lena Cowen Orlin, & Virginia Mason Vaughan, 78–88. London: Bloomsbury, 2013.

Wundt, Wilhelm Maximilian. "Selbstbeobachtung und innere Wahrnehmung." *Philosophische Studien*, vol. 1 (1888): 615–617.

Wundt, Wilhelm Maximilian. *Beiträge zur Theorie der Sinneswahrnehmung,* Leipzig: Winter, 1862.

Xenakis Iannis. «Notes sur un "Geste électronique"», *in* Jean Petit (éd.), *Le poème électronique Le Corbusier.* Paris: Éditions de Minuit, (1958): 226–231.

Xenakis Iannis. *Musique, Architecture,* Tournai: Casterman, 1971.

Yelmi, Pinar. "Protecting Contemporary Cultural Soundscapes as Intangible Cultural Heritage: Sounds of Istanbul." *International Journal of Heritage Studies* 22, no. 4 (April 2016): 302–311.

Youngblood, Gene. *Expanded Cinema*. New York: P. Dutton & Co., Inc., 1970.

Zelleke, Ghenete. "Harmonizing Form and Function: Mackay Hugh Baillie Scott and the Transformation of the Upright Piano." *Art Institute of Chicago Museum Studies* 19, no. 2 (1993): 160–173, 203–205.

Films:

Livet finner sted, Sven Erik Helgesen, 1992. 10:38-11:19. https://tv.nrk.no/program/FKUR30002291 accessed February 12, 2022.

Index

Color Plates

Plate 1: La Monte Young and Marian Zazeela, Re-Creation of *Dream House*, Church Street, New York City, 2015. Photgraph: Marian Zazeela. Public Domain. (Figure 1, p. 90)

Plate 2: Alvin Lucier performing *I am sitting in a room* in 2010. Public Domain. (Figure 2, p. 93)

Plate 3: The first acoustic model used by Yasuhisa Toyota for the Suntory Hall project, Tokyo, 1986. Nagata Acoustics. (Figure 1, p. 118)

Plate 4: Acoustic model (1:10 scale) of the Elbphilharmonie in Hamburg by Herzog & de Meuron, 2016. Nagata Acoustics. (Figure 3, p. 125)

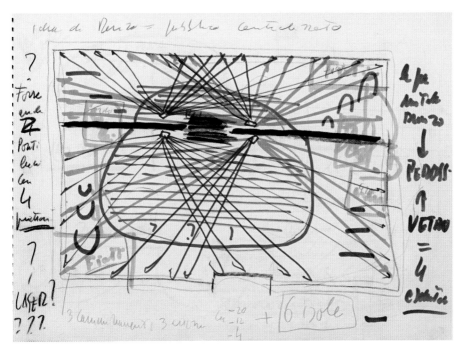

Plate 5: Luigi Nono, *Prometheus. Tragedy of Listening* (1984), Church of San Lorenzo, Venice. Plan studies of multidirectional light paths. 51.38.02_02 ALN, Archivio Luigi Nono, Venezia © Courtesy Eredi Luigi Nono. (Figure 2, p. 150)

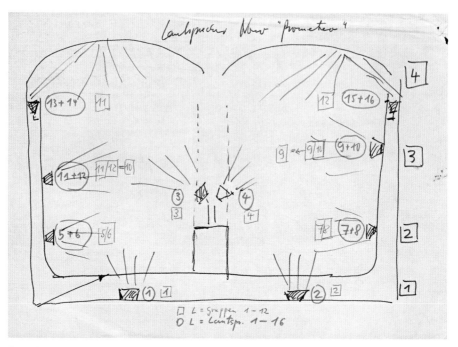

Plate 6: Luigi Nono, *Prometheus. Tragedy of Listening* (1984), Church of San Lorenzo, Venice. Sketch of the vertical section of the church by Nono, showing the position of the loudspeakers. 51.36.01_018_r ALN, Archivio Luigi Nono, Venezia © Courtesy Eredi Luigi Nono. (Figure 2, p. 150)

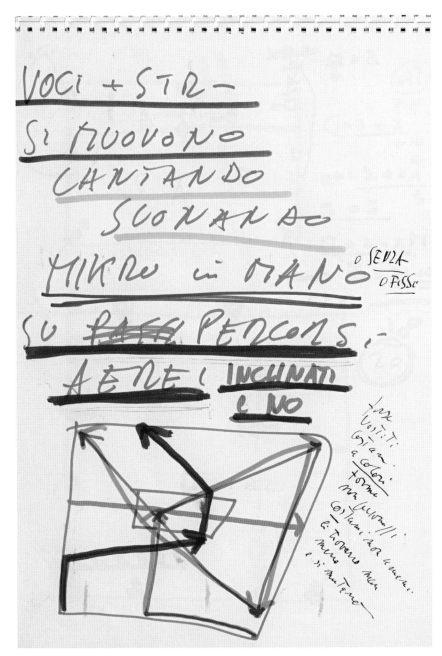

Plate 7: Luigi Nono. *Prometheus*. Preparatory sketch showing the sound paths. 51.35.01_08 ALN, Archivio Luigi Nono, Venezia © Courtesy Eredi Luigi Nono. (Figure 3, p. 151)

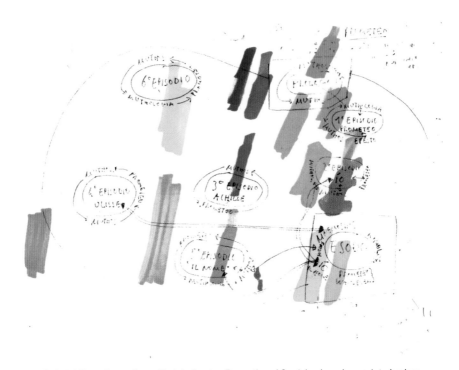

Plate 8: Luigi Nono. *Prometheus*. Sketch showing Prometheus' five islands and associated colors.
51.38.02_15v ALN, Archivio Luigi Nono, Venezia © Courtesy Eredi Luigi Nono. (Figure 3, p. 151)

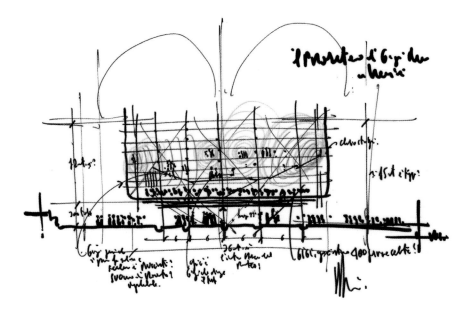

Plate 9: Preparatory sketch for the *Ark* by Renzo Piano (1984). © Courtesy of Fondazione Renzo Piano.

(Figure 4, p. 154)

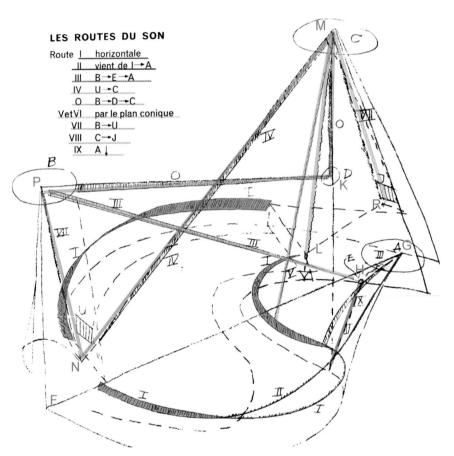

LES ROUTES DU SON

Route	I	horizontale
	II	vient de I→A
	III	B→E→A
	IV	U→C
	O	B→D→C
Vet VI		par le plan conique
	VII	B→U
	VIII	C→J
	IX	A↓

Plate 10: Iannis Xenakis, "Routes de Son" ["Sound Roads"] showing the placement of the loudspeakers across the main lines of the Philips Pavilion's geometry used for the music spatialization, as shown in Petit Jean (ed), *Le Poème Electronique-Le Corbusier* (Paris: Les editions de Minuit, 1958). © Archives Famille Xenakis. Colors and letters added by the author. Red letters coincide with the projections of generatives lines on the sketch of the first page of Xenakis' *Partition de Stereophonie*. (Figure 1, p. 162)

Plate 11: Liberation of Paris on August 25, 1944 (LOC). Open Source. (Figure 1, p. 206)

Plate 12: Fuente Invertida de Aschcott, Kassel, Germany. Photographer: Simenon. Open source.
(Figure 2, p. 209)

Plate 13: Border strip with house facades serving as the western border wall at Bernauer Straße, 1963-66. BWM image F-020564. (Figure 1, p. 217)

Plate 14: Ebertstraße, wall-peckers at work, February 1990. BWM image F-015772. (Figure 3, p. 220)

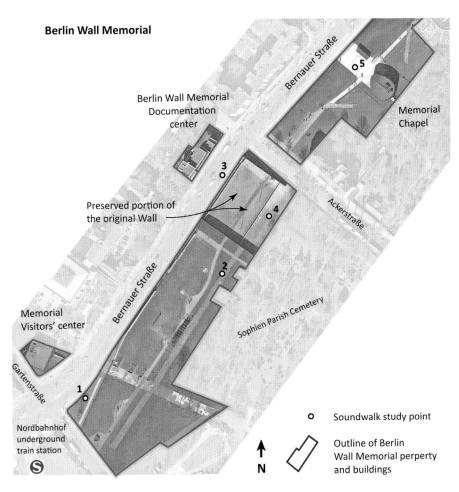

Berlin Wall Memorial

Bernauer Straße

○ **5**

Berlin Wall Memorial
Documentation
center

Memorial
Chapel

3
○

Preserved portion of
the original Wall ——

○ **4**

Ackerstraße

Bernauer Straße

2
○

Memorial
Visitors' center

Sophien Parish Cemetery

Gartenstraße

1
○

Nordbahnhof
underground
train station
Ⓢ

○   Soundwalk study point

↑
N

Outline of Berlin
Wall Memorial perperty
and buildings

Plate 15: Diagrammatic plan of the Berlin Wall Memorial, with preserved portion of the Wall and death strip in the center. © the author. (Figure 4, p. 221)

Plate 16: Alexander Petrounine using a spoon to explore soundscapes of Bogotá. Still from video, "Thinking through Things," https://www.tudelft.nl/index.php?id=45168. (Figure 1, p. 234)

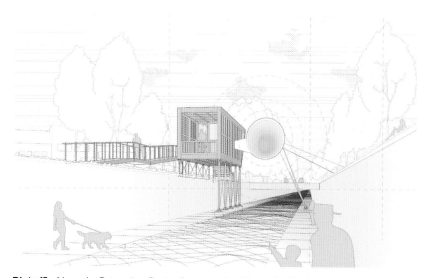

Plate 17: Alexander Petrounine, Design for a sound pavilion at the Rio Arzobispo, Bogotá. (Figure 2, p. 235)

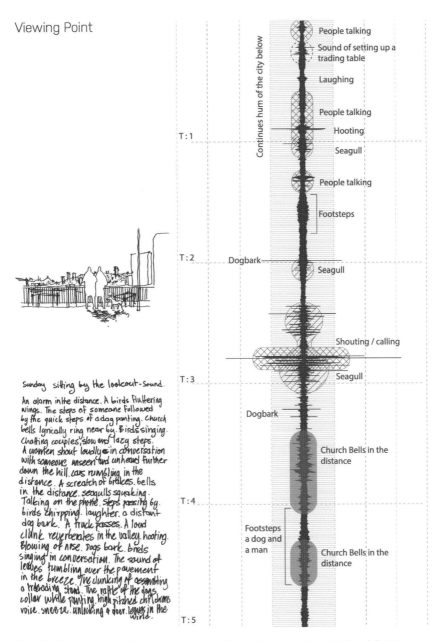

Viewing Point

Continues hum of the city below

People talking
Sound of setting up a trading table
Laughing
People talking
Hooting
T : 1
Seagull

People talking
Footsteps

T : 2
Dogbark
Seagull

Shouting / calling

T : 3
Seagull

Dogbark

Church Bells in the distance

T : 4

Footsteps a dog and a man
Church Bells in the distance

T : 5

Sunday sitting by the lookout - sound.

An alarm in the distance. A birds fluttering wings. The steps of someone followed by the quick steps of a dog panting. Church bells lyrically ring near by. Birds singing. Chatting couples, slow and lazy steps. A women shout loudly a in conversation with someone unseen and unheard further down the hill. cars rumbling in the distance. A screatch of brakes. bells in the distance. seagulls squaking. Talking on the phone. steps passing by. birds chirpping. laughter. a distant dog bark. A truck passes. A loud clunk reverberates in the valley. hooting. Blowing of nose. Dogs bark. birds singing in conversation. The sound of leaves tumbling over the pavement in the breeze. The clunking of assembling a trading stand. The raffle of the dogs collar while panting. high pitched childrens voice. sneeze. unlocking a door. leaves in the wind.

Plate 18: Michael de Beer, Soundscape analysis of Valparaíso, description, sketch and diagram.
(Figure 4, p. 237)

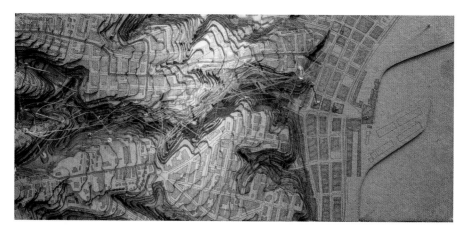

Plate 19: Michael de Beer, model of Valparaíso valley and sound study of varying conditions.
(Figure 5, p. 238)

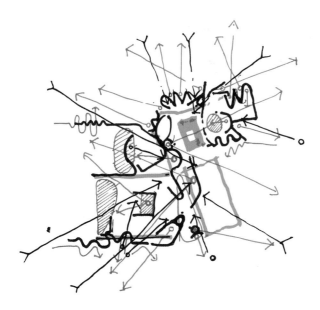

Plate 20: Michael de Beer, Synthesis of form and experience (Brown: Historic layout of site; Red: Sonic interaction; Black: Interacting sonic elements). (Figure 6, p. 239)